# Chinese Economic Growth and Fluctuations

Since the economic reform of the 1980s, the Chinese economy has boomed and has now become the second-largest in the world. Based on the constant and systematic researches of economic periodicity, this book studies Chinese economic growth and fluctuations.

As a famous Chinese economist, the author is the first to demonstrate investment periodicity in China. His groundbreaking studies on Chinese economic periodic fluctuation have significant impact at home and abroad. The first six papers collected in this book mainly examine issues on Chinese periodic fluctuation and macroeconomic regulation, including periodic fluctuations from 1953 to 1994, and a comparative analysis of five macroeconomic regulations since the reform and opening up in the late 1980s. The last seven papers appear in the author's collected works for the first time. They are focused on the new characteristics of Chinese macroeconomic operation and regulation after the financial crisis of 2007–08. In addition, this book reviews China's economic growth from 1949 to 2009 and provides some valuable suggestions on how to maintain the rising trend of the new economic cycle.

**Liu Shucheng** is the vice-director of the Academic Division of Economics, Chinese Academy of Social Sciences and the chief editor of *Economic Research Journal*. His research interests include macroeconomics and quantitative economics.

# China Perspectives

The *China Perspectives* series focuses on translating and publishing works by leading Chinese scholars, writing about both global topics and China-related themes. It covers Humanities and Social Sciences, Education, Media and Psychology, as well as many interdisciplinary themes.

This is the first time any of these books have been published in English for international readers. The series aims to put forward a Chinese perspective, give insights into cutting-edge academic thinking in China, and inspire researchers globally.

For more information, please visit https://www.routledge.com/series/CPH

## Existing titles:

**Regulating China's Shadow Banks**
*Qingmin Yan, Jianhua Li*

**Internationalization of the RMB**
Establishment and Development of RMB Offshore Markets
*International Monetary Institute of the RUC*

**The Road Leading to the Market**
*Weiying Zhang*

**Peer-to-Peer Lending with Chinese Characteristics**
Development, Regulation and Outlook
*P2P Research Group Shanghai Finance Institute*

**Chinese Economic Growth and Fluctuations**
*Liu Shucheng*

## Forthcoming titles:

**Government Foresighted Leading**
Theory and Practice of the World's Regional Economic Development
*Yunxian Chen, Jianwei Qiu*

**Free the Land**
A Study on China's Land Trust
*Jian Pu*

# Chinese Economic Growth and Fluctuations

## Liu Shucheng

LONDON AND NEW YORK

中国社会科学出版社

CHINA SOCIAL SCIENCES PRESS

This book is published with financial support from Innovation Project of CASS
Translator: Huang Rui

First published 2017 by Routledge

2 Park Square, Milton Park, Abingdon, Oxfordshire OX14 4RN

52 Vanderbilt Avenue, New York, NY 10017

*Routledge is an imprint of the Taylor & Francis Group, an informa business*

First issued in paperback 2020

*British Library Cataloguing-in-Publication Data*
A catalogue record for this book is available from the British Library

*Library of Congress Cataloging-in-Publication Data*
Names: Liu, Shucheng, 1945– author.
Title: Chinese economic growth and fluctuations / Liu Shucheng.
Other titles: Yun xing yu tiao kong.
English Description: Abingdon, Oxon ; New York, NY : Routledge, 2017. |
    Series: China perspectives series | Includes index.
Identifiers: LCCN 2016043229 | ISBN 9781138898684 (hardcover) | ISBN
    9781315708430 (ebook)
Subjects: LCSH: Economic development—China. | Business cycles—China. |
    China—Economic conditions—1949– | China—Economic policy—1949–
Classification: LCC HC427.9 .L597513 2017 | DDC 338.951—dc23
LC record available at https://lccn.loc.gov/2016043229

ISBN: 978-1-138-89868-4 (hbk)
ISBN: 978-0-367-52287-2 (pbk)

Typeset in Times New Roman
by Apex CoVantage, LLC

# Contents

# Figures

# Tables

# Acknowledgements

This book is a collection of evidence-based studies funded by the Innovation Program of the Chinese Academy of Social Sciences (CASS). It contains my experience regarding both the practices and the theoretical studies of China's economic development.

Here I would like to express my sincere gratitude to Ms. Huang Rui, the translator of this book, for her painstaking efforts devoted to the book; I also thank all of the colleagues at China Social Sciences Press for their professional and energetic support.

My particular thank goes to the CASS Innovation Translation Fund for having the book translated and published.

June, 2016

# 1 Issues on periodic fluctuation of China's economy

## Periodic fluctuation of China's economy

It is essential to predict and analyze the economic growth trend in certain years in terms of the timing to implement significant reform measures or make effective adjustments to the macro economy. The prediction for economic trends for a given year should not be made statically or in isolation from many other factors. It should particularly take account of the periodic fluctuation of national economies.

### Periodic fluctuation of China's economy

Since 1953, China has begun a massive economic construction. By 1994, it had experienced a total of nine economic periodic fluctuations in the past 42 years. China is now in the ninth cycle of economic fluctuation. In terms of the annual growth rates of major economic indicators such as national income, gross domestic product (GDP) and total industrial output value, the economic periodic fluctuation refers to fluctuation of the economy between periods of expansion (growth) and contraction (recession). The starting and ending years of the nine cycles are listed in Table 1.1, in which every five years on average is observed as a cycle.

### The economic periodic fluctuation in 1994 and 1995

China's economy began to recover in 1991. It has entered into the ninth cycle of economic fluctuation with the GDP growth rate to 8 percent. The economy expanded rapidly in 1992 with the GDP growth rate rising to 13.2 percent. It reached the peak in 1993 with the GDP growth rate reaching 13.4 percent. In 1994 it will sustain a rapid growth after the peak year. This implies that, on the one hand, economic growth began to fall in 1994 in comparison with that of 1993 and the peak of the ninth cycle was over and, on the other hand, the economy growth will still maintain at a reasonably high level although it began to fall. According to our projection, the GDP growth rate of 1994 will be around 11.5 percent. It was 12.7 percent in the first quarter and 12 percent in the second. It is expected to be 12.5 percent in the first half of the year and around 11 percent in the second half.

In view of the regular pattern of economic periodic fluctuation and the price movement, the economic growth rate of 1995 is expected to fall continuously but steadily. According to the calculation results of the model, it is estimated that the

*Table 1.1* Economic periodic fluctuation in China

| No. | Starting and ending year | Duration | Nature of fluctuation | Amplitude |
|-----|--------------------------|----------|-----------------------|-----------|
| 1 | 1953–57 | 5 years | Growing fluctuation | 9.6% |
| 2 | 1958–62 | 5 years | Classical fluctuation | 51.7% |
| 3 | 1963–68 | 6 years | Classical fluctuation | 24.2% |
| 4 | 1969–72 | 4 years | Growing fluctuation | 20.4% |
| 5 | 1973–76 | 4 years | Classical fluctuation | 11.0% |
| 6 | 1977–81 | 5 years | Growing fluctuation | 7.4% |
| 7 | 1982–86 | 5 years | Growing fluctuation | 5.9% |
| 8 | 1987–90 | 4 years | Growing fluctuation | 7.6% |
| 9 | 1991–94 (not completed) | | | |

GDP growth rate will fall to about 10 percent. The retail price increasing rate in the first quarter of 1994 reached 20.1 percent. It is expected to be between 16 percent and 18 percent in the second quarter, between 14 percent and 16 percent in the third quarter, and between 11 percent and 13 percent in the fourth quarter, manifesting a gradual fall quarter by quarter. It is estimated to be between 13 percent and 15 percent for the whole year of 1994. In order to keep the price inflation within 10 percent in 1995, the economic growth should continue to fall compared to that of 1994. According to our prediction, 1995 will be the trough of the ninth cycle of economic fluctuation if there are no major changes. China's economy will recover from 1996 and then enter into the tenth cycle of economic fluctuation.

The steady fall of economic growth at a high rate from the second half of 1994 to 1995 will provide a moderately hassle-free environment in which the supply and demand will remain balanced. This offers a remarkable opportunity for vigorously promoting enterprise reforms. Meanwhile, the level of the price increase will be relatively low from 1995 to 1996, which suggests a good opportunity for price reform for the factors of production.

## Comparative analysis of economic periodic fluctuation before and after the reform

Since the economic reform and the implementation of an open-door policy, some characteristics of the periodic fluctuation of China's economy have profoundly altered whereas some have not.

### What has changed

The changes of China's economic periodic fluctuation have affected two areas. First, as far as the nature of economic fluctuation is concerned, it has changed from being previously dominated by classical fluctuation to being dominated by growing fluctuation. The so-called classical fluctuation refers to the absolute decline in main economic indicators such as national income, GDP and total industrial output value in a trough, namely a negative growth. The so-called growing fluctuation refers to the fact that these main economic indicators do not decline in their absolute values in a trough, but show slowdown in the growth rate. This change has demonstrated that China's economy is stronger and that its strength in resisting recession is much more improved than in the past. Second, in terms of fluctuation amplitude, it has changed from the previously wild fluctuations to relatively mild ones. In the second cycle (1958–62) of the most aggressive fluctuation, the gap of the annual growth rate of the national income between the peak and trough went as high as 51.7 percent. Yet the gap in the eighth cycle (1987–90) after the reform was only 7.6 percent (see Table 1.1). It showed that economic growth in China was more stable than in the past.

There are two major explanations for the above changes. The first explanation focuses on the structural change of the economic system and operation brought about by the reform, including: (1) changes of ownership structure in industrial production. Non-state-owned firms have gradually increased their output value in the gross industrial output value, over 50 percent up to now, with a high growth rate. Replacing state-owned enterprises (SOEs), they have become the main source of industrial growth and economic fluctuation. Non-state-owned enterprises are subject to less intervention by the government and are more responsive to changes of supply and demand through market operation. They are more vigorous than SOEs during an excessive economic fluctuation, which will be beneficial for national economic growth and resistance to recession; (2) changes of ownership structure in agricultural production, which is accompanied by the changes of industrial structure. The implementation of the agricultural household responsibility system and the development of township and village enterprises (TVEs) have significantly promoted agricultural development in China. Prior to the economic reform the total agricultural output value appeared as a negative growth in seven years during the period of 26 years from 1953 to 1978. Since the reform, it has been a positive growth consecutively for 15 years from 1979 to 1993. This has guaranteed the steady development of national economy; and (3) changes of price structure. The price is increasingly regulated by the market and acts as a "cold" or "hot" indicator in economic periodic fluctuation. This is helpful for the government to strengthen macro control and reduce economic fluctuations.

The second explanation emphasizes the improvement of the government's regulation and control of the macro economy. The scale and extent of economic fluctuation are closely related to government regulations and control over the macro economy. An excessive rise in economic growth often inevitably leads to its drastic fall. The key reason for the sharp fluctuations of China's economy in the past was due to the excessive rise without realistic plans. Through decades of wild economic fluctuations since the founding of new China, the government has learned how to smooth economic periodic fluctuation.

### *What is unchanged*

There are few changes in the following aspects: The first are hard constraints in the sectors that are the bottleneck of China's economy. Throughout all the previous periodic fluctuations of China's economy, every rapid economic expansion had to come down in two-three years or three-four years. Apart from its origin of political and institutional systems and policy implementation, this phenomenon was also due to the hard constraints of "bottleneck sectors" such as agriculture (especially grain), transportation, energy and raw materials. This situation has not changed fundamentally yet and, correspondingly, the length of each economic periodic fluctuation still remains approximately five years. The second are soft constraints in institutional systems. One of the most imperative problems is lack of accountability and risk control mechanisms, which leads to purposeless investment impulses and constrains a smooth and steady economic development. The other is the lack of competition and elimination amongst SOEs. The fall and trough in an economic periodic fluctuation are often the chief moments in which renewing products, upgrading industries, surviving fittest enterprises, and promoting technology are undertaken. Nevertheless, China does little during these periods until entering the next cycle of economic fluctuation. In the beginning of the next cycle, it will exhibit a new round of rapid economic expansion without the advancement of quality development. This has restricted the effective supply of products and improvement of productivity. All these difficulties can only be solved through further reforms.

## Relations between economic fluctuation and price fluctuation

The relations between economic fluctuation and price fluctuation can be observed from three aspects.

### *Three positions*

Currently, there are basically three positions among scholarship on whether economic progress will inevitably bring a rise in price. The first position denies that. Those who hold this viewpoint argue, based on the comprehensive survey of 56 countries (regions) conducted by US economists J. Woods and J. Marshall, that only two countries, Egypt and Uruguay, present positive correlation between the two phenomena, whereas the rest or 54 countries (regions) show no correlation and, in some cases, even a negative correlation between the two. The second viewpoint is in favor of their correlation—rapid economic expansion is accompanied by a rise in price. Those who hold this viewpoint often take high-speed growth in Japan and South Korea as an example. The third perspective regards the relations of the two facts as being more complicated than simple correlation or non-correlation. There are various combinations of correlations at high, medium and low levels.

### *Long-, medium- and short-term observations*

Based on the statistical data of both developed and developing countries after World War II, in order to unambiguously understand the relations between economic growth and price increase, we need to distinguish different situations in the long-term, medium-term and short-term.

1   Long-term observation (for example more than 20 years) can be grouped into two categories. The first is to observe the relations between economic growth and price inflation at the absolute level. After World War II, GNP or GDP in most countries presented a rising trend, and so did the price level, which showed a positive correlation between the two facts. The absolute price level increased because of the absolute economic growth, demand increase and cost raise. The second is the observation of various correlations between economic growth and rise in price, derived from different combinations between the economic annual growth rate and inflation in different periods and under different situations. These combinations make the relationships increasingly blur and irrelevant as the observation period extends. This is the conclusion the two above-mentioned US economists have drawn.

2   Medium-term observation (for example 10 to 20 years) is designed to observe the relationships between economic average annual growth rate and average annual price increase rate in a medium term. Dividing the economic growth rate into three ranges – high, medium and low – and the price increase rate into three ranges as well, there will be nine different combinations between these ranges. For example, under a high-speed economic growth, there was a low level of inflation in the Federal Republic of Germany (from 1954–60, the average annual growth rate of GNP was 8.5 percent, and average annual consumer price index was 1.6 percent), a medium-level of inflation in Japan (from 1960 to 1970, the average annual growth rate of GNP was 11.4 percent, and average annual consumer price index was 5.6 percent), and a high-level of inflation in South Korea (from 1963 to 1973, the average annual growth rate of GDP was 9.8 percent, and average annual consumer price index was 13.8 percent). Under the low-speed economic growth, there are also different combinations with low, medium or high-level inflation because of different levels of industrialization, different fiscal and monetary policies and different industrial structures in various countries.

3   The short-term observation (for example within 10 years) is to observe relationships between economic growth and price increase in a particular economic periodic fluctuation. Economic fluctuation goes along with price fluctuation in the market economy. With the recovery of an economy from fluctuation, the price level increases slowly. Before and after the peak of economic periodic fluctuation, the price level increases quickly. In the trough of short-term fluctuation, the price increase falls subsequently because both economic fluctuation and price fluctuation are impacted by the quantifiable balance between supply and demand and by structural balance. Price fluctuation often lags behind economic fluctuation from six months to one year.

### *Economic fluctuation and price fluctuation in China*

Before the economic reform and at the beginning of the reform in 1985, economic fluctuation and price fluctuation in China presented a converse relationship in most years. During the 33 years from 1953 to 1985, there were 25 years in which economic fluctuation and price fluctuation were related conversely either in the absolute or relative level. The so-called absolute converse relationship refers to the two fluctuations in the opposite direction at an absolute level, namely the level of the economy rises and the level of prices falls; and vice versa. The so-called relative converse relationship refers to economic fluctuation and price fluctuation in the opposite direction at a relative level, namely the economic growth is faster than the previous year, but the rise in price is slower than the previous year; and vice versa. The relative converse relationship between economic fluctuation and price fluctuation lies in restriction on the demand under the rationing system where coupons were distributed to residents for purchasing basic necessities. In this circumstance, prices fluctuated when supply changed. Thus, when the economy grew, supply improved and price fell at the absolute level or relative level; and when the economy declined, supply was short; commodity was in severe shortage and price rose.

After 1986, dramatic changes have taken place in price formation as price controls were gradually lifted. Since the demand is no longer controlled by the rationing system, the price level goes up variously with changes in demand. When the economic growth rate rises, the rate of price increase also rises as demand increases. When the economic growth rate declines, the rate of price increase also falls as demand decreases. During the eight years from 1986 to1993, economic fluctuation and price fluctuation in China demonstrated changes in the same direction regardless of the absolute level or the growth rate.

As it should be, price fluctuation is influenced by, in addition to demand, multiple factors such as the price reform, costs, individual expectations and immature market. The rise in price in the first quarter of 1994 was related to a variety of factors such as wage expenditures, industrial producer costs, individual expectations in price increase and immature market. In view of this, it is necessary to adopt a holistic approach to the challenge.

(Originally published in *Brief Report of Chinese Academy of Social Sciences [Zhongguo Shehui Kexueyuan Yaobao]*, No.58, June 1994)

# 2  Macroeconomic prediction in China and proactive measures of firms in 1996

## Prediction of macroeconomic development in 1996

### *Difficulties in macroeconomic prediction*

It has been six years since we formally carried out macroeconomic prediction in 1990 in China. The forecast of economic trends for the five years from 1991 to 1995 was accurate. A case in point is that we predicted that the economy would recover in 1991, rapidly expand in 1992, reach the peak in 1993 and come down in 1994 and 1995, which had proved to tally with reality. However, it is particularly difficult in forecasting the economic trend in 1996 since it is a rather special year.

First, 1996 is special in China's economic cycles. China has experienced a total of nine economic cycles to date since the massive socialist economic construction started in 1953, in which five cycles took place prior to the economic reform and four cycles afterwards. Each round of cycle generally progresses in the sequence from recovery, expansion and peak, contraction or decline to the trough. It should be noted that the trough is only relative to the peak. It does not necessarily mean a low growth while the peak may not be a high-speed upsurge. The recovery and peak appear as an expansion of the economy while the decline and trough indicate a deterioration of the economy. This round of economic cycle, which is the ninth cycle since 1953 and the fourth since the economic reform, started in 1991 and has lasted for five years by the end of 1995. The year 1991 was the recovery year, and the economic growth rate, represented by gross domestic product (GDP), rose from 3.9 percent in the last trough in 1990 to 8 percent in 1991. The year 1992 was the expansion and peak year, and the GDP increased to 13.6 percent in 1992 and reached the peak in mid-1993. Then it began to decline slightly. The annual GDP growth rate of 1993 was 13.5 percent. It slipped to 11.8 percent in 1994. The estimated GDP increment in 1995 is around 10 percent. Briefly, during this cycle the first two and a half years were the stage of economic growth and the second two and a half years were the contraction stage. Reviewing the eight cycles during the past 38 years from 1953 to 1990, the average length of each cycle was 4.75 years, rounding up to 5 years. The question is: when will the trough of this round of the economic cycle occur, since it has already lasted for five years? Will it be 1995 or

1996? In other words, will 1996 be the outset of a new round of an economic cycle or the continuation of the last cycle?

Second, the year 1996 is distinct in terms of macroeconomic regulation and control. By the end of 1995, it had been two and a half years since the implementation of macroeconomic control, which is characterized by moderate austerity and represented by policy measures of rectifying economic order and curbing inflation. The bottlenecks in the areas of energy, transportation and raw materials have been alleviated. There are even overstocked means of production. In this case, should the austerity policy be continuously executed in 1996 or should it turn to an easier policy?

Finally, 1996, as the first year of the Ninth Five-Year Plan, is very distinctive. Should the economy expand rapidly when China enters a new planning period?

Different accounts and judgments for the above questions will directly affect the forecasting of China's economic tendency in 1996.

## *Three judgments of economic trends in 1996*

There are three different judgments when estimating the economic trends in 1996.

First, some researchers believe that the rates of economic growth and price increase (represented by the national commodity retail price index) still remain at a high level although the former dropped down to about 10 percent and the latter to approximately 15 percent in 1995. Correspondingly, the austerity policy on macroeconomic regulation should be retained and/or even be tighter. Consequently, the economic growth and price upsurge will obviously decline in 1996 in comparison with those in 1995.

Moreover, some scholars hold the view that the bottlenecks in the fields of energy, transportation and raw materials have been relieved and means of production are overstocked after implementing the austerity policy for two years. Considering various challenges that state-owned enterprises are facing, 1995 can be the end of this round of economic cycle. The economy should recover with the injection of new projects and enter into the new round of economic cycle in 1996 – the first year of the Ninth Five-Year Plan. Accordingly, the macroeconomic control should loosen up.

The third perspective, which takes the above two judgments into consideration, deems that the primary objective of macroeconomic control in 1996 is to carry on the restraint on inflation so as to further reduce economic growth in a balanced manner – neither declining too violently nor rebounding too robustly. For this consideration the moderate austerity policy should be continually taken in combination with control over demand and improvement in supplies. It is especially important to lay stress on structure adjustment and enhancement of the quality of economic growth. The year 1996 may become the trough of this round of cycle if the economic growth reduces to about 9 percent and the price rises to around 10 percent. This trough will without doubt show its own features. Taking into account the decline in price index lagging behind that of economic growth within an economic cyclical fluctuation, the price rise will hopefully reduce to a one-digit number in 1997 if no measures to stimulate price rise are announced and if no natural disaster strikes in 1996 and 1997. In this circumstance, 1997 may enter a new round of economic cycle.

Personally, I support the third judgment and will elaborate the justifications in the subsequent analysis.

### *Further analysis of the above-mentioned third judgment*

*Securing and consolidating an economic "soft landing" in 1996*

There are two criteria for securing the economic "soft landing". On the one hand, China's economic growth should come down to the level at which social production potential can afford it. In other words, it should be in the appropriate range that social material, financial and labor resources could support it. On the other hand, the price should decline to the proper level at which customers could bear. There are different quantitative criteria for the appropriate range and proper level under different economic circumstances. In accord with the economic situation in China, it is promising to keep the economic growth rate at 9 percent and inflation at a one-digit number, i.e. below 10 percent.

We should realize that it is valuable to steadily control economic growth and price rise to the target levels because the implementation of appropriate austerity and "soft landing" policies have achieved tangible results since mid-1993. The economic "soft landing" is still in process in 1996. Although the strong momentum of brisk price rise has been stunted, there is still a pressure of inflation with a fragile economic basis.

This is the second economic "soft landing" since the economic reforms and implementation of opening-up policies. The first took place in 1986 but that "soft landing" was incomplete. It was followed by high-pace economic growth in 1987 and 1988, which led to the rise of prices in 1988 and 1989 and was followed by unremitting improvement and rectification for three years. We should not forget the experiences and lessons drawn from the above. The nationwide commodity retail price increased by 18.5 percent in 1988 and 17.8 percent in 1989, witnessing a historical summit since 1952. The highest historical record of price index was 16.2 percent in 1961. This second economic "soft landing" is facing a price increase at 13.2 percent in 1993 and 21.7 percent in 1994, which broke the highest historical record. Consequently, in order to consolidate the outcome of the "soft landing" in the past two years and to accomplish the "soft landing", we should continue to regard the curbing of inflation as the chief target of macroeconomic regulations and appropriately implement austerity policies.

*Features of the trough in this economic cycle and its policy implications*

There are different views about when this round of economic cycle will reach its trough. Some believe that it could be in between the end of 1995 and the first quarter of 1996. The second group of commentators predict that it could be in the second quarter in 1996, whereas others argue that it could be at the end of 1996. The fourth view considers that it could occur within 1997. Many others believe it is difficult to make an explicit estimation. My opinion is that a comprehensive easy policy over macro economy is inappropriate no matter when the trough emerges and when the economy enters the next round of cycle.

Regardless at which year the economy reaches the trough, the trough will be characterized with "a high-level bottom". In other words, China's economic growth will stay at a relative high level in the trough. It is forecasted that the economic growth rate will come down to 9.4 percent in 1996, the trough of the cycle, which is the highest in comparison with those in the previous cycles. This is owing to the moderate austerity policy implemented from mid-1993 through prompt unveiling of measures, appropriate contraction and gentle decline of growth rate. The amplitude, the gap of the economic growth between the peak and the trough, is the smallest too as compared with other cycles. It was higher than 10 percent in the five rounds of cycles prior to the implementation of economic reforms and opening-up policies except for the first cycle with the amplitude of slightly lower than 10percent. This can be regarded as "drastic rise and fall". The amplitude of the economic growth rate of four rounds of cycles after the implementation of economic reform policies was below 8 percent. It will be around 4 percent in this cycle.

Due to these characteristics, a slim margin of elevation will remain for the recovery, expansion and peak of the next round of economic cycle. If the austerity policy is relaxed in every aspect, China's economy will become overheated soon afterwards. In order to avoid an overheated growth again, a "slow-rise and slow-fall" approach should be preserved regardless of when the economy enters the next round of cycle. That means China should get rid of the previous all-inclusive stress-free policy which fueled social demands by extensive investment and inflated consumption. Rooted in investment impetus inherent in the old system, this policy often kicks off an overheated economy and then undertakes economic adjustment. China is currently in the transition from an old economic system to a new one. The fact that the old investment impulse persists, together with the new consumption demands, will undoubtedly lead to a rise in total demand. In this circumstance, we should make substantial modifications on the out-of-date measures in economic expansion and implement the policy of combining appropriate control with emphatically and moderately loosened regulation and combining the control over demand with improvement in supply. The overall control to an appropriate extent implies that we should regulate the total demand and not loosen all control no matter which stage of economic cyclical fluctuation it lies in because there are hidden investment impetuses and consumption impulses at this transitional period. The regulation can be adjusted slightly depending on different situations. The emphatically and moderately loosened regulation means that we should guarantee the availability of capital for those national key programs and technical transformation projects in the bottleneck sectors, such as infrastructure in the Ninth Five-Year Plan, agriculture, energy, transportation and main raw materials, and provide support in the circulation fund to industrial and business firms with low asset-liability ratio, sound operation and management, readily salable products and ability to repay loans. We should lay the emphasis of macroeconomic regulation on the improvement of supply and control of total demands simultaneously, and not just work on the size of demand and total supply. Improving the supply means that the government should make an effort to promote structure adjustment and upgrade of industry, promote technical innovation and progress, enhance production efficiency and economic effectiveness, improve quality of products, diversify categories of products and enlarge effective supply through macroeconomic policies on banking, finance, price, distribution and foreign trade.

*Distinguishing two different industrial structural adjustments*
*and their related different extents*

Industrial structural adjustment is crucial for improving supply. It has been increased very slowly due to restriction of the economic system, pricing, perception and planning. There is often confusion in understanding the two different approaches to industrial structural adjustment. One is the adaptive adjustment where the constraint of bottleneck sectors such as agriculture, energy, transportation and main raw materials is relieved owing to the squeeze of total demand at the contraction stage of each economic cyclical fluctuation. But this type of adjustment is temporary and has a short-term effect. When entering the expansion stage of the next round of economic cycle, the bottleneck is uncovered and high-speed economic growth becomes impossible. The other approach is the radical adjustment where the thorough alteration in bottleneck sectors is carried out through continuous endeavors The current alleviation of bottleneck restraint in the above sectors in 1996, directly caused by the decline of economic growth for more than two years, is nothing but the adaptive adjustment. In the past, having noticed somewhat of an achievement of the adaptive adjustment, some people felt relaxed and believed that industrial restructuring was just about to be finished and that it was time to expand the economy all-around without realizing that the adjustment effect was short-term. Confusion of the two kinds of adjustments will no doubt hold up the radical adjustment of industrial structure.

With respect to the approach to economic planning, the government needs to leave leeway when drawing up plans. For example, whereas the projected economic growth is 8 percent, the actual rate may reach 9 percent or 10 percent. On the other hand, if drawing up production and development plans, particularly for those bottleneck sectors such as agriculture, energy, transportation and main raw materials, in accordance with the projected economic growth rate of 8 percent, these bottleneck sectors will never meet the demand of the actual economic operation and alter their choke point. There are two approaches to allow leeway. One is to define a bit lower level of targets in the plans and allow a margin to exceed the planned targets in operation. For some indicators like the economic growth rate, fiscal revenue and expenditure, and currency and credit revenue, this approach is applicable. The other is to draw up a slightly high (but appropriate) level of targets in the plans and leave room as a precaution. This approach is suitable for the bottleneck sectors. It is not workable to always impose a single measure in the first approach.

*The "Speed Effect" could not solve problems facing state-owned*
*enterprises*

Presently, state-owned enterprises are facing a number of difficulties such as product backlog, fund shortage, low efficiency, high asset-liability ratio and lack of vitality. The fundamental solution to these difficulties relies on deepening the economic reform. Resting on high-pace development, the so-called Speed Effect, is no longer applicable.

First, some difficulties have been induced by the Speed Effect in the past. Some enterprises don't grow through further reforms, management enhancement and technical progress. Instead, they are accustomed to surviving in the overheated economy without concern about product markets. Encountering emerging competition and market fluctuation, they find it hard to deal with difficulties. The fund shortage is closely related to the overheated economy, excessive issuance of currency and bank loan and financial disorder in the last cycle.

Second, the Speed Effect could only have an effect in the short term. When the economy is overheated, firms may feel easy in their operation. Soon after that they encounter the re-emergence of existing problems, to an even more severe extent. The Speed Effect covers up existing problems for the time being instead of solving them. In fact, the Speed Effect essentially bungles the opportunity of meeting the challenges facing enterprises.

Finally, the Speed Effect may offer loopholes for products, either counterfeit or inferior at a high price. Under the Speed Effect, unmarketable products may build up in a large quantity. It acts against deepening the reforms of state-owned enterprises and the transformation of the economic growth pattern. In this sense, the Speed Effect should be discarded.

*To ensure the first year as a good start of the Five-Year Plan*

Should the first year of each five-year plan be characterized by a rapid expansion of the economy with the massive input of new investment projects? According to the statistical data of the past eight five-year plans, the first year of the last five five-year plans with no new and large-scale projects did not have high-speed expansion whereas the first three five-year plans did. The year 1971 – the first year of the Fourth Five-Year Plan- was just in the contract stage of the cycle. The year 1976 – the first year of the Fifth Five-Year Plan, 1981 – the first year of the Sixth Five-year Plan, and 1986 – the first year of the Seventh Five-Year Plan were all at the trough stage. The year 1991 – the first year of the Eighth Five-Year Plan was at the recovery stage of that round of the economic cycle. There was no injection of new and large projects in all these years. As far as the three five-year plans after the economic reform were concerned, each first year – 1981, 1986 and 1991 – was in the process of improvement and rectification and in preparation for smoothly carrying out each particular five-year plan at that time. With this model, 1996, the first year of the Ninth Five-Year Plan, will not necessarily imitate a massive and rapid expansion of the national economy. The pace of economic growth and the quantity of new investment projects in the first year of every Five-Year Plan should depend on specific conditions and situations. We should not simply believe that every first year of a Five-Year Plan is deemed to develop extensively and hastily. From the implementation of the Ninth Five-Year Plan in 1996, we should carry out the Party's strategy – transforming China's economy from extensive to intensive growth and avoid reoccurrence of an overheated economy rapidly led by the headlong rush of investment and excessive and repetitive construction during the economic cyclical fluctuations of the past.

## Proactive measures of enterprises to macro economy

Economic periodic fluctuation reflects the changes in the macroeconomic climate, in which the recovery year can be compared to the "spring" of economy, the expansion and peak year to the "summer", the contraction or decline year to the "autumn" and the trough year to the "winter".

In the light of the previous analysis, 1996 will probably turn out to be the trough year of this round of the economic cycle. However, 1996 will be a warm "winter" of this economic cycle because the economic growth still is maintained at a relative high level, around 9 percent, and the overall macroeconomic environment and market situation are not fully deflated. Some consumer goods markets are steady and tend to be prosperous. For these reasons 1996 will be an extremely warm "winter". After entering the next round of cycle, if the economy presents a state of "slow-rise and slow-fall", there will appear a new "cool summer and warm winter". In line with the international experiences of large firms, we propose ten proactive measures under this circumstance.

### *Alternation and transformation from the "quantity-based" production and management modes to the "quality-based" and "service-oriented" modes*

The so-called "quantity-based" mode refers to the pure pursuit for an increase in quantity of products and neglect of the improvement of product quality, design of products and high quality of service.

Since the 1980s and 1990s, facing depressive a market and fierce competition, Western firms one after another have transformed from the "quantity-based" management style to the "quality-based" and "service-oriented" mode. Their experience is worth considering.

Harley-Davidson Motorcycle is a world-famous brand. The headquarters of Harley-Davidson Motorcycle is located in the state of Wisconsin in the United States. In the early 1980s, the company was verging on bankruptcy owing to failure in intense competition. Harley-Davidson rallied through improving its motorcycle quality on the one hand and introducing a range of other measures such as expanding service, creating "Harley Motorcycle Fans", publishing an exclusive Harley magazine, pushing out tailored garments for Harley motorcycles, holding social gatherings with beer and bands for Harley motorcyclists and organizing Harley motorcycle contests, on the other hand. As a result, sales increased impressively both home and abroad.

South Korean entrepreneurs hold that the survival and development of enterprises depend on the products market and the market scale rests with customers. Whether a firm is able to appeal to new customers and capture loyal customers ultimately relies on whether they can offer high-quality products and first-class service. It is the key point that firms provide timely and excellent service to customers so as to score a success in competition. South Korean enterprises not only adhere to the essential rule of "satisfying the customer", but also set a higher standard of "touching customer service". In summer, some manufacturers give out fans to customers free of charge to relieve the heat. In winter, attendants cheerfully serve a cup of hot drink for customers who arrive at the shop earlier than business hours. For those who buy big-ticket items, shops not only offer delivery service, but also take charge of installation and commissioning. If there is a fault with an article, shops will pay a visit to the customer's home to fix the problem shortly after receiving a telephone call.

### Setting up a four-season view of the economic cycle and being prepared to "subsidize shortfall with bumper harvest"

Since the external macroeconomic environment of firms and the market situations change like seasonal alteration, firms should prepare a cyclical view and advanced awareness of potential change. The "autumn and winter" should back up for the "spring and summer" and in the "spring and summer" we should make arrangements for the "autumn and winter".

In June 1995, we visited the world-renowned Simons company in Germany. Their experiences are worth studying. Simons divides their products into two categories. One is easily affected by economic cyclical fluctuation, accounting for 65 percent of the total products. The other is not affected by economic cyclical fluctuation, accounting for the remaining 35 percent. This reveals that two-thirds of their products are closely related to economic cyclical fluctuation. Based on this situation, they collaborated with the famous Munich Economic Institute and established the econometric model of prosperity analysis to track the variation of economic situations at all times. When a prosperous time is coming, they push sales of their products in a flourishing sales season and develop new products. When a recession is approaching, they accelerate technical progress, improve production efficiency including practicing strict economy, lowering costs and advancing product quality, push out new products in good time, and develop new markets. Senior executives and the director of the China division at Simons were enthusiastic in their "Desperate Measure" that competition is actually a contest of time and that firms should act faster and faster.

### Applying the latest technologies, focusing on the market demand and being flexible in production

The traditional production mode of Western firms is characterized by a massive quantity, single species, standardized and efficiency-centered production. Its most representative form is the assembly line. Nowadays, great changes in social demands have taken place with an increase of people's income and rapid progress of modern technology. People start to pursue diversification and individualization in individual lives. The traditional production mode becomes increasingly noncompetitive. Since the 1990s, the major Western economies have experienced recession and faced a global sluggish market. This made transformation of the traditional production mode inevitable. Manufacturing becomes increasingly flexible and automatically controlled – the automatic production line. Products with different models, specifications, designs and colors could be manufactured at the same time on the same production line. This new flexible manufacturing system originated with the Toyota Automobile Company in Japan and has been introduced to many firms in the countries like the United States, UK, Germany and South Korea.

The Timken Company in the United States, with a 96-year history, is world-renowned for its ball bearings. At the later stage of the economic recession and the early stage of economic recovery, the company acted to seek an effective way of dealing with and pulling through the next recession smoothly. In recent years, it set up two bearing factories with an application of high technology. What is remarkable about these two new factories is that they can alter products promptly according to different requirements of customers and different orders and manufacture any one product from more than 26000 categories of standard bearings at all times. In the past, only by producing hundreds of the same category of bearing could they make a profit. After applying high technology, small orders can bring profits for them, too. With this flexibility, they are able to switch to a new product whenever there is a new order and sell it immediately afterwards with almost no inventory. In this way they save a large amount of circulating funds and lowered the cost.

### *Employing competent people at a high salary*

The competition between firms is ultimately the contest of competent people, especially the competition among top talents. Possessing capable talents implies a leading status in the market race among firms. During the economic recession in the United States, some famous firms fired their general managers and did not hesitate to employ talented general managers at a high salary in order to deal with the crises and make a breakthrough.

Sears, Roebuck and Co., the world's largest and a century-old retail business, ranked among the 66 companies with assets of over US$1 billion in 1952. Nevertheless, under intense market competition, Sears's business has declined since 1983. In early 1992, the company faced enormous difficulties and had a heavy deficit. At this vital moment, the company director, Edward Brennan, with keen insight, invited Arthur Martinez, who was about to take up a position as the general manager of Borgne Retailer (literal translation), to act as the general manager of Sears with a total remuneration of US$9 million including salary, bonus and stock shares in three years. Mr. Martinez did not let down Brennan's trust after taking office and carried out a series of drastic reforms. Within only a few months, Sears was reborn and turned losses into profits after nearly ten years of consecutive deficit and decline. The company revitalized and retained the century-old reputation with stock appreciating repeatedly. According to the data of 50 worldwide largest retailers published by US Fortune magazine in 1993, Sears's assets reached up to US$90.8 billion, ranking first with a total annual profit of US$2.3 billion (ranking first as well), and a total annual sales of US$54.8 billion, ranking second. It had more than 400,000 employees. Sears's commercial network and centers spread throughout all US urban and rural areas and throughout Western Europe, North America and Latin America.

### Cutting down excess employees and reducing working hours

At the expansion stage, many foreign companies increase employment as production rises. When it is at the contraction stage, they cut down employees to reduce labor costs. This is a general approach to which Western entrepreneurs cope with economic recession. US firms not only dismissed a large amount of blue-collar workers, but also fired many white-collar staffs including senior and intermediate managers during this recession.

The practice of cutting down employees in Japanese firms includes impelling the old staffs to retire in advance, providing a large termination payment for voluntary retirees, training those under deposition and dispatching staffs to work in subsidiary corporations.

### Actively promoting the organizational and management reforms of enterprises

#### Merger and decomposition of enterprises

After the economic recession, some large US corporations merged so as to create a competitive edge. The most attractive merger to gain worldwide attention was when the Walt Disney Company purchased the American Broadcasting Company (ABC). Along with significant mergers, some giant enterprises sparked a flurry of decomposition or split ups as they suffered from their unwieldy size in competition. American Telephone and Telegraph Company (AT&T) is the pioneer of vertical integration management and divided the group into three parts to resume independent operation, which is regarded as a revolutionary business perception. International Business Machines Corporation (IBM), a world-renowned US company, encountered competition from small computer companies and fell into a morass in 1993. Confronting the new competitors, IBM took the measure of decomposition and split up the head office into several small "Big Blue" units. Its strategy was to create initiative and flexibility within each "Big Blue". The management and review of the small "Big Blue" units from the headquarters was limited to several important indicators such as the market share, new product development and investment efficiency. Time has shown that this move has enhanced IBM's vitality and made it more responsive to the market.

#### Remolding of administration and management

In the past, Western firms mostly adopted the pyramid-layered administrative mode in their organizational structure. This "vertical integration system" involves product development, production and after-sales service, all of which are segmented and react slowly to market variation. Currently, there has been a transformation from the "vertical integration system" to the "horizontal integration system". In some US enterprises, product development, production and after-sales service are unified and integrated into a "Cooperative Production Group". Such a group is called as the "Professional Management Team" among South Korean firms. Either the group or the team commits to the general manager at one end and is responsible for consumers at the other end. This shortens the product development and production cycle and reduces the gap between production and market. Chrysler Corporation, one of the three largest automobile companies in the United States, implemented the "horizontal integration system" in automobile technical development in 1992. Its professional panels included market investigation, sales, environmental protection, social development, international economic policy research and international cooperation. Benefiting from the new management mode, Chrysler almost shortened half the time for developing new automobile models at a significantly reduced cost.

*Involvement of employees in decision-making and management*

Weirton Steel Corporation is one of the world's leading steel producers. Since the late 1980s, its earnings were depressed. In order to extricate itself from this predicament, the company initiated the "Employee Ownership" by which employees participated in decision-making and management. As a result, its product costs were reduced prominently and profits increased. United Airlines transferred 35 percent of its stock shares to its employees for increasing employees' morale and sense of responsibility. This program helped the company resolve its financial difficulties.

### Reducing expenditures

Reducing expenditures and cutting down expenses are the measures referred to as the "Prompt Reaction" amongst Japanese firms when economic situations deteriorate. The measures consist of decreasing the salary or bonus of corporate leaders, cutting down the entertainment allowance, travel expense and conference expense, and saving water, electricity and paper. Toyota Motor Corporation distributed the catalogue *Selections of Reducing Expenses* to its employees instructing them how to exercise savings in everyday work.

### Vigorously developing multiple products tied up with original business

The ratio of non-household electrical appliances of Panasonic Corporation rose from 19 percent in 1978 to 55 percent in 1988 in its total electrical products, accounting for more than half of the total. Panasonic expanded to seven new fields like sound-tape and videotape, radio semiconductor, industry automation, office automation, car micro-electronics and air conditioning. Among 1993's 500 global large industrial firms, Nippon Steel & Sumitomo Metal Corporation in Japan ranked 45th in sales. It planned that its output value of iron and steel would account for 50 percent and that the output value of other products would amount to 50 percent in 1995. The other products consist of the five new domains such as products for daily life, products for social development, electronic products, communication and IT products and products of advanced materials.

### Contracting business

During the economic expansion, one after another Japanese firms took part in other businesses irrelevant to their own. For example, some feed firms invested in tourist resorts such as holiday villages. When the economy becomes deflated, many firms resolutely withdraw from other businesses and bring funds back to avoid further losses while concentrating their funding, manpower and material on their own advantageous products in order to keep their own domains.

### Focusing on marketing

*Advertisement – the trumpeter in the commercial war*

In the market economy, advertisement is a significant competitive device for firms to explore and capture markets and promote sales, for which it has been called the trumpeter in market competition. The 1950s and the 1960s were the golden age of advertising development in the United States after World War II. The total annual advertising expense in the United States exceeded US$100 billion since the mid-1980s. In 1989, the proportion of advertising expenditure in the GNP accounted for 2.4 percent in the United States, 1.3 percent in Japan and 0.14 percent in China.

*Promoting new products with great fanfare in various approaches*

In the 1980, Sony Corporation in Japan developed a new product – the Walkman, a small portable CD player. It is enormously popular across the world in today. However, consumers knew little about it when it was first manufactured. In order to create inroads into the US market, Sony decided not to advertise the product using old methods. Instead, it turned to a US public relations company, Gilze Limited Co (literal translation). This company launched Walkman through a range of large-scale activities. They broadly advertised introductory articles about Walkman in first-class magazines and newspapers throughout the United States, illustrating its unique functions. As it was approaching Christmas, they took this opportunity to roll out Walkman as the best Christmas present. Mannequins in the showcase of large department stores wore Walkmans. In addition, a silent disco contest was held in high-ranking clubs, during which every contestant wore a Walkman and danced with the music played by the Walkman. Moreover, during a subway strike in New York, subway drivers and citizens wearing Walkmans gathered in the street. People watched the scene on TV as there was a real-time report on the subway strike in TV news. Last, Johnny Carson, a US famous humorist, performed in an evening TV program in his prime time slot with a Walkman in hand. Soon after this grand-scaled promotion, 500,000 Walkmans were sold out. The US market was opened up with one stroke.

*Concessional sales*

US firms initiate various concessional sales enabling their products to hit the market. The traditional method is usually to cut prices down on the occasions of festivals and anniversaries, which are advertised in various newspapers. In Boston's shopping mall, Favrini sold clothing at different prices cut-down automatically according to manufacturing dates. For example, if today was September 1, the price label marked 25 percent off for clothing produced before August 1 and 50 percent off for clothing produced before July 1. This would effectively accelerate commodity circulation and sales. There is another new approach. Stores give out a discount voucher to customers. Purchasers buy designated goods such as toothpaste and perfumed soap with the voucher. Then they send the receipts to the manufacturer and get refunded. This approach is beneficial for all – the manufacturer, seller and purchaser. Manufacturers can make use of the time gap between selling and refunding to speed up production so as to decrease debts and interest expenditures. Stores are able to attract more customers by giving out vouchers, thus enhancing their popularity. Purchasers are delighted to buy goods with a refund. However, some customers in fact would not go for the refund as it is troublesome. In this way, manufacturers would be more profitable.

*Prolonging business hours*

Nissan Motor Co. Ltd in Japan, which ranked 12th according to sales volume among 1993's 500 global large industrial companies, decided that all retail stores would be open on Saturday and Sunday during this economic recession. The head office would dispatch personnel to carry through supervision and inspection.

[Originally published in *Study and Practice (Xuexi Yu Shijian)*, No.2, 1996]

# 3 New perspectives on initiating Chinese economy

## Current issues on initiating Chinese economy

Since the beginning of 1998, the central government has adopted various measures to expand the domestic demand (mainly referring to investment) and stimulate the economy to achieve the target of 8 percent economic growth. However, the anticipated effects may not be perfect in terms of the stimulation paths. The main issues are discussed below.

### *Limitation of initiating an individual industry*

The current economic stimulation relies mainly on investment, which focuses on public infrastructure and urban residential housing.

Generally speaking, the development of urban residential housing is able to drive the progression of more than 50 relevant industries, including building materials, further encouraging economic growth as a whole. Nevertheless, it is difficult for China's housing industry to bear that responsibility, because innovation of the original welfare housing allocation system is an indispensable condition, not a sufficient condition to housing commercialization. The sufficient condition is the improvement of residents' income. Only with a relatively high level of income, can residents afford housing without affecting their general consumption expenditure. However, the current wage structure and wage level in China can hardly support housing commercialization and sustain the housing industry as the pillar industry. If residents compress their normal consumption expenditure and squeeze their original purchasing power (savings) to a great extent to buy houses (their savings are far from enough to buy houses, and support from the savings of children, relatives and friends is needed), the general consumption demand will inevitably fall, further aggravating the weakness of the general consumption market (including general consumer goods and service consumption). Household consumption is the origin and end point of the whole social production and investment. If the flaccid situation of the consumption market lasts for a long time, social production and investment will lose their starting point and end point and the economic growth as a whole will not have adequate consumption market space. Reliance only on the housing industry cannot drive overall economic growth. Moreover, if the whole nation marches towards the same economic growth point, will there be a tide of swarming mass consumption? The housing industry is a special industry, as houses are peculiar consumer goods. When housing is over-demanded, there will be bubbles. As the bubbles break, they will lead to the supply exceeding the demand at a high price level.

As far as public infrastructure is concerned, the infrastructure construction is far from sufficient in terms of the whole nation. However, in some regions, some infrastructures, like highways, railways and airports, which were built several years ago, have not yet fulfilled their anticipated roles. New highways have very few vehicles running on them. Railways have been constructed, yet the economic development of the surroundings is hard to follow up. Airports have been built but have very few passengers. The low level of efficiency of the constructed infrastructure influences the initiative of building new projects. With the slow progress of new infrastructure construction, around 40 percent of which transforms into consumption, it is difficult to stimulate the current flaccid consumption market. The stimulation of the economy by the public infrastructure industry mainly comes from government behavior. In view of the these circumstances, a situation will appear in which the government engages in infrastructure construction with enthusiasm and the infrastructure utilization and consumption markets respond passionlessly.

### *Limitation of initiating the economy only by investment*

The stimulation of the economy should rely on stimulating both investment and consumption in terms of domestic demand. However, it is hard to initiate consumption considering the current situation in China. The traditional approach of raising wages is impracticable. It is difficult to raise the salary of those staff members who stay in their post, as a large amount of employees are being laid off. In view of the previous analysis of infrastructure and residential housing construction, it is hard to achieve an effect in the short term by relying on transforming partial investment into consumption. In addition, under the current residents' income level, no one can afford a consumption loan, and banks dare not grant loans. If consumption loans are extended to those minorities who have already obtained a high-income level, the income distribution gap will be further enlarged, leading to unfairness. Therefore, currently it is difficult to implement consumption loans in China. Besides, it is hard to develop the vast rural market with no further improvement of the peasants' income. In brief, it is difficult to initiate the whole economy by relying only on investment if consumption cannot be stimulated.

### *Four significant changes in the environment in comparison with all the previous initiations*

The first is the change in the market environment. The formation of a buyer's market helped China bid farewell to the long-standing phenomenon of short supply. But we should remember that it formed under the following circumstances. The GDP per capita in China has not yet exceeded US$1000, which signifies that China is still a low-income country. The current and anticipated residents' income growth represents a downward trend. The general consumer goods market with the current residents' income level and consumption level tends to become saturated episodically. There was indiscriminate investment and repetitive construction in the previous period of rapid economic growth, with the variation of the supply structure proving to be incompatible with that of the demand structure. Consequently, the buyer's market plays a restraining role in the demand, production and investment of general consumer goods and even in the economic growth as a whole.

The second is the change in the system environment. Profound and significant changes have taken place in the systems of economic growth, which are mainly reflected in two aspects. Enterprises transform their operation mechanism and gradually become independent decision makers, but their production and investment decisions are market-oriented and restricted by the market. Commercial banks transform their operation mechanism, in which their loan decisions are market-oriented and conditioned by the market as well. These changes play an active role in curbing the investment hunger and blind expansion impetus that existed under the old system. However, there is much to be undertaken for enterprises and commercial banks to foster entrepreneurs' and bankers' mentalities of pressing forward in the face of risk, cultivate an innovative consciousness and establish a corresponding incentive mechanism while adapting to the new environment of the market economy and setting up risk evasion awareness.

The third is the change in the employment environment. China is currently facing a huge employment pressure that it has never encountered before. There is a great contradiction involved in solving the large-scale employment problems and the transference of rural labor and meanwhile preventing the economy from overheating.

The fourth is the change in the international environment. For this economic initiation, foreign demand is not taken into account; we rely mainly on domestic demand.

Stated simply, we need to change the way of thinking and take action to stimulate the economy, neither expecting the process to be finished within one year nor merely relying on initiating an individual industry and investment.

## New perspectives on initiating the economy

The general thought on initiating the economy is to look for a new economically growing region instead of a new economically growing industry to gradually promote nationwide economic development and combine the industrial development with the regional economic development. For example, taking the Yangtze River basin as a new economically increasing region and focusing on its regulation and development will promote the development of new economically growing industries and drive the cross-century economic growth in China. The reasons are as follows.

1   From the early 1980s to the 1990s, rapid nationwide economic growth in China was realized mainly through regional development and combining industrial development with regional economic development.

Since the reform and opening up, the high-speed economic growth in China has been driven by four special economic zones (Shenzhen, Zhuhai, Shantou and Xiamen) along the east coast and five provinces (Guangdong, Fujian, Jiangsu, Zhejiang and Shandong) together with Hainan and Shanghai, which were added subsequently. Comrade Deng Xiaoping explicitly pointed out in his South Tour Talk that "looking backwards, one of my big errors in establishing four special economic zones was that I did not add Shanghai into it, otherwise the Yangtze River delta, the Yangtze River basin and even the nationwide economic reform situation would be different now". Deng Xiaoping predicted at that time that after exploiting the coastal special zones, provinces and Shanghai, the specific development route from the coastal regions to the inland areas would take Shanghai as the leading region, then the economy of the Yangtze River basin and the whole nation will be driven. At present, economic initiation is just a good opportunity to implement the strategic assumption of Deng Xiaoping. China is a country with a vast territory and a natural advantage, which some East Asian countries do not have, of being able to develop the economy from the east part to the west part and connect the eastern, central and Western parts by means of river basins. During the rapid economic growth from the 1980s to the 1990s, the government did not call on or induce residents to buy household electrical appliances, like color TVs, refrigerators and washing machines. However, the household electrical appliances industry naturally became the new economic growth point with the development of the eastern coastal areas and the improvement of residents' income level nationwide.

2   Taking the Yangtze River basin as the new economic growth region to initiate the nationwide economy, we are able to achieve the following combinations organically.

    1   A combination of short-term initiation and long-term development. This is a huge and complicated systematic project to regulate and exploit the Yangtze River basin. Based on the existing development program and construction basis, we can start with public infrastructure construction, the construction of small and medium towns along the Yangtze River and the regulation of the river and the two river banks (taking the European Rhine River and Danube River as models) and selectively carry out the exploitation following the pattern from easy ones to difficult ones within three years. At present, this will play a role in initiating the nationwide economy and will be connected with the promotion of cross-century (around ten years) economic growth in China.

    2   A combination of investment initiation and consumption initiation. In the first group of medium and small towns (not large cities) in the regulation and exploitation regions along the river, we will take the lead in implementing wage structure reform and ensuring a reasonable proportion between the salary income and the purchasing of housing and cars. Meanwhile, the execution of consumption loans for housing and cars will drive the development of the housing industry and the automobile industry. This may not be practicable nationwide, but can be started in

the local region of the Yangtze River basin, which will be both promptly effective and demonstrative to other regions.

3   A combination of solving the massive employment problem and initiating the economy. By employing a market mechanism, attracting laid-off employees and workers to participate in the regulation and exploiting the Yangtze River basin will help to solve the employment problems on a large scale.

4   A combination of initiating an individual industry and a region. The driving scope and strength of the Yangtze River basin as the new economic growth region far exceed those of the housing industry and public infrastructure.

5   A combination of the governmental leading role and the role of a market mechanism. In the regulation of the Yangtze River basin and the development zones, we would be the first to carry out various economic system reforms and implement the new system completely. This will be propitious in giving play to both the governmental leading role and the role of a market mechanism.

6   A combination of state-owned and private-owned capital and domestic and foreign capital. Massive investment capital can be raised in various ways to promote the growth and development of the capital market in China.

7   A combination of general technology and high technique. The exploitation of the Yangtze River basin is conducive to promoting both high technique development and gradual transference of general technology from the east to the west.

8   A combination of construction and environmental protection. We will transform the Yangtze River Basin into a large and beautiful tourism area.

[Originally published in *Brief Report of Chinese Academy of Social Sciences (ZhongguoShehuiKexueyuanYaobao),* No.162, July, 1998]

# 4 On new trends in economic growth and fluctuation in China

## Comparison of economic fluctuation in China before and after reform

Periodic economic fluctuation is neither a phenomenon initiated by human society nor a special category of a commodity economy or a unique feature of capitalist economies. As pointed out by Marx, this "peculiar course of modern industry, which occurs in no earlier period of human history, was also impossible in the childhood of capitalist production" (2001).[1] In terms of the general commodity economy, the antithesis of sales and purchase in terms of time and place, namely the disjunction between supply and demand, merely implies the possibility of periodic economic crisis or fluctuation. "The conversion of this mere possibility into a reality is the result of a long series of relations that, from our present standpoint of simple circulation, have as yet no existence" (Marx, 1867/2001).[2] In "a long series of relations" that induces periodic economic fluctuation to convert from possibility into reality, modern mechanical industry, which is physical and original, has gradually become the dominant force in social production. It makes the production scale expand and contract greatly in a sudden leaping pattern. This does not happen in societies in which agriculture, animal husbandry and workshop handicraft industries predominate as their production expansion and technical progress are rather slow. Animal husbandry especially, with its long production cycle and being easily affected by natural conditions to a great extent, is unlikely to expand and contract extensively with a sudden leap within a short period of time like industrial machinery production. Modern periodic economic fluctuation is generated on the basis of such industrial production. Without doubt, a series of internal factors, such as the economic system, scale of total supply and demand, productivity development level and industrial structure, as well as a train of external impacts, such as government macro regulating policy, significant scientific and technological progress, world economic upheaval and severe natural disasters, will exercise influences on periodic economic fluctuations, giving them different characteristics at different stages. Just as Samuelson, the famous US economist, pointed out, "no two economic cycles are quite the same. When economic cycles are not identical twins, they often have a family similarity" (2004, p. 468).[3]

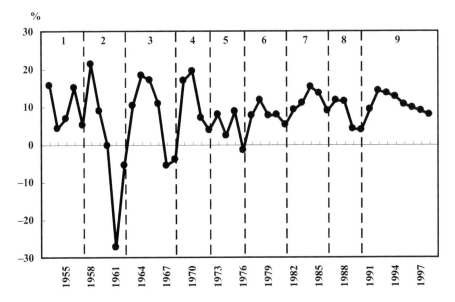

*Figure 4.1* Nine rounds of fluctuations of economic growth rate in China (1953–98)
Note. From previous years' *China Statistical Yearbook.*

National economic restoration in China was completed in the early 1950s. Since 1953, the new China started massive economic construction and entered into the industrialization process, which started what Marx called the "peculiar course of modern industry", with reciprocal alternating operations of social production expansion and contraction. The economic fluctuation in China, represented by the gross domestic product (GDP) growth rate, saw altogether nine rounds (see Figure 4.1 and Table 4.1) over 46 years from 1953 to 1998 according to the division method of "trough to trough". The first round was from 1953 to 1957, lasting five years; the second round 1958–1962, again over five years; the third round 1963–1968, six years; the fourth round 1969–1972, four years; the fifth round 1973–1976, four years; the sixth round 1977–1981, five years; the seventh round 1981–1986, five years; the eighth round 1987–1990, four years; the ninth round 1991–1998, eight years. (The first and fifth rounds implied two small fluctuations. The investigation of this article is cut off in 1998 as we have not gone through 1999.)

The average length of each round of fluctuation is 4.75 years from the first round to the eighth round, whereas the ninth round is eight years. Setting aside this issue for a moment, we turn to investigation of the characteristics of economic fluctuations presented in China before and after the reform, taking 1978 as the dividing line (see Figure 2). These are mainly reflected in the following four aspects:

*Table 4.1* Economic growth and fluctuation in China

| Serial No of Fluctuation | Year | GDP growth rate (%) | Serial No of Fluctuation | Year | GDP growth rate (%) |
|---|---|---|---|---|---|
|   | 1953 | 15.6 |   | 1977 | 7.6 |
|   | 1954 | 4.2 |   | 1978 | 11.7 |
| 1 | 1955 | 6.8 | 6 | 1979 | 7.6 |
|   | 1956 | 15.0 |   | 1980 | 7.8 |
|   | 1957 | 5.1 |   | 1981 | 5.2 |
|   | 1958 | 21.3 |   | 1982 | 9.1 |
|   | 1959 | 8.8 |   | 1983 | 10.9 |
| 2 | 1960 | −0.3 | 7 | 1984 | 15.2 |
|   | 1961 | −27.3 |   | 1985 | 13.5 |
|   | 1962 | −5.6 |   | 1986 | 8.8 |
|   | 1963 | 10.2 |   | 1987 | 11.6 |
|   | 1964 | 18.3 | 8 | 1988 | 11.3 |
| 3 | 1965 | 17.0 |   | 1989 | 4.1 |
|   | 1966 | 10.7 |   | 1990 | 3.8 |
|   | 1967 | −5.7 |   | 1991 | 9.2 |
|   | 1968 | −4.1 |   | 1992 | 14.2 |
|   | 1969 | 16.9 |   | 1993 | 13.5 |
| 4 | 1970 | 19.4 |   | 1994 | 12.6 |
|   | 1971 | 7.0 | 9 | 1995 | 10.5 |
|   | 1972 | 3.8 |   | 1996 | 9.6 |
|   | 1973 | 7.9 |   | 1997 | 8.8 |
| 5 | 1974 | 2.3 |   | 1998 | 7.8 |
|   | 1975 | 8.7 |   |   |   |
|   | 1976 | −1.6 |   |   |   |

## Peak Position

This refers to the economic growth rate of the peak year in each round of fluctuation, signifying the fluctuation altitude or the strength of economic expansion. However, an over-the-top peak position and over-intense expansion will be apt to result in a subsequent overly deep trough. An overly low peak position with feeble expansion illustrates slow economic growth. Thus, it is good to have a moderate peak position in each round of fluctuation. Before the reform, there were 5.5 rounds of fluctuations, in which the average peak position, namely the average economic growth rate of various peak years (1956, 1958, 1964, 1970, 1975, 1978), was 15.7 percent (see the top horizontal dotted line in Figure 4.2). After the reform, there were 3.5 rounds of fluctuations, in which the average peak position (1984, 1987, 1992) was 13.7%, percent, 2 percent lower than that before the reform, demonstrating that the economic growth in China after the reform reduced the blindness of expansion to some extent.

## Trough position

This refers to the economic growth rate of the trough year in each round of fluctuation, indicating the fluctuation depth or the degree of economic contraction.

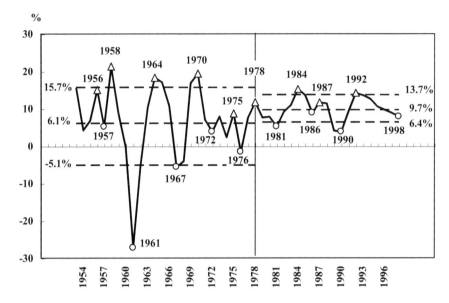

*Figure 4.2* Fluctuation curve of the economic growth rate in China (1953–98)

The status of the trough position is also termed the nature of fluctuation. When the trough position is negative, namely the economic growth rate of trough years is negative, GDP declines absolutely. This is called classical fluctuation. In the case that the trough position is positive, namely the economic growth rate of trough years is positive, this is called growing fluctuation. The fluctuations before the reform were mainly classical, whereas they transformed to the growing type after the reform. The average trough position before the reform, namely the average economic growth rate of the various trough years (1957, 1961, 1967, 1972, 1976), was −5.1 percent (see the bottom horizontal dotted line in Figure 4.2). After the reform, the average trough position (1981, 1986, 1990, 1998) was 6.4 percent, an increase of 11.5 percent compared to that before the reform. The distinct elevation of the trough position illustrates that the anti-recession power of China's economy has been enhanced.

## Mean level

This refers to the average economic growth rate each year in each round of fluctuation, manifesting the aggregate economic growth level. From 1953 to 1978, the average growth rate of GDP was 6.1% (see the middle horizontal dotted line in Figure 4.2). From 1979 to 1998, it was 9.7 percent, 3.6 percent higher than that before the reform, illustrating that the overall economic growth level in China has greatly improved.

## Amplitude

This refers to the fluctuating margin of the economic growth rate in each round of fluctuation, demonstrating the intensity of rise and fall. The amplitude can be divided into amplitude in the rising period and that in the falling stage. The former refers to the deviation between the previous trough and current peak. The latter refers to the deviation between the current peak and current trough. Before the reform, the average amplitude in the rising period was 19.3 percent, whereas it was 7.7 percent after the reform, showing a reduction of 11.6 percent. The amplitude in the falling stage before the reform was 21.7 percent, down to 6.8 percent after the reform, a decrease of 14.9 percent. The obvious diminution of amplitude signifies that economic growth in China has become more stable.

## The ninth round fluctuation: overlap and concurrence of three transitional periods

Let us turn to the ninth round fluctuation, which lasted eight years, longer than the previous eight rounds. The length of the falling phase of the economic growth rate extended to six years from the average of 2.5 years in the past. In this round of fluctuation, the rising stage was from 1991 to 1992 and the falling phase was from 1993 to 1998, during which economic operation in China successfully achieved a "soft landing" (Liu Guoguang, & Liu Shucheng, 1997)[4] from 1993 to 1996. Subsequently, economic growth and fluctuation in China presented new features. The economy maintained rapid growth against the background of the Asian financial crisis and international financial turmoil. China did not experience severe negative growth like some other Asian countries; nor indeed did China recommit the same error of the violent ups and downs common to all previous fluctuations. Although the economic growth rate was at a high rate (greater than 7 percent), it had been declining for several consecutive years.

The reason why the economic growth rate fell continuously or found it difficult to recover after the "soft landing" is that a series of new circumstances and issues emerged in economic operation in the preceding years. In addition to the international influences of international financial turmoil and worldwide economic structural adjustment, domestically we are facing the overlap and concurrence of three periods – the deepening stage of system transition, an adjustment phase after long-term high-speed growth and a transformation period from all-around shortage to a conditional buyer market. In other words, it is the overlap and concurrence of three transformational periods in terms of the background system, growth trend and market environment.

### *Deepening stage of economic system transition*

The upward and downward turns in economic fluctuation, namely when it is initiated and brakes, are asymmetric. In the original planned economic system and at the beginning of system transition, it was easy to start up but difficult to brake, whereas it was just the opposite as the reform of the economic system deepened substantively and the market mechanism was increasingly enhanced.

Softened financial constraints constituted the cause of the easy initiation and difficult braking of economic fluctuation in the original planned economic system and at the beginning of system transition. Before and at the beginning of the economic system reform, investment was state finance-based with the free utilization of budgetary funds. After preliminary reforms in the middle of the 1980s, state-owned enterprises introduced a system by which government appropriations are replaced by loans in fixed-assets investment and implemented full credit in circulating funds. Thus, investment turned to a bank-based model. However, bank capital was used with only nominal compensation. In reality, it was not necessary to pay it back. Thus, banks took on the role of quasi-finance. Investment diverted from the former "state finance common rice wok" to the "banking common rice wok". In this way, when the economy needs to be triggered, various regions, sectors and state-owned enterprises fall over each other to compete for bank capital, as long as it is loosened, leading to immediate economic start-up. But when the economy is asked to slow down, they are unwilling to stop for fear of suffering losses. The overall high-speed economic expansion then has to brake sharply until it is difficult to continue. In other words, the capital sluice gate was easy to open but difficult to shut in the original system. In terms of all previous economic initiations since the founding of new China, the economic growth rate leaped upwards greatly at the beginning of each start-up. From 1954 to 1992, there were 17 years (see Table 4.1) in which economic growth rate increased, of which there was a rise slightly below 3 percent in four years, accounting for 24 percent of the total number of years with a rising economic growth rate. There were as many as 13 years (76 percent of the total) that saw an increase of 3 percent or above and nine years (53 percent of the total) in which there were significant rises of 5 percent or above. This generated an investment famine phenomenon, the impetus for blind expansion and violent ups and downs in economic fluctuation.

Haberler, the famous US scholar who studied the economic fluctuation issue, indicated the asymmetric feature under a market economy and argued that economic fluctuation was easy to brake but difficult to start up with the market mechanism increasingly enhanced. He pointed out,

> an expansion can always be stopped and a contraction process started by a restriction of credit by the banks. A contraction, however, cannot always be ended promptly merely by making credit cheap and plentiful. There is thus a certain asymmetry between the upper and the lower turning-points which necessitates some departures in the method of exposition from that adopted in the corresponding section on the down-turn.
>
> (Haberler, 2011, p. 378)

Hardened capital constraints become the reason for the easy braking and difficult initiation of economic fluctuation while the market mechanism functions. Loans must be paid back and investment profit must be considered. When economic fluctuation is in the trough stage, investment prospects are not bright. No matter whether banks or enterprises are concerned, all will play safe in lending and borrowing money. But when economic expansion is required to brake, they all fear suffering losses owing to a delayed braking. This suggests that the capital sluice gate is easy to shut but difficult to open under the market mechanism.

In terms of the current situation in China, during the process of "soft landing" or after a "soft landing", the financial marketization reform, especially heeding the warning of the Asian financial crisis, is accelerating and transforming softened capital constraints to hardened capital constraints. It can remove the system foundations of long-term investment famine and the impetus for blind expansion and restrain violent ups and downs of economic fluctuation, but it gives rise to lack of adaptability in certain respects. From the perspective of enterprises, they are accustomed to the "common rice wok", whether financed by the state or banks, and are unable to adapt to the hard constraint at the moment that loans must be paid back. State-owned enterprises are heavily burdened with historic debts and unable to go forward without them. The motivation mechanism corresponding to economic benefit and risk liability has not been established. Enterprises, as individual investment entities, lack experience and this, together with the consecutive decline in the economic growth rate and deflation, leading to the lack of good investment prospects, means that they are not inclined to borrow money from banks. From the perspective of banks, they have become used to the role of cashier, without responsibility for profit or loss, and have not yet gained the capability of actively searching for investment projects on their own initiative and judging investment profit. They are still heavily laden with bad debts. The incentive mechanism related to economic efficiency and risk responsibility has not been set up. Banks, as commercial management bodies, also lack sufficient experiences and this, together with poor investment prospects, means that they are not apt to lend money. From the perspective of the capital market, it is still developing and far from maturity. Direct financial sources are very limited.

Integrating the above analysis with the existing characteristic of asymmetry in that economic fluctuation is easy to brake but difficult to start up under the market mechanism, together with the capital constraint just starting to harden in China, the economic stimulation after the "soft landing" is the first such occasion under the condition of marketization reform, especially under the substantively deepened reform in finance setting against the background of the overall immature market mechanism. This needs a process of adaptation and perfection in various respects. In this case, the economic stimulation is even more difficult. As a result, we can draw the implication for policy enlightenment that stimulating the economy merely by relying on reducing the interest rate and releasing the supply of money or on finance will not work effectively in the current system in China. To ensure that the economy increases steadily, we must promote microcosmic subjects to become more mature, something that the socialist market economy requires, and especially activate the initiatives of social and private investments and small and medium enterprises' investments through further deepening the reforms of state-owned enterprises and the financial system.

### Adjustment phase after long-term high-speed growth

During the 26 years from 1953 to 1978 before the reform, the average annual growth rate of GDP in China was 6.1 percent. Within the 12 years from 1979 to 1990 after the reform, it was up to 9 percent. From 1991 to 1995, which was before the "soft landing" succeeded, namely during the Eighth Five-Year Plan, it was even as high as 12 percent. In the 20 years from 1979 to 1998, it was 9.7 percent.

Since the reform and opening-up policy, with the long-term high-speed economic growth in China, it is inevitable that an imbalance will be gradually accumulated in certain economic structures, of which the most important is the imbalance in the final use structure of aggregate social product, namely the imbalance between accumulation and consumption.

The final use structure of aggregate social product refers primarily to the respective proportion of capital formation and final consumption in GDP, namely the proportional relationship between the capital formation rate and the final consumption rate. This is the most fundamental and comprehensive proportional relationship that determines whether social reproduction is able to operate smoothly and is a more basic structural issue at a higher level in comparison to other structural issues (for example industrial and product structures from the supply side and consumption and investment structures from the demand side) (Further Initiation, 1999; On How to Further Stimulate Economy, 1999).[5] When the investment benefit is fixed, long-term and high-speed economic growth necessarily depends on a high capital formation rate and a corresponding low final consumption rate. If the capital formation rate is over the top and the final consumption rate is overly low, this will cause an imbalance in the final use structure of aggregate social product, leading to a limited consumption market and further inducing investment to lose its objective. Social reproduction as a whole is unable to run normally.

Figure 4.3 provides three curves showing the final consumption rate, the capital formation rate and the net export and error rate from 1952 to 1996, calculated according to the constant price of 1952 in China. As shown in the figure, the final consumption rate presents a downward trend from 1981 to 1996, with 1981 being 61.2 percent and 1996 declining to 51.4 percent, a reduction of 9.8 percent. It is necessary to explain that absolute final consumption is constantly increasing in relation to long-term high-speed growth. What we would mention here is that its relative proportion in GDP is reduced. Correspondingly, the average capital formation rate from 1981 to 1996 was up to 41 percent and even reached as high as 42 percent in 1993, 43 percent in 1994 and 45 percent in 1995. Figures 4.4 and 4.5 present the curves of the aggregate consumption rate (including the statistical error rate) and the domestic gross investment rate of China, South Korea, Thailand and Japan from 1962 to 1996, drawn from the data of the World Bank. Looking at China's neighboring countries, the aggregate consumption rate of South Korea and Thailand presents a long-term downward tendency, while their gross investment rate takes on a long-range upward trend. This illustrates that China, like South Korea and Thailand, has adopted a growth pattern of a "high investment rate and low consumption rate". However, the aggregate consumption rate of South Korea gradually took on an upward trend after it declined to 61 percent in 1988. The aggregate consumption rate of Thailand also maintained a steady state after it reduced to 64 percent in 1991. In China, the aggregate consumption rate decreased to 56 percent in 1996, which was extremely low, not just in Asia, but in the world. According to the data of the relevant countries provided by the World Bank, the country with the lowest aggregate consumption rate in 1996 was Singapore with 49.5 percent. China was slightly higher than Singapore, but lower than Malaysia (58.1 percent), Thailand (64.7 percent), South Korea (65.8 percent)

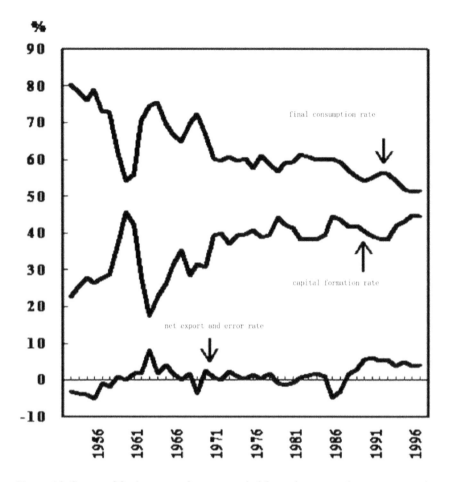

*Figure 4.3* Curves of final consumption rate, capital formation rate and net export rate in China

Note. Calculated according to constant price of 1952 and employed the final consumption index and gross capital formation index. The indices originate from the *Historical Data of GDP Accounting in China* edited by the National Economic Accounting Department of the State Statistics Bureau, Northeast University of Finance & Economics Press, 1997.

and Indonesia (66.8 percent).A growth trend of a "high investment rate and low consumption rate" emerged in Japan from 1965 to 1970, during which period the domestic gross investment rate increased from 31.88 percent to 39.02 percent and the aggregate consumption rate declined from 66.72 percent to 59.7 percent. Subsequently, its domestic gross investment rate appeared to take a downward trend and aggregate consumption rate took on an upward tendency.

There is an adjustment process to regain the normal proportional relationship of the final use of aggregate social product during which the speed of economic

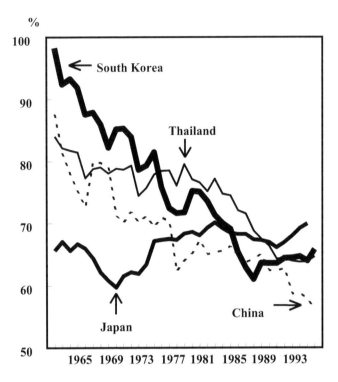

*Figure 4.4* Aggregate consumption rate of various countries

Note. From China Economic Information Network.

growth will temporarily reduce, but will lay a good foundation for future steady development. It is necessary to improve the investment benefit, control and reduce the capital formation rate (please note: it is not to reduce absolute investment), raise the final consumption rate so as to develop the domestic consumption market and create space for investment revival. Thus, we can draw the policy implication that in order to raise the final consumption rate, we should improve the income level of urban medium- and low-income people and farmers' disposable income from the income end and establish as soon as possible a social security system that favors the reduction of residents' expenditure anticipation to activate current savings from the expenditure side.

### Transformation period from all-around shortage to a conditional buyer market

The long-term high-speed economic growth in China since the reform and opening-up policy necessarily enhanced the comprehensive national strength greatly and basically changed the long existing commodity shortage of the past. It is

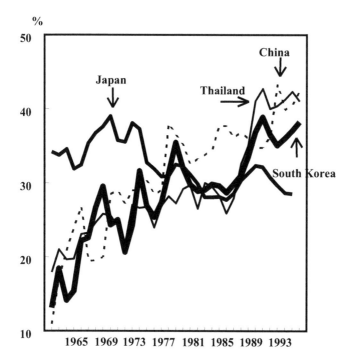

*Figure 4.5* Domestic gross investment rate of various countries
Note. From China Economic Information Network.

fundamentally and historically significant that the buyer market emerges with conditional structural and regional supply exceeding demand.

The so-called conditional supply exceeding demand refers to the buyer market at the low-income end, with GDP per capita of around US$800 in China, identical to the low-income level in the world. The current supply exceeding demand relates to the general consumption of food, clothing and daily necessities episodically reaching saturation level in terms of the current and anticipated income level and expenditure level. It emerges in the trough phase of economic fluctuation.

The so-called structural supply exceeding demand is caused by the production capacity surplus generated from blind investment and repeated construction during high-speed growth. The structural variation in supply neither adapts to the structural variation in demand in the upgrading process from low-grade to high-grade foods, clothes and daily necessities, from food, clothes and daily necessities to dwelling and transportation, from commodity consumption to service consumption and from general products to products of high quality, multiple varieties, high tech and high added value, nor meets the needs of fierce market competition. Thus, the structural supply exceeding demand is far from reaching the overall supply exceeding demand.

The so-called regional supply exceeding demand relates to the saturation phenomenon of urban consumption of general consumer goods. The rural demands for these goods have not been satisfied owing to the constraints on farmers' income and limitations from supply and service aspects.

The formation of the conditional buyer market has made economic stimulation quite difficult. On the one hand, the economic growth speed is not as high as that under severe shortages in the past. On the other hand, the economic growth pattern is required to transform from quantity-based expansion to quality-based and benefit-based improvement. Hence, we derive the policy implication that we must rely on technical advancement and knowledge innovation and promote the adjustment and upgrading of industrial structure and product structure with the aim of making a breakthrough in supply. Meanwhile, developing the tertiary industry vigorously is an important approach to promote economic growth and solve the issue of social employment when residents' income is constantly increasing, yet not reaching a higher and more prosperous level.

## Future economic growth and fluctuation trends in China

As remarked earlier, a series of profound and significant changes have taken place in the domestic and international environment of economic operations in recent years in China. However, we should not forget that some long-term and significant factors have not fundamentally been changed.

1   Basic development factor. Currently, GDP per capita is still very low in China, one of the low-income countries in the world. Economic development is still confined to the process of industrialization and modernization.
2   Urban and rural dualistic structure and employment factors. At present industrialization is advancing rapidly, whereas urbanization is rather slow, with a large amount of the labor force still remaining in the countryside. The contradiction in the urban and rural dualistic structure is becoming prominent. The transfer of a large amount of the rural labor force and the increment of urban laid-off staff brings not only pressure but also impetus to economic growth.
3   The territory factor. China has a vast territory with a huge and potential domestic market, providing a wide space for the gradual process of the industrial structure.

These three factors induced China's economy to maintain rapid growth at the beginning of the twenty-first century. We must persist in the fundamental guiding ideology of "development is the absolute principle" that Deng Xiaoping put forward (*Selected Works of Deng Xiaoping,* 1994)[6] to promote development through reform and make adjustments and overcome various difficulties during the process.

Under the general premise of development, the fluctuation in the economic growth rate in China may appear as a new trend of changing from acuteness to smoothness in the next few years, namely "slow rise and slow fall", "long-term rise and short-term fall". In the previous eight fluctuations from 1953 to 1990, the fluctuation trajectories, on the whole, are manifested as "violent ups and downs" and "short-term rise and short-term fall". Violent ups and downs refer to the fluctuations in amplitude, with a high peak position and a low trough position. The two trough positions in 1981 and 1990 after the reform were as low as 5.2 percent and 3.8 percent, respectively. Short-term rise and short-term fall relate to the fluctuation in time, with both a short rising period and a short falling period. In the ninth round of fluctuation from 1991 to 1998, new changes emerged. The past violent ups and downs changed to "violent ups and slow fall" with a high peak position and a higher trough position. The past short-term rise and short-term fall has turned into a "short-term rise and long-term fall", with a short rising period and a long falling period. Summarizing China's historical experiences and lessons – and drawing on those from other countries – we should try to achieve a new sound trajectory of economic growth and fluctuation in the next few years crossing the century. Transforming the past "violent ups and downs" and "violent ups and slow falls" to "slow rise and slow fall", will deform the previous striking contrast between peaks and troughs and great fluctuations over the years into indistinct peaks and troughs and small fluctuations. Converting the previous "short-term rise and short-term fall" and "short-term rise and long-term fall" to "long-term rise and short-term fall", will extend the prosperous rising period and shorten the falling phase.

We are aware that the US economy has presented a trend of an alleviated level of fluctuation since the 1980s. After World War II, the United States experienced three long prosperity phases in terms of economic fluctuation. The first was from February 1961 to December 1969, lasting 106 months (8.8 years); the second was from November 1982 to July 1990 with a duration of 92 months (7.7 years); the third one was from April 1991 to October 1999, 103 months (8.6 years) and maintaining a growth trend in terms of the period of this study. The interval between the latter two prosperity phases was as short as several months. Connecting the latter two phases from November 1982 to October 1999 together, they lasted a total of 17 years. According to the analysis of Steven Weber, a US scholar, ("The End of the Business Cycle?", 1997)[7] six factors in the contemporary economy contributed to the trend of an alleviated level of fluctuation in the US economy. First, there was the globalization of production, inducing supply and demand to cross borders and connect with each other in the global arena. Second, there was the globalization of finance, resulting in the flow of capital across national borders and the diversification of capital resources. Third, in terms of the industrial distribution of employment, it transferred from the manufacturing industry to the service industry. The employment pattern shifted from the lifelong type to the periodic model. Thus, this slowed down employment fluctuation. Fourth, the government vigorously implemented a market liberalization policy. Fifth, the rapid economic development of Asian emerging market countries generated huge demand and provided a wide market. Sixth, the rapid innovation in information technology greatly accelerated information transmission and improved information quality, enabling enterprises to make more scientific management decisions. Especially, modern information systems helped enterprises set up precise supply chains and closely connect product supply with market demand, to a great extent diminishing the disjunction between supply and demand in terms of time and place and reducing the impact of stock variation on production as a whole.

Without doubt, an alleviated level of economic fluctuation is not identical to nonexistence of fluctuation in economic operation in the future. When the US economy was in its first long-term phase of prosperity in the 1960s after World War II, there was a popular book entitled "*Has the Business Cycle been Out-of-Date?*" in which the writer's viewpoint was positive. However, four economic recessions followed in 1970, 1974–75, 1980 and 1982. In the long-term phase of prosperity in the 1990s, Steven Weber wrote an article entitled "*The End of the Business Cycle?*" His answer to his own question was that economic cyclical fluctuation would tend to be alleviated, rather than being no longer in existence. This conclusion is believable and will be verified by China's future economic fluctuation.

[Originally published in *China Social Sciences (ZhongguoShehuiKexue)*, No.1, 2000, Anniversary Issue of the 20th Anniversary]

## Notes

1 K. Marx. (2001). *Capital* (Vol. 1, p. 908). ProQuestebrary. Retrieved June 4, 2015, from: http://site.ebrary.com.ezproxy.cityu.edu.hk/lib/cityu/reader.action?docID=2001687)
2 K. Marx. (2001). *Capital: A Critique of Political Economy, the Process of Production of Capital* (Vol. 1, p. 164). S. Moore & E. Aveling (Trans.). London: Electric Book Co. (Original work published 1867)
3 P. A. Samuelson & W. D. Nordhaus. (2004). *Economics* (18th ed., p. 468). New York: McGraw-Hill Irwin.
4 See Liu Guoguang & Liu Shucheng. (1997, January 7). On Soft Landing. *The People's Daily*, p. 9.
5 Wang Luolin, Liu Shucheng, &Liu Rongcang. (1999, March 10). Further Initiation of Economy with Focus on Raising Final Consumption Rate. *The Economic Information Daily*; On How to Further Stimulate Economy. (1999). *The Finance & Trade Economics*, p. 4.
6 *Selected Works of Deng Xiaoping* (1st ed., Vol. 3, p. 365). (1994). The Bureau for the Compilation and Translation of Works of Mars, Engels, Lenin and Stalin under the Central Committee of the Communist Party of China (Trans.). Beijing: Foreign Languages Press.
7 Weber, S. (1997, July/August). The End of the Business Cycle? *Foreign Affairs*.

# 5 Analysis of the economic trends in China, 2003–04

**Features of the economic growth of 2003 in China**

In 2003, two indicative features of economic growth in China were the GDP and GDP per capita and the economic growth rate.

*GDP and GDP per capita*

The gross domestic product (GDP) of China increased from 360 billion yuan in 1978 to 1000 billion yuan in 1985 through seven years of endeavors at the beginning of the reform which was introduced in the 1980s. It reached 2000 billion yuan in 1990 through another five years of efforts. After the middle of the 1990s, it increased continuously each year, reaching 3000 billion yuan, 4000 billion yuan, 5000 billion yuan, and reached 10000 billion yuan in 2002. In 2003, it was up to 11000 billion yuan (see Figure 5.1). According to the latest announced statistical data of the International Monetary Fund (IMF), China's GDP ranked seventh in the world in 2003, when the countries ranked in the top ten were, respectively, the United States, Japan, Germany, the UK, France, Italy, China, Canada, Spain and Mexico.

In terms of the GDP per capita in China, it continuously remained below US$300 (see Figure 5.2) from the beginning of the 1980s to 1987. In 1984, the GDP per capita was US$297 (calculated according to the foreign exchange rate of 1984). In the same year, Deng Xiaoping, in two of his speeches, proposed: "China is still very poor at present. Gross national product per capita is only US$300. Our target is to reach US$800 per capita by the end of the century. US$800 is nothing for economically developed countries. But for China, this is a great ambition" (May 29, 1984, *Selected Works of Deng Xiaoping*, Vol. 3, p. 57).

> The lowest target we proposed for the four modernizations is to secure a well-off livelihood for the people. I first mentioned this to the former Prime Minister Masayoshi Ohira during his visit here in December 1979. The so-called well-off refers to the annual gross national product per capita reaching US$800.
>
> (June 30, 1984, *Selected Works of Deng Xiaoping*, Vol. 3, p. 64)

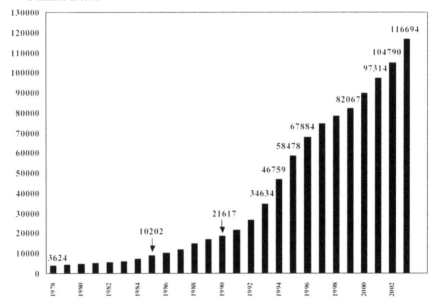

a hundred million

*Figure 5.1* Gross domestic product in China (1978–2003)

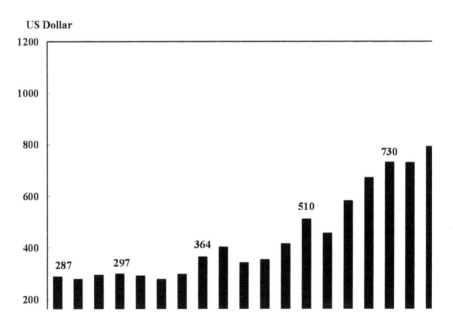

US Dollar

*Figure 5.2* Gross domestic product per capita in China (1981–2003)

Through efforts over more than 20 years following the reform and opening up, the GDP per capita in China reached US$856 in 2000 (calculated according to the foreign exchange rate of 2000), realizing the magnificent strategic conception of Deng Xiaoping at the beginning of the reform and opening up. It broke US$1000 and achieved US$1090 by 2003 (calculated according to the foreign exchange rate of 2003), thereby reaching an important stage.

The World Bank divides countries and regions into three categories – low income, middle income and high income – in the annually published "World Development Report", in which middle income is divided into lower-middle income and upper-middle income. As per the foreign exchange calculation approach of the World Bank, those with a GNP per capita below US$545 in 1988 were low-income countries. China just fell into this range, with a GNP per capita at US$330 in that year. Those with a GNP per capita above US$756 in 1999 were lower-middle income countries. China first entered into the category of lower-middle income countries with GNP per capita at US$780 in that year, ranking 140th among 206 countries and regions in the world. Although the income level per capita in China had improved remarkably compared with the past, it still fell behind in the world ranking. There is a long way to go on the path to its future development.

It is an important stage when GDP per capita exceeds US$1000, as it indicates that a country's economic development is entering a vital period. On the one hand, it may be a golden era for development. With the upgrading of its consumption structure, the subsequent upgrading of its industrial structure and the acceleration of industrialization and urbanization, a national economy may continuously experience rapid growth over a comparatively long period of time. On the other hand, it may be a period characterized by prominent economic and social contradictions. With the continuous expansion of total supply and demand, resource consumption will increase and the contradiction of resource restraints will become more prominent. Profound changes will take place in its social structures. Especially as income disparity is widening, the conflicts between various interest groups may become aggravated. There may appear to be two development prospects for a country reaching the stage at which it achieves a GDP per capita of US$1000. Seizing such an opportunity will enable its economy to develop steadily and rapidly and gradually realize modernization. If the contradictions cannot be tackled properly, its economy may stagnate for a period of time, even leading to social instability, such as occurred in many Latin American countries.

In conclusion, the first feature of the economic growth in China in 2003 was that GDP per capita exceeded US$1000, demonstrating the long-term economic growth trend in China; that is, the economy would still maintain rapid growth over a comparatively long period of time. Since the reform and opening up, the economy has maintained a growth rate of 9 percent. From now on, until 2020, an even longer period of time, it will continue to sustain a development trend of fairly rapid growth. As for the appropriate rate of economic growth, it can be explored further. The sixteenth congress of the Chinese Communist Party proposed that we should build a more comfortably well-off society by 2020. The gross domestic product will quadruple by then, compared with 2000, with a target of annual economic growth rate remaining at 7.2 percent. Thus, there is still a great deal of room for development. We should especially place stress on the overall coordinated development of the economy and society, and avoid a situation in which the more the economy develops, the more prominent the social contradictions become. In October 2003, the Third Plenary Session of the 16th Central Committee of CPC timely proposed a scientific outlook on development.

### Economic growth rate

In 2003, the economic growth rate (GDP growth rate) in China reached 9.1 percent. Reviewing the situation since the 1990s, the economic growth rate was just at a trough period with a rate of 3.8 percent in 1990 (see Figure 5.3). Following the rapid growth of more than 10 years from the early stage of the reform and opening up in the 1980s, the economy in China was in a period of adjustment. The economic growth rate increased to 9.2 percent in 1991, entering the rising stage of a new round of economic cycle. During such an economic situation, Deng Xiaoping's South Talk in early 1992 opened up new prospects for the reform, opening up and modernization construction. However, since it was just around 10 years after the reform and opening up, the original planned economic system still had not been fundamentally transformed, and dysfunction in the original system, such as the hunger for investment, the over-anxiety for success and the overall

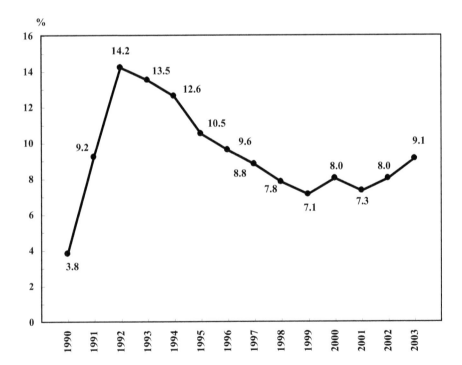

*Figure 5.3* Growth rate of gross domestic product in China (1990–2003)

mere pursuit of high speed had not been overcome, leading to economic growth exceeding 10 percent and reaching a peak of 14.2 percent. The supply of coal, electricity, oil, transportation and important raw materials was short, which was accompanied by financial disorder, presenting an obviously overheated economy. This overheated situation continued during the first half of 1993. By the middle of 1993, the central government took prompt action to resolutely adopt moderately tight regulation measures for a "soft landing", such as the publication of 16 measures to restore financial order, control the scale of fixed-assets investment and so on. Through four years of efforts, the economic growth rate and the rate of price increases both fell back within 10 percent in 1996. The economic growth rate varied from 13.5 percent in 1993, 12.6 percent in 1994, 10.5 percent in 1995 to 9.6 percent in 1996, falling, on average, 1 percent annually. With the decline of the economic growth rate, the rise rate of commodity retail prices also fell from a peak of 21.7 percent in 1994 to 6.1 percent in 1996. This demonstrated the success of the "soft landing".

In general, the economy should be maintained steadily at a certain level or it should gradually recover after the successful adjustment of a "soft landing". Nevertheless, it continued to decline consecutively over three years in 1997, 1998 and 1999. In this way, the economy declined for a total of seven years consecutively, during which the former four years involved proactive adjustments of "soft landing" and the latter three years dealt with the impact of an international crisis and the insufficiency of effective domestic demand. Since the great crisis from 1929 to 1933 and the World War II, there had not been a financial crisis as severe as the Asian financial crisis. By taking Thailand as the breakthrough point, international financial speculators sabotaged the outcome of rapid growth over a period of more than 10 years in Thailand overnight. The East Asian regions, from the "Four Tigers" to the "Four Dragons" and Japan, which entered into a stage of high-speed growth successively in the middle of the 1950s, were all shot down like a flock of wild geese. The approach that should be used to deal with such a severe financial crisis was to temporarily implement a tight credit and monetary policy. China was comparatively less impacted due to its economic adjustment of the "soft landing" over the course of four years, together with the incomplete convertibility of Renminbi acting as a firewall. However, the surrounding countries were all greatly and adversely affected. At a time when Hong Kong had just been returned to China, it was extremely important for us to maintain the prosperity of Hong Kong and to withstand the impact of the financial crisis. Under such circumstances, it was impossible to employ the approach of loosening credit to stimulate the economy after the "soft landing". Meanwhile, with the deepening of economic reforms, the original welfare measures in the residents' consumption and expenditures were becoming market-oriented. The cost of education was higher than before. People needed to purchase houses by themselves. Laid-off workers needed to accumulate unemployment compensation for themselves. Endowments had gradually turned toward a market orientation as well. Therefore, everyone was saving for their children's education, life after being laid-off, housing and their endowments, causing insufficiency in the effective domestic demand. Coping with this insufficiency and the impact of the Asian financial crisis, the central government started to carry out positive fiscal policy and moderate monetary policy in 1998. Through several years of endeavors, the economy recovered from 7.1 percent at the trough to 8 percent in 2000. However, influenced by the US economic adjustment (including the impact of the September 11th event) and the simultaneous low economic growth and recession of the major developed countries, the economic growth rate in China was again reduced to 7.3 percent in 2001 and returned to 8 percent in 2002. It was hard won that the economic growth rate in China maintained a relatively stable level of 7 percent to 8 percent from 1997 to 2002. In comparison with the major countries in the world and the surrounding countries and regions over the same period, the economic growth trend in China outshone the others, which merely referred to a comparison of the tendency for economic fluctuation. The economic growth rate in China reached 9.1 percent in 2003, beginning a new upward trend. The Central Economic Working Conference held in November 2003 pointed out that "currently the economic development in China is in the rising stage of the economic cycle."

To sum up, the second feature of the economic growth in 2003 in China was that the economic growth rate reached 9.1 percent, signifying a medium- and short-term periodic fluctuation trend. This ended the situation in which there was an average decline of 1 percent annually for seven consecutive years, from the second half of 1993 when implementing the "soft landing" policy to 1999 and the high trough, with an economic growth rate of 7 percent to 8 percent for six consecutive years from the 1997 Asian financial crisis to 2002. The economy entered into a rising stage in a new round of economic cycle. In addition, an economic growth rate of 9.1 percent showed that economic development in China has reached a critical juncture. The macroeconomic regulation could result in three probabilities. First, if the macroeconomic control was too loose, economic growth could very quickly exceed 10 percent, such as occurred in the beginning of the 1990s, leading to an overheated economy and the need for a subsequent extensive adjustment. Second, if the macroeconomic regulation was too tight, the economic growth may contract and return to below 8 percent. Third, if the macroeconomic control was appropriate, it would extend the rising stage of the economic cycle and sustain the economic development steadily and rapidly.

The economic growth rate reached 9.8 percent in the first quarter of 2004 on the basis of an economic growth rate of 9.6 percent in the third quarter and 9.9 percent in the fourth quarter of 2003, respectively, with a continuous high-level macroeconomic operation. On the one hand, the increase in the economic growth rate from 7–8 percent to 9 percent during the period of 1998–2002 was hard won, demonstrating that the economic operation had entered into a rising stage in a new round of the economic cycle and showing the overall prospective national economic situation. On the other hand, the economic growth rate, in excess of 9 percent, was already close to 10 percent, the upper warning limit. According to the practical experiences since the reform and opening up, especially in terms of the current resource supply of coal, electricity, oil, transportation and important raw materials, the potential economic growth rate is approximately 9 percent, with an appropriate range between 8 percent and 10 percent. If it is lower than 8 percent, the economy is over-stretched, with an unsettled unemployment problem. If it is higher than 10 percent, the bottleneck constraint is severe, causing difficulties for macroeconomic regulation. In other words, the upper warning limit of the economic growth rate can be controlled at 10 percent. If it is exceeded, the economy may change from partially overheated to completely overheated, thus leading to violent ups-and-downs. From the third quarter of 2003 to the first quarter of 2004, the economy was almost in this situation, with partially overheated industries, overly-active investment demand and overly-speeded loans. Therefore, the Party Central Committee and the State Council resolutely implemented a series of timely macroeconomic regulation measures. The economic growth rate in the second quarter of 2004 will still be high, which is related to the low economic growth base of 6.7 percent in the second quarter of 2003, when the country was fighting against SARS. It will cool somewhat in the third and fourth quarters of 2004. For the whole year, if the macroeconomic regulation is appropriate, the economic growth rate will be slightly lower than that of last year, but will still maintain good development momentum of over 8 percent.

Concerning the argument, during the two sessions in March 2004, regarding whether the economy in China is overheated, we can sum them up as 10 different viewpoints. We will not make comments on them here, but merely report them on-the-spot. First, Professor Wu Jinglian believed that, currently, there was a phenomenon of overall overheated economy in China. Second, Professor Zhang Zhuoyuan thought that the whole economic situation was becoming better, but an overheated tendency had emerged. Third, Professor Lin Yifu held that local investment was overheated, and that it was necessary to avoid future deflation. The above three viewpoints are all related to an overheated economy to different extents. Fourth, Professor Xiao Zhuoji proposed that an overheated economy, a real estate bubble and RMB appreciation could not be easily defined according to the economic situation in 2003–04. Fifth, Professor Li Yining believed that it was not a problem for the current economy in China to be a bit heated, but it would be troublesome if it was a bit cold. Sixth, Zhao Long's point of view was that consumption was cold, and the investment was heated in China's economic operation. Seventh, Professor He Keng thought that the problem of the current economy in China was not overheating, but lay in the unapparent alteration of the cold feature of the macro economy and the failure of the final consumption stimulation. The sixth and seventh viewpoints are both related to coldness. Eighth, Ma Kai, the director of the State Development and Reform Commission, in answering reporters' questions during the two sessions, proposed that the Chinese economy in 2003–04 was not simply overheated or non-overheated, but was much more complicated in its practical operation. The ninth and tenth viewpoints are the extensions of this discussion; there was deflation in 2003, with no inflation involved during the discussion of the problem of an over-heated economy. In 2004, the discussion extended to the inflation problem. Ninth, Zhou Xiaochuan, the president of the central bank, believed that, currently, an inflation trend had already become very obvious. Tenth, Professor Yao Jingyuan held that there was no foundation for the emergence of inflation in the economy in China.

## Ways to grasp the current economic trend

In order to grasp the current economic trend properly, we should be careful not to fall victim to the following four types of confusion.

First, do not confound long-term trends with the medium- and short-term periodic fluctuation trends. The GDP per capita in China has reached the level of US$1000 and industrialization and urbanization accelerated with the upgrading of the consumption structure and the rapid development of the heavy chemical industry. These factors demonstrate the long-term trend, i.e. the economy in China may increase rapidly in the future (for example, for the next 20 years). In 2003, the economic growth rate reached 9.1 percent, indicating a medium- and short-term periodic fluctuation tendency. In analyzing the economic trend, some scholars only carried out a long-term trend analysis, instead of medium- and short-term ones, which we believe is not feasible. The long-term growth trend is achieved through the medium- and short-term periodic fluctuations (for example, short-term fluctuations of about five years or medium fluctuations of around 10 years) without excluding the possibility of greater fluctuations during the process. Long-term steady and rapid growth is realized through the constant enhancement and perfection of macro regulation and through medium- and short-term steady and fast growth, rather than automatically.

Second, do not confuse the current point in time with a future one. Currently, the consumption prices of residents have not yet increased excessively. But this judgment is not identical to and cannot replace a future one. There is a transmission process in inflation. The transmission will be very rapid if there is no necessary macro regulation. The overall level of residents' consumption will not increase severely if the appropriate macro control is implemented for certain sources, namely, control of the fixed-assets investment scale and the corresponding credit scale. It will be too late if the macro regulation is carried out at a time when the presence of inflation is already very obvious. We should conduct a dynamic analysis of inflation and should not rest only on the present static analysis. Taking preventive measures is preferable.

Third, do not mix speculative demand with normal demand. The practice in the market economy countries demonstrates that initial recovery growth in certain industries during economic periodic fluctuations will evolve into overheated increases promoted by high demand and high prices, which leads to huge profits. They will stimulate speculative demand, which further advances prices. Speculative demand for steel, iron ore and real estate has appeared in some regions. The speculative demand is actually fictitious and drives prices to increase, which brings about price bubbles. We should not mistake such speculative demand for normal market demand.

Fourth, do not confuse macro regulation with macroeconomics. Some scholars put forward that the so-called "overheating" is an aggregate concept of the macro economy (namely, total social demand increases excessively and outstrips total supply). The statement "partially overheated" cannot be employed. The so-called "overheating" is definitely an aggregate concept in macroeconomics. However, macro regulation is not identical to macroeconomics. It is a practical issue with multi-disciplinary application, including both aggregate issues and structural issues, such as industrial structure, business structure, enterprise structure, regional structure and price variation structure. The so-called "overheating" is not just an issue of macroeconomics, but is further an issue of economic cycle theory.

Economic cycle studies not only deal with aggregate issues such as total demand and total supply, but also stress research of the production structural imbalance and investigate "partial recession" led by excessive investment and expansion (namely, the so-called "partially overheated") of a certain business, sector and industry and a further induced decline in total demand and a universal economic contraction. Hence, the concept of "partially overheated" is applicable in economic cycle theory.

## Proper recognition of the background features of a new round in the economic cycle

With the view of properly grasping the current macroeconomic trend, we must correctly recognize the background features of a new round in the economic cycle. We should consider the following points:

First, the system's foundation has changed, but the basic mechanisms of economic cyclical fluctuation have not been altered. It is still necessary to avoid the phenomenon of an overheated economy and violent ups-and-downs. In the original planned economic system, violent economic ups-and-downs led by an overheated economy emerged many times (see Figure 5.4). Before the Cultural Revolution, there were three time periods with violent economic ups, with the economic growth rate respectively reaching 21.3 percent in 1958, 18.3 percent in 1964 and 19.4 percent in 1970, approaching or exceeding 20 percent. After the

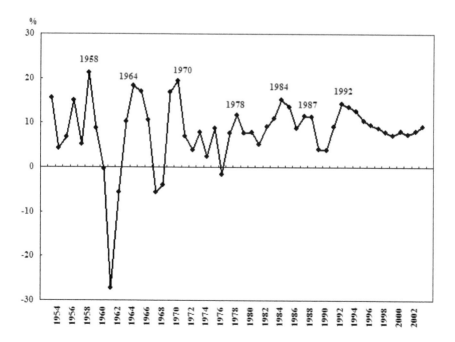

*Figure 5.4* Growth rate fluctuation of gross domestic product in China (1953–2003)

Cultural Revolution, there were also four time periods with an economic growth rate of, respectively, up to 11.7 percent in 1978, 15.2 percent in 1984, 11.6 percent in 1987 and 14.2 percent in 1992, all exceeding 10 percent.

Currently, the socialist market economic system in China has preliminarily been established. The new round in the economic cycle is the first one under the socialist market economic system. It is inevitable to consider whether there will be an overheated economy under market economic conditions and whether there will be violent economic ups-and-downs led by an overheated phenomenon, in other words, whether it is necessary to avoid an overheated economy under market economic conditions. In fact, an overheated economy, economic cyclical fluctuations and violent ups leading to violent downs are the original phenomena that emerge under the market economy and during the industrialization process. In 1825, the first overall economic crisis took place in the UK, thus starting the course of economic cyclical fluctuation under the market economy. In the first 40 years of the twentieth century, four violent ups-and-downs, with gaps of 19.8 percent to 21.5 percent between the peaks and the troughs, took place in the United States (see Figure 5.5). After World War II, the US government carried out macro regulation by employing fiscal and monetary policies, and narrowed the amplitude of economic fluctuations, together with the upgrading of industrial structures.

Regardless of whether there is a market economy or a planned economy, the basic mechanism is the same, i.e. there is a logical economic decline after the economy

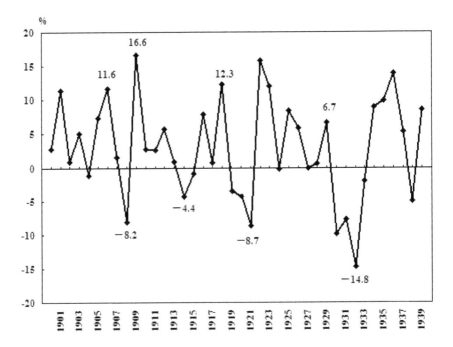

*Figure 5.5* Growth rate fluctuation in the gross national product in the United States (1900–39)

rises in its practical operation. The difference is that there are different features in terms of the specific formation mechanisms (for example initiation and restraint mechanisms) and forms of expression (for example amplitude) of economic cyclical fluctuations due to the different economic systems. Historical experiences and lessons from violent economic ups-and-downs can be drawn from the original planned economic system in China and the market economic system in Western countries. With the preliminary establishment of the socialist market economic system in China, its economic operation bears features of a planned economic system that had existed before the transition, such as the blind expansion impetus of local governments, and those of a market economic system, such as diversification in the ownership of enterprises and the marketization of the behavior of enterprises. Therefore, both types of experiences and lessons regarding violent economic ups-and-downs are worth learning conscientiously. Particularly, the more violently the economy increases, the more severe the proportional imbalance of the economic structure becomes. This leads to violent downs when adjustments are made.

The history of the Chinese and foreign economic cycles reveals that the core of the violent ups-and-downs is the intensity of fluctuations in fixed-assets investment. The violent ups generally originate from sharp increases in investment. Investment increased the least in 1999, with a social fixed-assets investment growth rate of merely 5.1 percent. It sped up continuously after 2000 and reached 43 percent in the first quarter of this year, in which certain industries appeared to exhibit the phenomenon of partial overheating. In 2003, the annual growth rate of fixed-assets investment was 26.7 percent, during which investment in the coal industry increased 52.3 percent, textile industry 80.4 percent, automobile industry 87.2 percent, electrolytic aluminum 92.9 percent, iron and steel industry 96.6 percent and cement 121.9 percent. As the effect of macro regulation is gradually visualized, it is estimated that the growth speed may slow down in April. At present, we should attach great importance to the fact that investment growth is excessively fast, the construction scale is oversized, blind investment and repeated construction at a low level in certain industries and regions are quite severe, the supply shortages in coal, electricity, oil, transportation and important raw materials are further intensified and monetary credit growth is once again accelerating.

Second, the consumption structure has changed, but there is still consumption restraint from the demand side. After more than 20 years of development, industrialization and urbanization will accelerate in the twenty-first century. The upgrading of the consumption structure represented by housing and automobiles becomes a significant motivation for promoting economic growth over a certain long period of time in the future. However, the GDP per capita in China has currently reached the stage of US$1000. The overall purchasing power was still comparatively low in the medium and short term. The upgrading of the consumption structure has just started and will be realized over a long period of time through different stages. Currently, it is a time in which industrialization and urbanization are accelerating, or objectively, the amplitude of economic fluctuation is enlarging. We should enhance and improve macro regulation measures to develop the economy steadily and rapidly, and we should not believe that the acceleration of industrialization and urbanization will automatically and smoothly promote fast and steady growth in the economy.

Third, the supply-demand relationship has changed, but a bottleneck restriction on the supply side still exists. Although total supply exceeded total demand several years ago, bottleneck restrictions in coal, electricity, oil, transportation and important raw materials will emerge once the economy is overheated. In particular, grain was a bottleneck that had previously been universally neglected. During the rapid economic growth, lawbreaking and deregulation in the occupation of cultivated land were prominent, leading to a reduction in the grain yield. Since 1999, the planting areas for grain crops have continuously diminished from 1.7 billion mu in 1998 down to 1.49 billion mu in 2003, the lowest since the founding of the new China. Meanwhile, the grain yield has decreased from 512.3 billion kg, the highest in 1998 to 430 billion kg in 2003, the lowest since the 1990s. Therefore, intensifying land management and deepening the improvement and rectification of the land market are strongly emphasized in this macro regulation.

Fourth, the price trend has changed, but the excessively rapid economic growth will still lead to inflation. Some hold the opinion that the deflation of consecutive years has not yet ended and that rapid economic growth will not initiate new inflation. Thus, there is no need to worry about an overheated economy. We believe that the variation relationship between economic growth and price movement is equidirectional under a market economy in terms of the general law of economic cyclical fluctuation. The overall price level increases as the economic growth rate rises. It declines (or there is a decline in the rise rate of the overall price level or an absolute decline in the overall price level) as the economic rate decreases. Frequently, there is a slight time lag of the variation between them. When entering a rising stage in the economic cycle, an acceleration in the speed of economic growth will still follow the general variation law between economic growth and price movement, and will correspondingly lead to an increase in the overall price level. There is a transmission process from an increase in the economic growth rate to an increase in the overall price level, including a transmission process from the primary product price, the intermediate product price to the final product price, from the factory price, the wholesale price to the retail price, and from the agricultural product to foodstuff. Whether the transmission process will give rise to an all-round increase or a severe increase in the overall price level depends on the origin and mainly rests with the investment scale and a further corresponding expansion of the credit scale. A "partial overheating" will bring on local and structural price increases. If this develops into a globally overheated situation, it will cause all-around inflation or even severe inflation. This is the typical manifestation of the law of the economic cycle. If the macro regulation is appropriate and proceeds well in 2004, the overall annual consumption price level for residents will hopefully be controlled within 3 percent. If we allow the market price to increase arbitrarily, the severe lagging rise in the overall price level will be out of control.

## Macroscopic proactive measures

In the Government Work Report (2004), macroscopic regulation was regarded as the first among nine tasks. It was proposed that we should "strengthen and improve macroscopic regulation to maintain steady and fast economic development".

The basic goal of macro regulation is "to protect various initiatives to accelerate development with good direction and exertion, so as to achieve steady and fast economic development and avoid violent economic ups-and-downs." The appropriate macro regulation should include both control and expansion, and should imply the following points.

In terms of the aggregate structure of the two domestic demands, investment and consumption, we should implement both regulation and expansion. Partially overheated investment demand should be controlled. Consumption demand still needs to be expanded.

In terms of the internal investment structure, we should carry out both regulation and expansion. Partially overheated industrial investment, investment with high energy consumption and high pollution, and investment in image projects, high standard residential housing and the construction of towns with land enclosures should be regulated. Agricultural investment and investment in the tertiary industry that absorbs employment and various social undertakings still need to be increased.

In terms of the internal consumption structure, we should practice both regulation and expansion. Extravagance and waste, corruption and degeneration, recreational activities and tours at the public expense should be controlled. The income and consumption of farmers and the urban medium- and low-income population still need to be enlarged.

In terms of the regional structure, we should effectuate both regulation and expansion. Considering the imbalance in regional development, partially overheated regions should be regulated. The old industrial bases, such as the western and northeastern regions, still need to expand investment.

We should make some adjustments in the utilization direction, while continuously implementing active fiscal policy. The long-term constructive public debt has decreased from a total of 150 billion yuan in previous years to 110 billion yuan in 2004. It is vital that the target for public debt in 2004 has shifted from the previous goal of mainly preventing an economic downturn and spurring economic growth to a focus on promoting economic structural adjustments and an all-round coordinated development of the economy and society. Concerning monetary policy, we should properly control the monetary credit scale and optimize the credit structure in order to give full play to the monetary policy, so as to support economic growth and prevent inflation and financial risks.

## Enterprise proactive measures

Under the market economic system, enterprises are the main bodies in the market, bearing the sole responsibility for their profits or losses. Therefore, they must establish their own precautionary mechanisms to cope with the risk of market fluctuation. These mechanisms can preliminarily be summed up as four types.

First, store up during fat years to make up for lean ones. Enterprises should not spend all of the money earned during times when the market situation is good and should save it in various forms in case the market suddenly changes.

Second, develop innovation products. Enterprises should practice strict economy, reduce energy consumption, lower costs, improve productivity and develop varieties of high-quality innovation products so as to remain invincible in the face of fierce market competition and market variation. The reason why the German company SIEMENS has been long-lasting is that they divide various products into two categories. One is closely related to economic fluctuation. The other is unrelated to economic fluctuation. The latter products earn stable and low profits, whereas the former products have a very high profit during the rising stages of economic fluctuation and may incur losses during the falling stages. Thus, it is necessary to promote technical progress and constantly develop innovative products. Once the market fluctuates, replacing old products with newly developed products will continuously increase the level of profits.

Third, carry out diversified operations. For example, in the German Benz Co., automobile investment only occupies one-fourth of its total capital and investments in other industries account for three-fourths (another three industries respectively take up one-fourth). This is simply to prevent fluctuations in the automobile industry from having great fluctuations in the company's total profits.

Fourth, implement coordinated operations with upstream and downstream products. It was reported that while general investors poured into the steel industry with enthusiasm and grabbed the domain of steel industrial investment, Baoshan Iron and Steel Group, one of the Chinese steel magnates, did not make use of its strength to stimulate heated investment and made investments, other than in the steel industry, in upstream products, such as iron ore and coal mining, and downstream products, such as the design of new automobile steel plates, preliminarily forming a safe industry chain in the upstream and the downstream. This was much more important than blindly grabbing its domain of steel industrial investment. The steel industry will enter into a new round of adjustment after the "heated" steel industry investment subsides. Those who obtain a secure industry chain will gain the market and consolidate their competitiveness; otherwise, they may be sifted out.

[Originally published in *Beijing Finance (Beijing Jinrong)*, No.6, 2004]

# 6 Comparative analysis of five macroeconomic regulations in China

Since the reform and opening up, the Chinese government has carried out five retrenchment macro regulations (see Figure 6.1) according to the different economic operation trends and systematic environment. The detailed time brackets are, respectively, from 1979 to 1981, from 1985 to 1986, from 1989 to 1990, from the second half of 1993 to 1996 and from the second half of 2003 to 2004 (the previous macroeconomic regulation from 1998 to 2002 was the expansive type). In comparison to the previous four retrenchment macroeconomic regulations, the fifth one presents new characteristics in various aspects. It is of great significance for us to properly recognize the new characteristics, ideas and mechanisms of the current macro regulation so as to implement a series of decisions by the central government.

## Against different economic operation trends

First, the previous four macro regulations were all directed against the peaks at that time, the violent ups with the economic growth rate of over 11 percent that had emerged in the economic fluctuation. The economic growth rates reached 11.7 percent in 1978, 15.2 percent in 1984, 11.6 percent in 1987, 11.3 percent in 1988 and 14.2 percent in 1992, respectively. Second, the previous four macro regulations were all aimed at an overall overheated economy or an overheated economic aggregate. The first period having an overheated economy was originally reflected in the excessive investment and the serious imbalance between major sectors of the national economy. Subsequently, the financial expenditures towards consumption greatly increased and caused vast fiscal deficits, leading to excessive distribution of the national income. The second to the fourth periods of an overheated economy were dual expansions in investment demand and consumption demand, which brought about an excess of the total social demand over the total social supply. Third, the previous four macro regulations were directed towards fighting severe inflation. The nationwide rate of the increase of commodity retail prices reached 6 percent in 1980 (this was the first peak since the reform and opening up and the greatest increase after 1962), 8.8 percent in 1985 (this was the second peak since the reform and opening up), 18.5 percent in 1988 (this was the third peak since the reform and opening up), 13.2 percent in 1993 and 21.7 percent in 1994 (this was the fourth peak since the reform and opening up and the peak since the founding of the new China). Each of the four peaks was higher than the previous one (see Figure 6.2). In brief, the four previous violent economic ups were all adjusted passively when they were unable to continue.

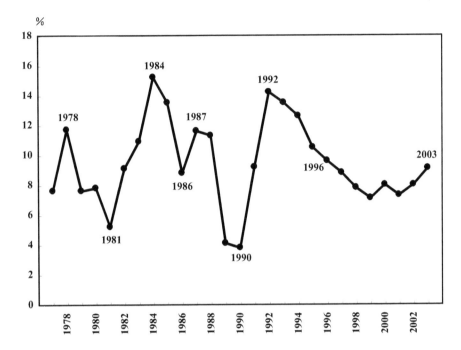

*Figure 6.1* Fluctuation curve of the economic growth rate in China (1977–2003)

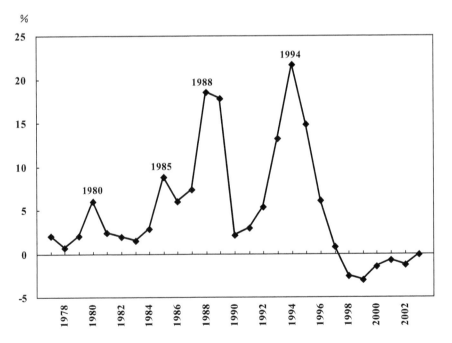

*Figure 6.2* Commodity retail price rate of increase in China (1977–2003)

The fifth macro regulation was directed against the prevention of violent economic ups and the induced violent economic downs, rather than the violent ups with the economic growth rate of over 11 percent (the economic growth rate was 9.1 percent in 2003). It was aimed at the phenomenon of partially overheating in some industrial investments, rather than an all-around overheated economy or overheated aggregate and the dual expansions of investment and consumption demands. It pointed at the appearance of the price increase pressure instead of the severe existing inflation. In a word, the fifth macro regulation was promptly enacted for some overheated industries. It was a preventive and precautionary active adjustment for the whole economic operation.

## On a different economic systematic basis

The four previous macro regulations took place during the process of the gradual transformation of the original planned economic system and the unfinished "basic transition". The fifth macro regulation was the first retrenchment macro regulation after the preliminary establishment of the socialist market economic system in China, in which the diversification of the stakeholders was fully displayed and reflected in academic circles and the news media, forming a diversity of various opinions and undoubtedly enhancing the great difficulties in the macro regulation. In fact, each macro regulation among the five since the reform and opening up needed to have a unified recognition, which was very difficult; the fifth one, in particular, was even more difficult than the others.

The first macro regulation was directed against the overheated economy in 1978. The Third Plenary Session of the 11th Central Committee of CPC, the great historically significant conference held in December 1978, put forward that the Party's work focus should shift to the socialist modernization construction and proposed that the serious imbalance between major sectors of the national economy had not completely changed and that the infrastructure must be actively carried out in proper sequence without a rush, according to the actual capability. In March 1979, Li Xiannian and Chen Yun wrote a letter to the Party Central Committee on the finance and economics work and clearly brought forward that the imbalance between major sectors of the national economy was quite severe, and that it was necessary to take two to three years to make adjustments. In the same month, the Political Bureau of the Central Committee decided to spend three years in implementing the adjustment. The Central Working Conference, which specifically discussed economic issues, was held in April 1979 and formally advanced that China would spend three years to make adjustments to the national economy and implement the new eight character principles of "Adjustment, Reform, Rectification, and Improvement" (the eight character principles proposed in 1961 were "Adjustment, Consolidation, Supplementation and Improvement"). However, in 1979 and 1980, the central authority and the local governments had different understandings of the adjustment, causing poor implementation. The total infrastructure scale had not been reduced, because the local government and enterprises, with enlarged financial authority, blindly launched new projects. That caused vast financial deficits and an excessive amount of currency issuance.

For this reason, the Party Central Committee again held a working conference in December 1980. Deng Xiaoping sharply pointed out that

> after the Third Plenary Session of the Eleventh Central Committee in December 1978, Comrade Chen Yun took charge of the financial and economic work and proposed the policy of readjustment, which was adopted by the Central Working Conference in April last year. The policy was not effectively implemented, however, because Party members did not have a profound or unanimous understanding of the issues involved. A change in this situation took place only very recently.
>
> (Selected Works of Deng Xiaoping, 1984, p. 335)[1]

The Central Working Conference decided to make greater adjustments to the national economy in 1981 after two years of adjustments in 1979 and 1980. So far, the first adjustment of the national economy since the reform and opening up was effectively carried out.

The second macro regulation was aimed at the overheated economy in 1984. The State Council issued a notice in November 1984 requiring various regions and sectors to strictly control fiscal expenditures and the credit supply. In March 1985, the "Government Working Report" proposed that we should strengthen and perfect the effective control and management of the macro economy and resolutely prevent the blind pursuit of and competition for rapid growth. However, the overheated situation was not controlled that year. Many regions and units still launched new projects. To this end, the 7th Five-Year Plan was approved in March 1986 and was divided into two stages: a first stage of two years and a second stage of three years. The adjustment in the first stage of two years stressed solving the oversized scale of fixed-assets investment and the excessively violent growth of the consumption fund. However, after the industrial production growth rate fell in the first quarter of 1986, many people thought that the economic growth declined and strongly required the money supply to be loosened, so as to stimulate the economy. Since 1986 was the first year of the 7th Five-Year Plan, the enthusiasm of speeding up development in various regions was strong. Under various pressures, the adjustment that was made in 1986 was not in place and concealed the probability of further inducing a new phenomenon of overheating.

The third macro regulation was directed at the overheated economy from 1987 to 1988. At that time, the state budgetary infrastructure investment was controlled to a certain extent, but the expansion of the extra-budgetary investment scale was far from under control and became increasingly intensified. The Third Plenary Session of the 13th Central Committee of CPC, held in September 1988, formally proposed that we should shift the focus on reform and construction over the next two years toward improving the economic environment and rectifying the economic order. Nevertheless, in 1989, some regions and sectors lacked an understanding of the necessity of improvement and rectification, which caused the macro regulation measures to be ineffectively implemented. The Fifth Plenary Session of the 13th Central Committee of CPC, held in November 1989, approved the "Decision of the CPC Central Committee on Further Rectification and Deepening Reform" and further put forward that we should spend a period of three years or more on substantially finishing the tasks of improvement and rectification. Thus, the third adjustment of the national economy since the reform and opening up was effectively carried out.

The fourth macro regulation was directed against the overheated economy from 1992 to the first half of 1993. In June 1993, the central government announced the "Opinion of the CPC Central Committee and the State Council on Current Economic Situation and Enhancement of Macro Regulation", took 16 measures and formally started to carry out macro regulation with a focus on rectifying the financial order and with the first task of fighting inflation. During the regulation process, academic circles once again raised an argument of whether the macro regulation should make inflation control its primary task or give priority to the continuous acceleration of growth and employment enlargement. Some scholars brought forward that a double-digit inflation rate was nothing to be feared, and that a double-digit economic growth rate was amazing. Meanwhile, there were constant demands by some regions and enterprises for the money supply to be loosened. However, the macro regulation eliminated various barriers, and through more than three years of efforts, successfully achieved a "soft landing" in 1996. This laid a good foundation to resist the risks of the subsequent explosion of the Asian financial crisis.

The fifth macro regulation was directed at preventive and precautionary control, rather than at an all-around overheated economy and serious existing inflation. The complicated interest pattern generated by the diversified stakeholders under the market economy, such as the central government and local governments at various levels, macro regulation sectors and other sectors, the central bank and commercial banks and securities companies, overheated industries and non-overheated industries, upstream industries and downstream industries, state-owned enterprises and private enterprises, large-scale enterprises and small- and medium-sized enterprises, the coastal areas and inland regions and high, middle and low income groups, reflected different interests and opinions. As a result, economic circles raised the most heated arguments, which lasted for more than 20 years, about judgments regarding the economic situation and the ways and approaches of macro regulation. Some stated that "this is a game of unprecedented scale". It seems that heated arguments regarding the macro regulation, especially fast and precautionary regulation under a market economy, are unavoidable in the future.

## Different ways and measures

1   In regard to the ways by which the regulation was implemented, the first to the third macro regulations were implemented hesitantly, with poor execution in the first two years of the initial adjustment of the national economy. Resolute and massive adjustments were subsequently made. Drawing on the lessons from the first three macro regulations, the fourth one was carried out vigorously and effectively upon making the decision in favor of improvement and rectification. The fifth macro regulation was a fast and precautionary one and was thus adopted in a progressive way, which was manifested in

observations, alerting and progressive reinforcement, giving consideration to accurately grasping the timing of the regulation, and its pace and strength, and taking swift and effective measures on the definite issues.

2   Concerning the scope of the regulation and compression, the adjustments of the last year (1981) of the first macro regulation and the last year (1990) of the third macro regulation were all conducted regarding investment and consumption for an overall strengthened austerity, which made the economic growth rate decline greatly and rapidly (the economic growth rate decreased to 5.2 percent in 1981 and 3.8 percent in 1990). The fourth macro regulation, which started in June 1993, also implemented an overall retrenchment on investment and consumption, but in a moderately austere way with moderate retrenchment monetary policy and fiscal policy, making the economic growth rate steadily and gradually decline from a peak of double-digits to an appropriate growth range of within 10 percent. The fifth macro regulation was appropriate and discriminatory, without sudden braking and rigid uniformity, other than the overall austerity. The monetary policy has gradually transformed from a steady one several years ago to a moderate retrenchment. The fiscal policy has also progressively shifted from an active one several years ago to a neutral one. The fifth macro regulation gave consideration to strictly controlling excessive investment and blind development in some industries and practically strengthening and supporting the weaknesses in economic development. It firmly controlled the expansion of investment demand and made efforts to increase consumption demand. It stressed the current prominent problems and long-term development. It regulated quite well what should happen in the macro scope and gave full play to the role of market mechanisms. In a word, the fifth macro regulation was aimed at sustaining the economic development steadily and rapidly at an appropriate growth range and striving to extend the rising stage of the economic cycle through proper speed control, rather than causing the economic growth rate to decline and land greatly from a peak at double-digits. On the whole, the economy was operated within the appropriate growth range (8 percent to 10 percent), with neither a "hard landing" nor a "soft landing".

3   With respect to the regulation measures, the economic adjustment is generally divided into three types – complete market adjustment, complete government adjustment and market adjustment plus government adjustment – in which government adjustment, namely government macro regulation, generally adopts three main measures – economic measures, legal measures and administrative measures. The economic measures refer to the government's employment of various economic leverages (for example prices, interest rates, tax rates, foreign exchange rates, etc.) to regulate the economic activities of market participants indirectly through market mechanisms. The legal measures refer to the government's application of various related laws and regulations and relevant state policies and stipulations to control the economic activities of market players through legal force. The administrative measures refer to the government's exercise of administrative authority to adjust the economic activities of enterprises or individuals directly through mandatory

instructions. The first to the third macro regulations mainly adopted administrative measures, such as administrative fiscal policy, coercively controlling the financial expenditures (cutting investment expenditures and curbing consumption expenditures) and administrative monetary policy, compulsorily regulating the credit supply. We ended the fiscal subsidies and bank loans to state-owned enterprises with bad management and long-term deficits and reorganized and rationalized small, backward enterprises. The fourth macro regulation shifted from the pure dependence on administrative measures utilized in the past to the concentration on the application of economic and legal measures, for example carrying out regulation by applying market monetary policy, such as interest rates, deposit reserve ratios and open market operations. The fifth macro regulation emphasized economic and legal measures at the very beginning and was complemented by necessary administrative measures. Currently, since the socialist market economic system has preliminarily been established in China, the economic operation bears both the characteristics of the original planned economic system before the transition (for example the blind expansion impetus of some local governments, soft budget constraints with no liability for loss in the practice in some enterprises) and those of a market economy system (for example the diversification of enterprise ownership, the marketization of enterprise behavior) and further has features of an immature market economy (for example the nonlegalization and irrationalization of enterprise behavior). Under such circumstances, it is advisable that we should comprehensively apply the economic, legal and administrative measures directed against the existing problems to ensure the desired effects of the macro regulation. Without dispute, macro regulation will employ economic and legal measures more frequently in the future along with the constant perfection of the socialist market economic system, the gradual maturity of the market economy and the promotion of legal construction.

## Different foreign economic relationships

The former four macro regulations did not attract international attention. But the fifth one drew extensive concern internationally, because foreign economic relationships in China have been increasingly enlarged with the deepening of the reform and opening up. Comparing 1992 with 2003, the import scale expanded from below US$100 billion (US$80.6 billion) to over US$400 billion (US$412.8 billion), an increase of four times. The actual foreign direct investment in China grew from around US$10 billion (US$11 billion) to more than US$50 billion (US$53.5 billion), an increment of four times as well. The state foreign exchange reserves in China increased from below US$20 billion (US$19.4 billion) to around US$400 billion (US$403.3 billion), a growth of 19 times. China became the world's third-largest importing country in 2003, the aggregate amount of which merely occupied 3.4 percent of the world's total imports. However, in terms of the increment, China's import growth accounted for approximately more than one-third of the global increment. Overseas related institutions, investors and news media have raised an extensive debate about whether the Chinese economy is overheated, how to carry out macro regulation, and especially, what the macro regulation's effect will be. In terms of the macro regulation's effect, the overseas debate is divided into an optimistic school and a pessimistic school. The optimistic school believed that slowing down measures were adopted much earlier than 10 years ago, when the economy was overheated at that time. This would sustain the current economic growth for a longer time and establish a significant basis for extending the economic cycle. The pessimistic school mainly worried that the sharp economic slowdown led by the macro regulation would result in a "hard landing" and have an impact on the world economy, especially on that of the surrounding countries and regions. "The Wall Street Journal Asia" pointed out that "the optimists are still more numerous than the pessimists."

[Originally published in *Economic Perspectives(JingjixueDongtai)*, No.9, 2004]

## Note

1 *Selected Works of Deng Xiaoping* (1st ed., Vol. 2, p. 335). (1984). The Bureau for the Compilation and Translation of Works of Mars, Engels, Lenin and Stalin Under the Central Committee of the Communist Party of China (Trans.). Beijing: Foreign Languages Press.

# 7 Analysis of national and international economic trends, 2008–09

## Features of China's economic situation in 2008

The economic trends in 2008–09 refer to the extension of the economic situation in 2008 as there was inertia in economic operation and the stepwise development of economic trends in 2009. We first examine the features of the economic situation of China in 2008.

Significant changes took place in the national and international economic environments in 2008, an extraordinary and marvelous year in China's economic development process. We sum up China's economic situation in 2008 as consisting of the following four features:

### Overlap of fourfold international and national adjustments

In 2008, the most prominent feature of China's economic situation was the overlapping of fourfold international and national adjustments, namely the overlap between the adjustment following the long-term rapid growth of the national economy and the national economic periodic adjustment, the overlap with the US economic periodic recession and the adjustment led by the US subprime mortgage crisis and the further overlap with the worldwide adjustment induced by the international financial crisis that evolved rapidly from the US subprime mortgage crisis.

For more than 30 years, since the reform and opening up, China's economy has increased rapidly, on average by 9.8 percent annually in the long run, but, at the same time, it has accumulated many problems. In particular, the inveterate extensive economic growth mode and the economic structural contradictions have not changed fundamentally. The extensive economic growth mode is mainly displayed in the high energy consumption, high material consumption, high pollution, low labor cost, low resource cost, low environmental cost, low level of technical content and low price competition. The extension of this growth mode is precisely to compete internationally through the low cost, leading to a high degree of external dependence in the economic expansion. The economic structural contradictions are primarily reflected in uncoordinated structures between primary, secondary and tertiary industries, an imbalance between internal and external demand, an irrational proportion between investment and consumption and imbalanced development between urban and rural areas and between various regions. Both the growth mode and the economic structure are severely conditioned by energy, mineral resources, land, water and the ecological environment, influenced by an increase in various costs, restricted by the low domestic consumption demand and easily affected by the risk of the international economic and financial crisis.

The adjustment for these long-term cumulative issues during the economic development is interwoven with the periodic adjustment of this round of economic cycle after many consecutive years of growth. In 2000, the economic growth rate in China (the GDP growth rate) surpassed the trough of the last cycle (the ninth cycle since 1953), specifically exceeding the 7.6 percent of 1999 and recovering to 8.4 percent, entering a new round (the tenth cycle) of economic cycle. The economic growth rate was 8.4 percent in 2000, 8.3 percent in 2001, 9.1 percent in 2002, 10 percent in 2003, 10.1 percent in 2004, 10.4 percent in 2005, 11.6 percent in 2006 and 13 percent in 2007, respectively, following a rising trend from above 8 percent to 13 percent for eight consecutive years (see Figure 7.1). The rising stage of the economic growth rate had generally been as short as one or two years during the previous economic cycles, whereas it lasted for eight years in this round, which has never occurred in the history of economic development since the founding of new China. However, the issues, such as the overly rapid economic growth and the increasing pressure of price inflation, in the many consecutive years of growth need to be addressed urgently. The economic growth rate fell to 9 percent in 2008, being 10.6 percent in the first quarter, 10.1 percent

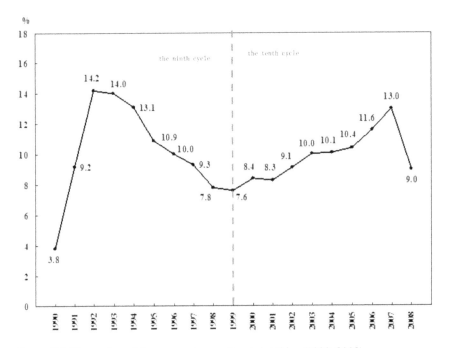

*Figure 7.1* Fluctuation of the economic growth rate in China (1990–2008)

in the second quarter, 9 percent in the third quarter and 6.8 percent in the fourth quarter, respectively.

The previously described adjustment made for the long-term and periodic issues requires the economic growth speed to be decreased properly. In the summer of 2007, the US subprime mortgage crisis caused the US economy to enter a periodic recession and adjustment (the eleventh recession since 1949), which evolved rapidly into a severe and once-a-century international financial crisis in September 2008 and further enabled the world economy to enter a major adjustment with an apparent slowdown in economic growth and the external demand of China to decline drastically. According to the latest data and the prediction announced by the International Monetary Fund on 28 January 2009, the economic growth rate of China, the United States and the world in 2008 and 2009 presented a downward tendency (see Table 7.1 and Figure 7.2). The economic growth rate in China fell from 13 percent in 2007 to 9 percent in 2008 and is estimated to drop to 6.7 percent in 2009, whereas the economic growth rate in the United States decreased from 2 percent in 2007 to 1.1 percent in 2008 and is estimated to descend to −1.6 percent in 2009. On the grounds of the latest report published by the US Department of Commerce at the end of January 2009, the GDP of the United States grew at an annualized rate of −3.8 percent in the fourth quarter of 2008, which was the greatest decline for 27 years since the first quarter of 1982. The world economic growth rate dropped from 5.2 percent in 2007 to 3.4 percent in 2008 and is estimated to fall to 0.5 percent in 2009. The report of the International Monetary Fund stated that "the world economic growth rate is predicted to decrease to 0.5% in 2009, which will be the lowest since the Second World War". The economic growth rate in Japan fell from 2.4 percent in 2007 to −0.3 percent in 2008 and is estimated to drop to −2.6 percent in 2009. The economic growth rate in the euro area descended from 2.6 percent in 2007 to 1 percent in 2008 and is estimated to fall to −2.0 percent in 2009. Among the "BRICs" countries, the economic growth rate in India fell from 9.3 percent in 2007 to 7.3 percent in 2008

*Table 7.1* Economic growth rate of the world and related countries (1998–2010)
Unit: %

| Year | China | World | US | Japan | Euro Area | India | Russia | Brazil |
|------|-------|-------|------|-------|-----------|-------|--------|--------|
| 1998 | 7.8   | 2.5   | 4.2  | −2.0  | 2.8       | 6.0   | −5.3   | 0.1    |
| 1999 | 7.6   | 3.5   | 4.5  | −0.1  | 3.0       | 6.9   | 6.4    | 0.3    |
| 2000 | 8.4   | 4.7   | 3.7  | 2.9   | 3.8       | 5.4   | 10.0   | 4.3    |
| 2001 | 8.3   | 2.2   | 0.8  | 0.2   | 1.9       | 3.9   | 5.1    | 1.3    |
| 2002 | 9.1   | 2.8   | 1.6  | 0.3   | 0.9       | 4.6   | 4.7    | 2.7    |
| 2003 | 10.0  | 3.6   | 2.5  | 1.4   | 0.8       | 6.9   | 7.3    | 1.1    |
| 2004 | 10.1  | 4.9   | 3.6  | 2.7   | 2.1       | 7.9   | 7.2    | 5.7    |
| 2005 | 10.4  | 4.5   | 3.1  | 1.9   | 1.6       | 9.1   | 6.4    | 3.2    |
| 2006 | 11.6  | 5.1   | 2.8  | 2.2   | 2.8       | 9.7   | 6.7    | 3.8    |
| 2007 | 13.0  | 5.2   | 2.0  | 2.4   | 2.6       | 9.3   | 8.1    | 5.7    |
| 2008 | 9.0   | 3.4   | 1.1  | −0.3  | 1.0       | 7.3   | 6.2    | 5.8    |
| 2009 | 6.7   | 0.5   | −1.6 | −2.6  | −2.0      | 5.1   | −0.7   | 1.8    |
| 2010 | 8.0   | 3.0   | 1.6  | 0.6   | 0.2       | 6.5   | 1.3    | 3.5    |

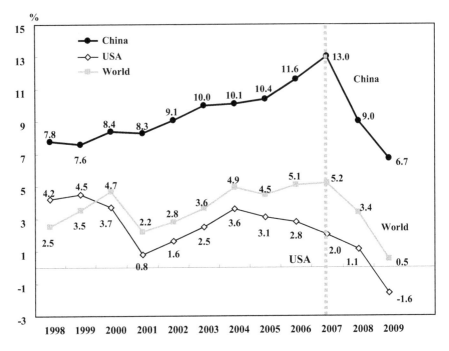

*Figure 7.2* Economic growth rates of China, the United States and the world (1998–2009)

and is estimated to drop to 5.1 percent in 2009; the economic growth rate in Russia fell from 8.1 percent in 2007 to 6.2 percent in 2008 and is estimated to drop to −0.7 percent in 2009; and the economic growth rate in Brazil rose slightly from 5.7 percent in 2007 to 5.8 percent in 2008 and is estimated to drop to 1.8 percent in 2009.

The expansion effect of the multiple international and domestic adjustments produces enormous pressures in two aspects. On the one hand, it increases the pressure in the transformation of the economic growth mode and the structural adjustment. This requires the economic growth to transform from relying mainly on investment and exports to relying on consumption, investment and export coordination, from depending primarily on the secondary industry to depending on the collaboration of the primary, secondary and tertiary industries and from relying mainly on increasing material and resource consumption and low-cost expansion to relying primarily on scientific and technological progress and the construction of an innovation-oriented country and a resource-efficient and environment-friendly society. On the other hand, it further intensifies the pressure of the economic downside in China. The financial crisis in 2008–09 was the most severe in the world since the Great Depression during the period from 1929 to 1933. In particular, it has not yet reached its lowest point and its impact on finance and the real economy is continuously spreading and deepening.

### Economic growth presenting a trend of high rises in the first half and low rises in the second half in 2008

In 2008, some economic indicators fell rather gently and slowly in terms of the total year-on-year monthly growth rate, but they dropped greatly in terms of the same-month year-on-year growth rate, presenting a trend of high rises in the first half and low rises in the second half in 2008.

*Industrial added value of the nationwide enterprises above the designated size*

In 2008, the industrial added value of the nationwide enterprises above the designated size declined mildly and slowly (see Figure 7.3) in terms of the total growth rate from January to December on a year-on-year basis, falling from the highest point of 16.4 percent in the period from January to March to 12.9 percent in the period from January to December and merely decreasing by 3.5 percent. However, in terms of the same-month year-on-year growth rate, it fell rapidly from 16 percent in June to 5.4 percent in November, dropping by 10.6 percent, resembling a high-platform dive. In comparison with the historical data, this was the lowest growth for 17 years after the decrease to 5 percent in December 1991, excluding the data from January and February, which are greatly influenced by the seasons in each year. It was even lower than the monthly growth in 1998 and 1999 when they received a great impact from the Asian financial crisis. The year-on-year growth rate of the industrial added value in December was 5.7 percent,

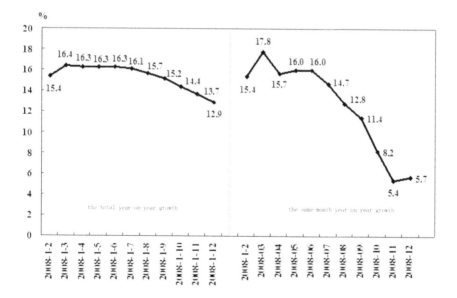

*Figure 7.3* Growth rate of the industrial added value for the nationwide enterprises above the designated size

0.3 percent higher than that of November, preliminarily showing a certain containment of the trend of a sharp drop in growth.

*Export growth rate*

In 2008, the export growth rate fell rather gently and slowly in terms of the total year-on-year monthly growth rate, decreasing from the highest point of 22.9 percent in the period from January to May to 17.2 percent in the period from January to December and merely declining by 5.7 percent (see Figure 7.4). However, in terms of the same-month year-on-year growth rate, it fell from 26.9 percent in July to 19.2 percent in October and further dropped rapidly to −2.2 percent in November. It descended by 29.1 percent from July to November, even more like a high-platform dive. The export growth rate in December further declined to −2.8 percent. In comparison with the historical data, the year-on-year export growth rate of −2.2 percent in November was negative for the first time in seven years after the decrease to −0.5 percent in June 2001.

*Import growth rate*

In 2008, the import growth rate fell rather gently and slowly in terms of the total year-on-year monthly growth rate, descending from the highest point of 31.1 percent in the period from January to July to 18.5 percent in the period from January to December and declining by 12.6 percent (see Figure 7.5). However, in terms of the same-month year-on-year growth rate, it fell from 40.0 percent in May to 15.6 percent in October and further dropped rapidly to −17.9 percent in November.

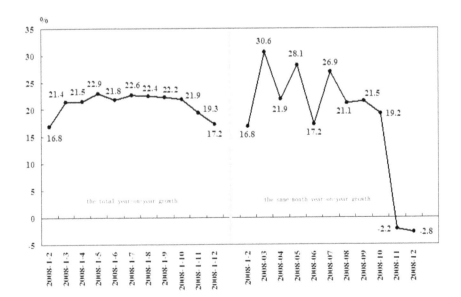

*Figure 7.4* Export growth rate

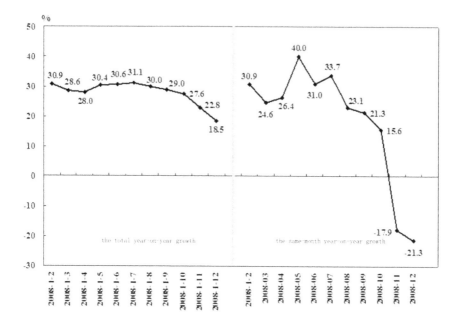

*Figure 7.5* Import growth rate

It decreased precipitously by 57.9 percent from May to November. The year-on-year import growth rate in December further declined to −21.3 percent.

### Imbalance of the economic growth in various regions

In 2008, the fluctuation of the economic growth was very imbalanced in various regions, among which the growth in the eastern coastal region decreased very early and considerably. Examining the growth of the industrial added value of the enterprises above the designated size in various regions from 2001 to 2008 (hereinafter referred to as "industrial growth"), Figure 7.6 depicts the fluctuation curve of the nationwide industrial growth. On the whole, this growth was basically in the rising stage during the period from 2001 to 2007 (see the trend line in Figure 7.6), during which it continuously maintained high growth at a rate of 16 percent to 18 percent from 2003 to 2007. The peak of the industrial growth reached 18.5 percent in 2007 and fell to 12.9 percent in 2008, decreasing by 5.6 percent.

The fluctuation of the industrial growth in various regions can be divided into the following four types:

Type 1 is a round-arched fluctuation. In some regions, the rising stage of the fluctuation of the industrial growth occurred two or three years ago and the fluctuation has been in the falling stage in the recent two or three years, thus presenting a round-arched fluctuation, under which the industrial growth fell greatly from the peak in previous years to that in 2008. Twelve regions out of thirty-one provinces,

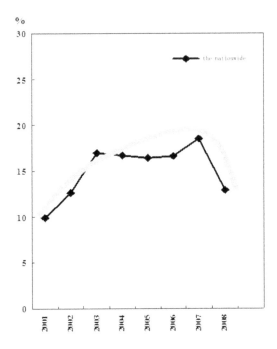

*Figure 7.6* Fluctuation curve of the nationwide industrial growth

autonomous regions and municipalities in China (excluding Hong Kong and Macao) presented this type of fluctuation. They consisted of seven regions in the eastern coastal areas, Zhejiang (see Figure 7.7), Jiangsu (see Figure 7.8), Guangdong (see Figure 7.9), Shandong (see Figure 7.10), Beijing, Shanghai and Hebei; and five regions in the west, Guizhou, Tibet, Gansu, Ningxia and Inner Mongolia.

The industrial growth in Zhejiang reached a peak of 23.7 percent in 2003, began to fall in 2004 and decreased greatly to 10.1 percent in 2008, declining by 13.6 percent. Moreover, the growth in 2008 was even lower than that in 2001 (12.5 percent). The industrial growth in Zhejiang was higher than that of the whole country during the period from 2001 to 2006, whereas it was lower in 2007 and 2008.

The industrial growth in Jiangsu reached a peak of 23.4 percent in 2004, began to fall in 2005 and decreased to 14.2 percent in 2008, falling by 9.2 percent.

The industrial growth in Guangdong reached a peak of 22.4 percent in 2004 as well, experienced a falling stage from 2005 to the present and declined to 12.8 percent in 2008, decreasing by 9.6 percent.

The industrial growth in Shandong reached a peak of 28.4 percent in 2005, began to fall in 2006 and decreased to 13.8 percent in 2008, declining by 14.6 percent.

Type 2 is a dual-peak fluctuation that starts to fall. In some regions, the fluctuation of the industrial growth has implied two small cycles since 2001, presenting a dual-peak fluctuation, in which once the first small cycle was over, during the second small cycle, the industrial growth rose in the last one or two years and

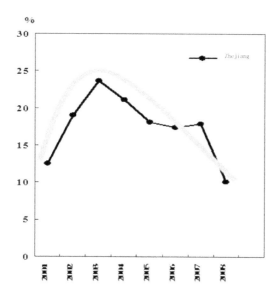

*Figure 7.7* Fluctuation curve of the industrial growth in Zhejiang

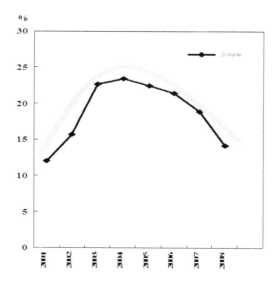

*Figure 7.8* Fluctuation curve of the industrial growth in Jiangsu

began to fall in 2008. Twelve regions presented this type of fluctuation. They con-sisted of five regions in the middle of China, Hubei (see Figure 7.11), Hunan (see Figure 7.12), Anhui, Shanxi and Jiangxi, and Fujian (see Figure 7.13), Hainan, Sichuan, Yunnan, Chongqing (see Figure 7.14), Liaoning and Jilin. Except for

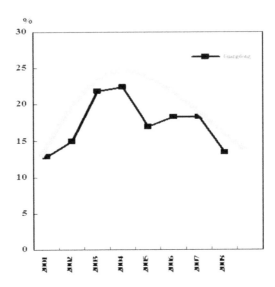

*Figure 7.9* Fluctuation curve of the industrial growth in Guangdong

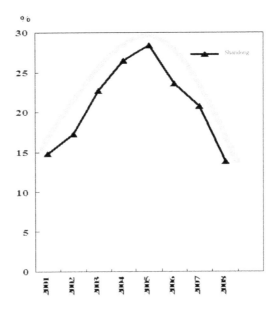

*Figure 7.10* Fluctuation curve of the industrial growth in Shandong

Hainan and Shanxi, the industrial growth of the remaining 10 regions fell by a small amount from the peak to that in 2008 during the second small cycle.

Taking Hubei as an example, the two peaks of its industrial growth appeared in 2004 and 2007, respectively. The industrial growth was 23.6 percent in 2007 and 21.6 percent in 2008, merely falling by 2 percent.

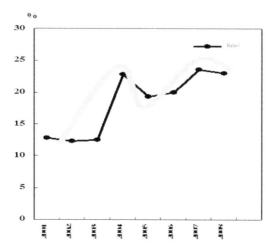

*Figure 7.11* Fluctuation curve of the industrial growth in Hubei

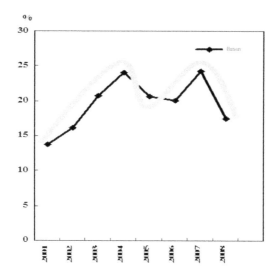

*Figure 7.12* Fluctuation curve of the industrial growth in Hunan

Type 3 is a crescent-shape fluctuation. In some regions, on the whole, the fluctuation of the industrial growth remained in the rising stage from 2001 to 2007 and started to fall in 2008, presenting a crescent-shape fluctuation. The industrial growth also fell by a small amount from the peak in 2007 to that in 2008. The three regions that presented this type of fluctuation were Guangxi (see Figure 7.15), Henan (see Figure 7.16) and Heilongjiang.

Taking Guangxi as an example, the industrial growth rose from 8.6 percent in 2001 to 26.5 percent in 2007 and decreased to 22.6 percent in 2008, falling by 3.9 percent.

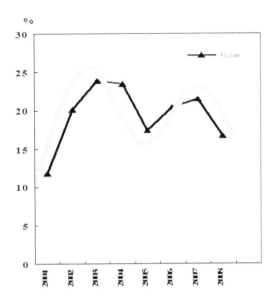

*Figure 7.13* Fluctuation curve of the industrial growth in Fujian

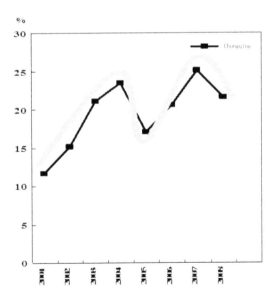

*Figure 7.14* Fluctuation curve of the industrial growth in Chongqing

Type 4 is a dual-peak fluctuation that is still rising. In some regions, the fluctuation of the industrial growth implied two small cycles, presenting a dual-peak fluctuation, in which the first small cycle was over. However, the industrial growth rose in 2008, rather than descending during the second small cycle. The four regions that presented this type of fluctuation were Shaanxi

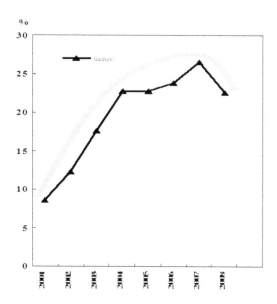

*Figure 7.15* Fluctuation curve of the industrial growth in Guangxi

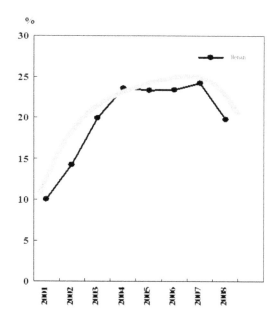

*Figure 7.16* Fluctuation curve of the industrial growth in Henan

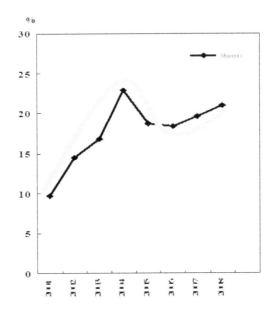

*Figure 7.17* Fluctuation curve of the industrial growth in Shaanxi

(see Figure 7.17), Qinghai (see Figure 7.18), Xinjiang (see Figure 7.19) and Tianjin (see Figure 7.20).

Taking Shaanxi as an example, the growth trough for the industrial added value of enterprises above the designated size was 18.4 percent during the second small cycle in 2006 and reached 21 percent in 2008, rising by 2.6 percent.

We can conclude from the preceding analysis that the fluctuation of economic growth has been very imbalanced among various regions in recent years. In particular, some eastern coastal regions have already experienced the adjustment process, with their growth speed falling before the international financial crisis broke out. On the other hand, we can perceive that the whole macro economy is still able to maintain a certain level of steady growth in the current and future adjustment and is unlikely to fall greatly owing to the imbalance of the economic growth and the different times necessary for adjustment in various regions.

### *Rapid fall-back in the price increase*

*Monthly rate of residents' consumption price increase*
*on a year-on-year basis*

The price increase fell back rapidly in 2008, which provided space for the implementation of an expansionary macro regulation policy. This round of the residents' consumption price increase started with 4.4 percent in June 2007 (see Figure 7.21) and subsequently maintained a high rate ranging from 6.2 percent to 6.9 percent for five consecutive months from August to December. It rose to a high level above 8 percent during the period from February to April in 2008,

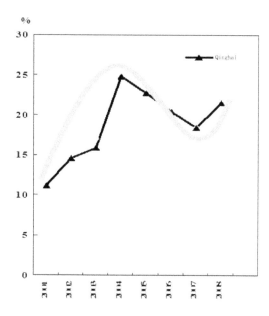

*Figure 7.18* Fluctuation curve of the industrial growth in Qinghai

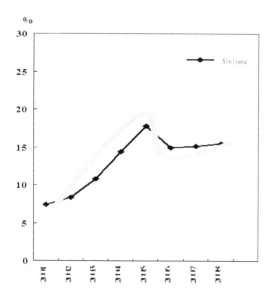

*Figure 7.19* Fluctuation curve of the industrial growth in Xinjiang

which was the highest increase for nearly 12 years since the monthly rate of residents' consumption price increase reached 8.9 percent in May 1996 on a year-on-year basis. Thus, curbing price inflation became a prominent issue in macro regulation. After May 2008, the price increase fell month by month and dropped to 1.2 percent in December. The annual rate of the price increase in

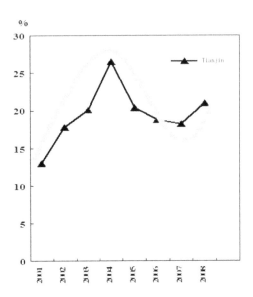

*Figure 7.20* Fluctuation curve of the industrial growth in Tianjin

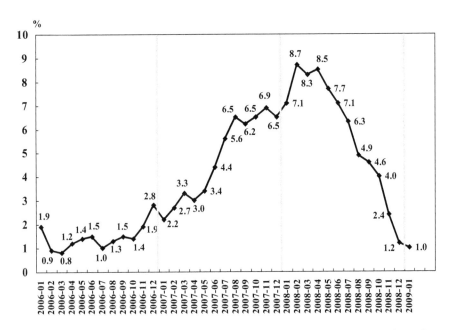

*Figure 7.21* Year-on-year rate of the monthly increase in residents' consumption price (January 2006–January 2009)

crops

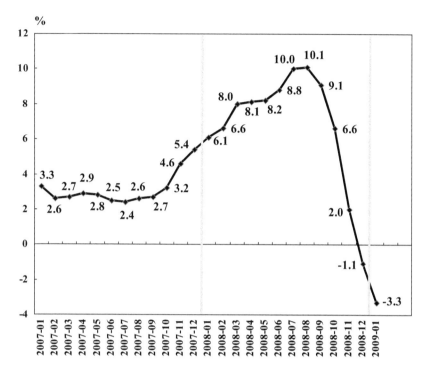

*Figure 7.22* Year-on-year rate of the monthly increase in the ex-factory price for industrial products (January 2007–January 2009)

2008 was 5.6 percent. In January 2009, the rate of the price increase decreased to 1 percent.

*Monthly rate of the ex-factory price increase for industrial products on a year-on-year basis*

The ex-factory price for industrial products rose from 2.6 percent in August 2007 to as high as 10.1 percent in August 2008 (see Figure 7.22). It started to fall in September 2008, dropped to −1.1 percent in December and continuously decreased to −3.3 percent in January 2009, showing an absolute decline in the ex-factory price for industrial products.

## Analysis of the national and international economic trends in 2009

*Uncertainties in the international economic trends*

The international economic trend is still very uncertain in 2009. There are different views on when the impacts of the US subprime mortgage crisis and the international financial crisis on the world's economic growth will reach the bottom. Summing up various predictions and analyses (Finch, 2008),[1] the following six scenarios may occur in relation to the international economic trend:

The first is a V-shape fluctuation (reaching the bottom). After the world economy has experienced a short-term drastic decline, the rescue plan of various countries will have been proved to be successful. The world economy will reach the bottom in 2009 and may recover at the beginning of 2010.

The second is a U-shape fluctuation (wide bottom). After the world economy has experienced a severe decrease, it is unable to recover immediately after reaching the bottom. Instead, a very wide bottom is drawn out. For example, the world economy will experience a downturn for a period of three to five years and will recover afterwards because banks will still be reluctant to increase their lending and give a lower interest rate to borrowers with the aim of avoiding risks although the interest rate will decrease. In the meantime, the governments of various countries will be unable to put forward any more effective stimuli.

The third is a W-shape fluctuation (dual bottom). The world economy will touch the bottom twice, that is, it will experience a depression twice. After going through the first depression, it will fall into the second depression while it is just recovering owing to the possible impact of oil production reduction or new agricultural drought. Meanwhile, if inflation emerges in the first resurgence, the policy of raising interest rates will cause borrowers to lose confidence because they will suffer as a result of paying their debts. The rate of housing property repossessions and the quantity of bankrupt companies will rise again.

The fourth is that it is still hard to discuss the bottom (no bottom).While entering 2009, the internationally prevalent thought is that the crisis is still continuing and the second financial tsunami is approaching. Thus, it is hard to talk about the bottom in the short run. On the one hand, following Lehman Brothers' bankruptcy on 15 September 2008 and the first financial tsunami that swept over the world, the losses of the European and US financial magnates and the international financial market turmoil have become increasingly severe again since the beginning of 2009. On the other hand, the international financial crisis has greatly influenced the real economy. Conversely, the depression of the real economy has transmitted to finance and constantly increased the risks for banks, contributing to the second financial crisis. To take strict precautions against the upgrading of the financial crisis, the United States and some European countries have recently initiated a second upsurge of government bailouts.

The fifth is an L-shape fluctuation (long bottom). After the world economy has experienced a decline, it is difficult to recover in the medium and short term and a long bottom will be dragged out, for example, over 10 years. Just as shown in Japanese banking following the crisis, inflation will transform into long-term deflation. The bankruptcy rate of enterprises will hit a new peak with increased unemployment and bankruptcy in banks and insurance companies. The stock index will drop significantly and be hard to revitalize.

The sixth is a great depression. For example, the war in the Middle East causes the world oil price to rise to the highest level and forces the central banks of various countries to raise the interest rate one after another to guard against the risk of inflation, thus resulting in a severe economic depression in most large countries. The bank system in some countries will crash, preventing people from saving and withdrawing cash. The unemployment rate will exceed that of the 1930s. The world total output will maintain a constant decreasing situation in the long term, thus producing massive social upheaval and political convulsions. Since December 2008, the spreading and deepening of the international financial crisis has led to a tide of social protests in European countries. On 29 January 2009, the first massive strike broke out in France since the financial crisis.

At present, the first prediction is dominant; specifically, the world economic trend will present a V-shape fluctuation, reaching the bottom in 2009 and recovering in 2010. For example, according to the latest prediction by the International Monetary Fund on 28 January 2009, the world economy will recover gradually in 2010. The world economic growth rate will recover from the trough of 0.5 percent in 2009 to 3 percent in 2010. In the same period, China's economy will recover from 6.7 percent to 8 percent; the US economy from −1.6 percent to 1.6 percent; the Japanese economy from −2.6 percent to 0.6 percent; the economy in the euro area from −2 percent to 0.2 percent; the Indian economy from 5.1 percent to 6.5 percent; the Russian economy from −0.7 percent to 1.3 percent; the Brazilian economy from 1.8 percent to 3.5 percent; developed economies from −2 percent to 1.1 percent; and new and developing economies from 3.3 percent to 5 percent. However, the International Monetary Fund emphasized its prediction that the world economy would recover gradually in 2010 but that the prospect was very uncertain. The report issued by the World Bank on 9 December 2008 also predicted that the world economy would recover in 2010.

### Uncertainties in the national economic trends

Affected by the uncertainties of the international economic trends, the economic trend in China remains very uncertain in 2009, which is reflected in the predictions for China's economic growth rate in 2009 made by various related institutions and scholars. Many different forecasts can be summed up as the following seven types (see Table 7.2):

The low prediction involved three groups: the first group predicted that the GDP growth rate of China in 2009 would be 5 percent, which was announced by Royal Bank of Scotland; the second group predicted that the GDP growth rate of China in 2009 would be 6.7 percent, which was announced by the International Monetary Fund; and the third group predicted that the GDP growth rate of China in 2009 would be 7–7.5 percent, which was announced by the Deutsche Bank and the World Bank.

*Table 7.2* Predictions of the GDP growth rate of China in 2009

| Serial No | State | GDP Growth Rate | Forecaster |
|---|---|---|---|
| 1 | First group of low prediction | 5% | Royal Bank of Scotland |
| 2 | Second group of low prediction | 6.7% | International Monetary Fund |
| 3 | Third group of low prediction | 7%–7.5% | Deutsche Bank, World Bank |
| 4 | First group of medium prediction | 8%–8.4% | Hang Seng Bank, United Nations Development Program |
| 5 | Second group of medium prediction | 8.5% | Bank of China (Hong Kong) Limited |
| 6 | First group of high prediction | Slightly above 9% | Certain institutions and scholars in China |
| 7 | Second group of high prediction | Around 10% | Certain institutions and scholars in China |

Two groups made a medium prediction: the first group predicted that the GDP growth rate of China in 2009 would be 8–8.4 percent, which was announced by the Hang Seng Bank and the United Nations Development Program; and the second group predicted that the GDP growth rate of China in 2009 would be 8.5 percent, which was announced by the Bank of China (Hong Kong) Limited.

The high prediction concerned two groups: the first group predicted that the GDP growth rate of China in 2009 would be slightly above 9 percent, which was announced by some domestic institutions and scholars; and the second group predicted that the GDP growth rate of China in 2009 would be around 10 percent, which was also announced by some institutions and scholars. They believed that China's economic growth would start to recover in the first quarter of 2009 and might achieve a high level in the fourth quarter. The annual growth rate might reach around 10 percent. However, the economy might become overheated in the first quarter of 2010 (Wang Hongru, 2009).[2]

It is important to note that the International Monetary Fund made predictions for the world economy and that of each country for 2009 five times. The predictions for China's economic growth rate in 2009 are as follows:

The first time was in April 2008 with a predicted rate of 9.5 percent;

The second time was in July 2008 with a predicted rate of 9.8 percent, 0.3 percent higher than the last time.

The third time was in October 2008 with a predicted rate of 9.3 percent, 0.5 percent lower than the last time.

The fourth time was in November 2008 with a predicted rate of 8.5 percent, 0.8 percent lower than the last time again.

The fifth time was in January 2009 with a predicted rate of 6.7 percent, 1.8 percent lower than the last time again.

This further demonstrates that China's economic trend in 2009 is very uncertain. Following the latest announced prediction of 6.7 percent made by the International Monetary Fund on 28 January, its president, Kahn, answering the questions of reporters from Xinhua News Agency on 2 February, stated that China's growth target of 8 percent was challenging, but it might be realized considering China's considerable potential for stimulating the economy. He emphasized that China's economic performance in the past had already exceeded people's expectations.

It is necessary to clarify that the United Nations Development Program published a report entitled "World Economic Situation and Prospect in 2009" in January 2009 and designed three prediction programs. According to its first benchmark program, the economic growth rate in China in 2009 would be 8.4 percent. In the light of its second, optimistic program, the growth rate could reach 8.9 percent. In accordance with its third, pessimistic program, the growth rate would be 7 percent.

*Hopefully the national economic growth will present a trend of low rises in the first half and high rises in the second half in 2009*

Some experts' and scholars' analyses indicated that the GDP growth would hopefully present a V-shape rebound. It might continue to decline and seek a bottom in the first quarter of 2009 and tend to be steady and recover in the second quarter because the state published a series of regulatory measures for expanding the domestic demand in the fourth quarter of 2008. The effects would be revealed gradually. Meanwhile, many enterprises may reduce their accumulated inventories by the end of the second quarter. The GDP growth rate is estimated to reach around 7–7.5 percent in the first half of 2009 and may be above 8 percent in the second half of 2009, hopefully taking the lead in escaping from the economic downtrend and realizing the earliest recovery among the world's large economies. It is promising to ensure that the annual GDP growth rate will reach 8 percent.

Some experts and scholars made different predictions and believed that the economic fluctuation in China might produce a W-shape recovery involving seeking the bottom twice (Shi Beibei, 2009),[3] because the trend of low rises in the first half and high rises in the second half in the year-on-year quarterly economic growth rate in 2009 actually implied the base effect of the trend of high rises in the first half and low rises in the second half in the year-on-year quarterly economic growth rate in 2008 and the quarterly economic growth in 2009 would still fall compared with that of the recent quarter. In the meantime, the slowdown of enterprises' investment was just starting and would last for about a year and a half. Therefore, the GDP growth rate touched the bottom in the fourth quarter in 2008 for the first time and rebounded to a certain extent in 2009, but it might seek the bottom again in the first half of 2010.

*Facing obvious deflation pressure*

Experts and scholars pointed out that the inflation pressure had decreased, as shown by the price increase in residents' consumption falling from 8.7 percent in

February 2008 to 1.2 percent in December. However, there is obvious deflation pressure in 2009. In terms of the annual price increase in residents' consumption, on the whole, there are three predictions. The first one is −0.2−−0.5 percent; the second one is 1–2 percent; and the third one is around 4 percent because some experts and scholars believe that we should not rule out the possibility of a rebound in inflation along with the development of massive investment.

### Gloomy export trend

The impact of this financial crisis on the decrease in China's external demand is much greater than that of the Asian financial crisis in 1997 and 1998 because the US and European developed economies grew positively at that time. Currently, the three large economies, the United States, Japan and Europe, will all fall into negative growth simultaneously in 2009 and the world economic growth rate will drop to as low as 0.5 percent, which will be the lowest growth rate since World War II. Against this background, it will be impossible for the exports in China to increase more than 20 percent annually or even to exceed 30 percent, as it did in the period from 2002 to 2007. Specifically, experts and scholars have made different predictions about China's export increase in 2009. They can be summed up as follows: 1) zero growth; 2) negative growth; 3) feeble growth, for example 2–3 percent; and 4) medium and low growth of around 5–10 percent.

### Significant adjustments to the macro regulation policy

Three significant adjustments were made to the macro regulation policy within the short time of one year at the Central Economic Working Conference at the ends of 2007 and 2008 to cope with the complicated and changeable trends of the national and international economy in a timely and effective manner.

The first significant adjustment was carried out at the Central Economic Working Conference at the beginning of December 2007. Directed against the rapid economic growth and the increasing inflation pressure, the primary task of macro regulation was adjusted from preventing rapid economic growth from transforming into an overheated economy to avoiding both an overheated economy transformed from rapid economic growth and obvious inflation evolving from a structural price increase. Correspondingly, a steady monetary policy was adjusted to a tight monetary policy.

Following the first significant adjustment, certain fine adjustments were made to the operation of macro regulation in accordance with the constant changes in the domestic and international economic situation. First, by the end of January 2008, it was put forward that "we should scientifically grasp the pace and strength of macro regulation". When the Central Economic Working Conference closed in December 2007, the prevalent expectation for the macro regulation policy in 2008 was in particular that the monetary policy would become tighter. However, entering 2008, the world economic growth was faced with many uncertain factors, such as slowing down due to the spread of the impact of the US subprime mortgage crisis. On 31 January 2008, the *People's Daily* published the speech delivered by President Hu Jintao in the third group study among the members of the Political Bureau of CPC Central Committee and asserted that "we should properly hold the world economic trend and its impacts and fully recognize the complexity and changeability of the external economic environment to scientifically grasp the pace and strength of macro regulation". On the second day, 1 February 2008, the *China Securities Journal*, *Shanghai Securities News* and *Securities Times*, respectively, published commentaries entitled "Scientifically Grasp the Pace and Strength of Macro Regulation" and believed that the macro regulation policy might be finely adjusted and become loose. Second, on 5 March 2008, the *Government Work Report* proposed that the rapid economic growth should be prevented from transforming into an overheated economy and the obvious inflation evolving from a structural price increase should be avoided, taking these as the primary tasks of macro regulation in the economic work in 2008. Particularly, it put forward the idea that

> in view of many uncertain factors in the development of the current domestic and international economic situation, we should closely follow up and analyze new situations and new issues and make a correct assessment to take corresponding measures timely and flexibly from the reality and grasp the pace, stress and strength of macro regulation properly with the purpose of maintaining steady and rapid economic development and avoiding violent ups and downs.

Third, on 29 March 2008, the *Key Work of the State Council of 2008* proposed that "we should guard against an economic decline". "We need to prevent a rapid economic growth from transforming into an overheated economy to curb inflation and avoid an economic downturn and violent ups and downs" (Key Work of the State Council of 2008, 2008).[4]

The second significant adjustment was made at the Conference of the Political Bureau of Central Committee on 25 July 2008. The prime task of macro regulation was adjusted from the prevention of an overheated economy and obvious inflation to the maintenance of steady and rapid economic development and the control of an overly rapid price increase. The difference was the change from the prevention of an overheated economy to the maintenance of steady and rapid economic development, implying the prevention of an economic downturn.

The third significant adjustment was made after October 2008, transforming from the maintenance of steady and rapid economic development and the control of an overly rapid price increase to an assurance of development, an expansion of domestic demand and a structural adjustment. In September 2008, the US subprime mortgage crisis evolved rapidly to become the most serious global financial crisis in a century. China's economy was affected to a great extent. However, the issue of price increase was no longer a prominent contradiction as it declined month by month from May 2008. First, on 17 October 2008, the executive meeting of the State Council proposed to adopt a flexible and prudent macroeconomic policy to ensure development. Second, on 5 November 2008, the executive meeting of the State Council put forward the implementation of a proactive fiscal policy and a moderately easy monetary policy and published 10 important measures for expanding the domestic demand and promoting economic growth, with a proposal for a massive investment program of construction projects of the central government amounting to 4000 billion yuan within two years (among which the investment of the central government amounted to 1180 billion yuan, driving local and social investments and reaching a total of 4000 billion yuan). Third, on 28 November 2008, the conference of the Political Bureau of CPC Central Committee proposed to take the maintenance of steady and rapid economic development as the primary task of the economic work in 2009 and better combine the assurance of development, the expansion of domestic demand and the structural adjustment. Fourth, from 8 December 2008 to 10 December 2008, the Central Economic Working Conference further stated explicitly that the overly rapid economic slowdown had become a prominent issue in the current economic operation. It was necessary to take the maintenance of steady and rapid economic development as the primary task of the economic work in 2009. The conference raised four guiding principles for working hard to ensure development. In detail, they were to take an expansion of the domestic demand as a fundamental method, accelerate the transformation of growth mode and the structural adjustment as a major direction, undertake a deepening reform in key regions and links and an improvement in opening wider to the outside world as a strong impetus and improve people's livelihood as a supreme goal and ultimate objective to ensure development.

## Issues for further research

### *Successfully dealing with the relationship between government and market*

To cope with the international financial crisis, the governments of various countries apparently intensified their interference in the economy. An international commentary pointed out that 2008 would be a turning point in the transformation of the Western mainstream economic theory and policy from laissez-faire to government intervention.

From the perspective of the history of Western economics, facing different economic issues at different times, the evolution of the decision regarding government intervention or laissez-faire for market development has been a mainstream issue and has experienced four periods from the fifteenth century to date.

The first period was from the fifteenth century to the seventeenth century, when mercantilism was the mainstream economic thought popular in Western Europe at that time. In the late period of Western Europe's feudal society and during the nascent stage of the budding and gradual growth of the capitalist mode of production, mercantilism advocated proactive interference in the economy by a state and the intensification of state power of feudal centralization to develop a commodity economy and break the feudal separatist rule, with the purpose of expanding foreign trade and implementing protective tariffs to protect domestic industries.

The second period was from the eighteenth century to the 1930s, when mainstream economic theory transformed to bourgeois classical economics and the subsequent neoclassical economics. They advocated economic liberalism and opposed state intervention in the economy with the view of liberating the productive forces from the fetters of the feudal system and further developing them. They held that all protective policies and restrictive measures must be eliminated regardless of domestic trade or foreign trade and believed that a capitalist market economy is able to be self-regulated and self-balanced and solve an economic crisis by itself.

The third period was from the 1930s to the 1970s, when the mainstream of the economic theory transformed to Keynesianism. The Great Depression that took place in the period from 1929 to 1933 broke the long-term dominance of the classical market equilibrium theory and enabled a rapid rise of Keynesianism, which advocated smoothing economic fluctuations through government intervention owing to the defects of a market economy.

The fourth period was from the 1970s to 2008, when the mainstream economic theory transformed to modern neoclassical economics. Under the impact of the oil crisis that occurred in the 1970s and the predicament of the severe economic stagflation, along with the failure of Keynesianism, various modern forms of neoclassical economics advocating the free development of a market economy, an opposition to government intervention and deregulation of government control, rose in succession.

Nevertheless, the international financial crisis that broke out in September 2008, like the Great Depression in the period from 1929 to 1933 and the oil crisis in the 1970s, flung down a challenge to the original mainstream economic theory of opposing government intervention. Facing a severe crisis, many countries shifted the focus of their economic policy to massive government intervention for market rescue. An international commentary pointed out that a turf war was being carried out again between government and market and the pendulum between them was swinging back.

We believe that the government function in managing an economy and the fundamental role of the market in resource allocation supplement and complement each other in the condition of modern market economy. Thus, it is possible to dispense with neither the government, "the Visible Hand", nor the market, "the Invisible Hand". To perform the nation's economic function and guarantee national economic safety, rational and perfect government intervention is all the more necessary to make up for the deficiencies of a market economy and protect the normal operational order of a market mechanism. In particular, in coping with the most severe international financial crisis in a century, the function of the government, "the Visible Hand", will inevitably be strengthened. However, the market economy is still the basis of economic activities and operation. The fundamental role of the market, "the Invisible Hand", in resource allocation will not change. In the conditions prevailing in China, we should continuously enhance and improve the government function in managing the economy and simultaneously recognize that the socialist market economic system has just been established in China. Thus, the market development is immature and the function of the market mechanism is imperfect. We must firmly insist on the reformation of the socialist market economy in the current assurance of development and expansion of domestic demand. We need to eliminate the systematic and mechanism obstacles that restrain the expansion of domestic demand and establish a system or mechanism that encourages enterprises' rational investment and supports residents' rational consumption through deepening the reform. The expansion of the domestic demand and the assurance of development and employment ultimately rely on enterprises, residents and the whole society. Taking the fund sources of the social fixed-assets investment as an example, the proportion of the state budgetary fund fell from 28.1 percent in 1981 at the beginning of the reform and opening up to 3.9 percent in 2007, decreasing by 24.2 percent, whereas the proportion of the self-financing fund of various regions, sectors, enterprises and institutions rose from 55.4 percent to 77.4 percent, increasing by 22 percent in the same period. Presently, the government's direct investment merely accounts for a very small proportion of the whole social investment. An investment expansion mainly relies on enterprises and the whole society, that is, it depends on the exertion of the fundamental role of the market in resource allocation. Currently, due to the severe employment situation nationwide, governments at all levels are actively creating conditions for expanding employment. However, to solve an employment issue extensively, they must rely more on numerous small and medium-sized enterprises and the whole society.

### Wisely managing the relationship between prosperity and adjustment during the economic periodic fluctuation

For thirty years, since the reform and opening up, China has achieved the great historical transition of a highly centralized planned economic system into a vibrant socialist market economic system. However, a market economy fluctuates, rather than remaining calm and tranquil. Various stages of the economic periodic fluctuation or various economic situations, such as prosperity and adjustment, ascent and descent, expansion and recession, easing and tightening, prosperity and crisis, inflation and deflation, are inherently interrelated with a certain interchangeability. In a sense, each time of prosperity breeds the next adjustment and every adjustment breeds the next time of prosperity.

In the current international and domestic economic situation we are able to gain the following enlightenment from this relationship. First, every adjustment and crisis frequently breeds new opportunities for development in the survival of the fittest and brings about new breakthroughs in science and technology, products and management. This is what we call "a crisis implies an opportunity". Currently, in coping with various difficulties and challenges, we should be fully confident and transform pressure into power and challenge into an opportunity to identify and cultivate new sources of economic growth in adversity. Second, we need to avoid blind excessive expansion and newly created bubbles during the implementation of a loose policy and the promotion of expansion. In resolving the immediate issues, we should attend to the implied and hidden issues, follow up the situation closely and discover new circumstances and new incipient tendencies in a timely manner to avoid great accumulated problems, remembering the common saying that one tendency covers up another. One significant lesson learned from the US subprime mortgage crisis is that, with the purpose of preventing a severe economic recession and stimulating economic recovery, an excessively loose policy with a lack of regulation was implemented in 2001, the trough of the last economic cycle. This led to the real estate bubbles prior to and after the economic peak in 2004 and ultimately resulted in the severe crisis in 2007 and 2008. At present, the academic sphere and the society are worried about the massive investment program of 4000 billion yuan within two years in China. They are worried about whether the massive investment will give rise to a new round of overheated economy and inflation rebound. Since many construction projects involve problems of land utilization, they are concerned about whether the warning limit of 1.8 billion mu of arable land can be maintained. As a result of the extensive mode of expansion that some local governments and enterprises may follow, they are worried that excessive consumption of energy resources, destruction of the ecological environment and low-level redundant development will make energy conservation, emission reduction and pollution control more difficult. They fear that government-oriented investment will create various forms of corruption.

*Handling the relationship between investment and consumption well*

The problem of disproportionate investment and consumption, specifically the high investment rate and the low consumption rate, has remained unresolved for many years in China. Since the start of the new century, the consumption rate constantly decreased from 62.3 percent in 2000 to 48.8 percent in 2007, falling by 13.5 percent during the acceleration of industrialization and urbanization, whereas the investment rate rose from 35.3 percent to 42.3 percent, increasing by 7 percent, and the net export rate climbed from 2.4 percent to 8.9 percent, rising by 6.5 percent in the same period. Numerous measures have been taken to expand consumption, such as improving the income of medium- and low-income residents, perfecting various social security systems, cultivating new hot consumption spots, steadily increasing the consumption of big-ticket items like housing and automobiles and expanding the consumption of public services like education, health and culture so as to ensure development and expand the domestic demand. However, it is worthwhile discussing the issue that an expansion in investment will still cause the investment rate to increase during the acceleration of industrialization and urbanization and the upgrading of the consumption structure to housing and transportation at the present stage in China.

Along with the enhancement of China's overall national power, we attach great importance to various projects that are related to the direct improvement of people's livelihood in this investment expansion, such as increasing the government's investment in and construction of welfare-oriented housing, which is different from its previous investments. We need to clarify the special relationship between investment and consumption in housing construction. Housing construction is added as "investment" to "fixed capital formation" of the gross domestic product by the expenditure approach according to the international unified prescribed statistics of the national economic accounting. Although the self-used houses that residents purchase are complete consumption in terms of residents' life, they are merely added annually to "final consumption" as a small depreciation cost in the above statistics. For example, for a house that is worth 900,000 yuan and takes 3 years to build, 300,000 yuan will be added annually, on average, to the "fixed capital formation" of the gross domestic product by the expenditure approach. Although the residents spend 900,000 yuan purchasing the house, an annual depreciation rate of 2 percent over a period of 50 years means that only 18,000 yuan per annum will be added annually to "final consumption" in the statistics of the gross domestic product by the expenditure approach. In brief, housing, acting as a special commodity, is added as "investment" in annual statistics, which is more than that of "consumption" in the statistics. The investment rate will be relatively high when a country is experiencing a high tide of housing construction. In the long run, the consumption rate will increase in terms of statistics following the expansion of residents' housing quantities.

At present, the measures taken for the expansion of consumption are not strong enough relative to the expansion of investment in the process of expanding the domestic demand.

### Properly dealing with the relationship between domestic demand and external demand

According to the analysis of the International Monetary Fund, the world economic growth continuously maintained a high level of around 5 percent from 2004 to 2007, representing the greatest growth since the 1970s. China grasped this opportune time tightly and promoted economic growth by giving play to the comparative advantages and making full use of the external demand. From 2005 to 2007, the proportion of the net export increment of goods and services in the increment of the gross domestic product by the expenditure approach in China, namely its contribution rate, increased rapidly and reached around 20 percent. Affected by the current international financial crisis, the world economic growth slowed down rapidly, leading to a sharp reduction in the external demand. This objectively provided a strong forced impetus to expand the domestic demand and adjust the structures. To maintain steady and rapid economic growth in the long run, we must lay the basic footing of economic growth by expanding domestic demand. However, this does not necessarily mean that we will give up utilizing external demand. The current economic globalization trend based on the rapid development of science and technology and a global flow of productive factors in the world will not change. We should integrate the domestic and international politics, make full use of both domestic and international resources and combine the expansion of the domestic demand with a stabilized external demand to promote China's international competitiveness and counter-risk ability constantly by continuously leveraging China's comparative advantages so as to further enhance China's economic strength.

[Originally published in Economic Blue Book, Spring Issue, *Analysis of Economic Prospect in China-Spring Review of 2009*, Social Sciences Academic Press, 2009]

## Notes

1 Finch, J. (2008, October 20). What May Happen Next? Chinese version published in *News for Reference*, originally published in *The Guardian*, UK, 18 October 2008; Special issue "Will the Second Financial Crisis Attack the World?" (2009, February 5). *News for Reference*.
2 Wang Hongru. (2009, January 5). Economic Observation: Conjecture of the GDP Growth in 2009. *The China Economic Weekly*.
3 Shi Beibei. (2009, January 23). Ma Jun, an Economist of Deutsche Bank: W-Shape Recovery Emerging in China's Economy. *The Shanghai Securities News*.
4 Key Work of the State Council of 2008. (2008, April 3). *The People's Daily*.

## References

Beibei, Shi. (2009, January 23). Ma Jun, an Economist of Deutsche Bank: W-Shape Recovery Emerging in China's Economy. *The Shanghai Securities News*.
Hongru, Wang. (2009, January 5). Economic Observation: Conjecture of the GDP Growth in 2009. *The China Economic Weekly*.

# 8   Review and prospect
## The 60-year economic growth curve
## of new China

At the time of the sixtieth anniversary of the foundation of the People's Republic of China, when China's economy became stabilized and gradually recovered in coping with the impact of the most serious international financial crisis in a century and when it is about to step into a crucial period of overall resurgence, this article intends to carry out a review and present the prospect for China's 60-year economic growth curve and will be divided into four parts. The first part summarizes the profound changes that have occurred in the growth curve over 60 years and generalizes five features. The second part analyzes the seven great changes taking place in the economic structure that is implied by the growth curve since the reform and opening up, which will be significant promoting factors for future sustainable growth in China's economy. The third part illustrates that a new round of the economic cycle is approaching. The fourth part stresses that we should draw from the historical experiences and lessons to endeavor to extend the rising stage of the new round of the economic cycle. Thus, we must grasp its fluctuation profile and appropriate growth range well. In particular, the author analyzes the significant role of urbanization and the housing industry in the new economic cycle and further investigates ways to resolve the issue of increasing housing prices effectively.

### Profound changes in the 60-year growth curve

New China has experienced 60 years of brilliant history and achieved splendid accomplishments in economic development that are of worldwide interest. The annual economic growth rate has also experienced numerous rounds of fluctuations. Figure 8.1 presents the fluctuation curve of the economic growth rate over 60 years (from 1950 to 1952, the curve shows the growth rate of the gross social production value; from 1953 to 2009, it represents the growth rate of the gross domestic product; the 8 percent growth rate in 2009 is estimated by the author).[1]

On 1 October 1949, the founding of new China opened up a new epoch in Chinese history. The national economy recovered rapidly through three years of efforts in 1950, 1951 and 1952, during which the growth rates of the gross social production value were respectively 22.6 percent in 1950, 20.1 percent in 1951 and 23.8 percent in 1952. This was the recovery growth in the early decades of the founding of new China. Since 1953, China has engaged in massive economic

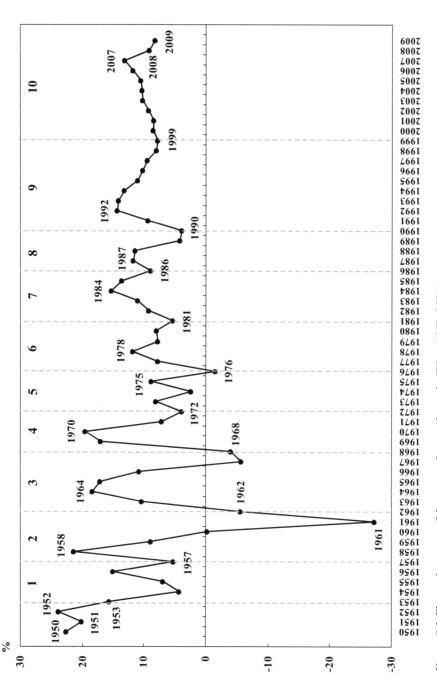

*Figure 8.1* Fluctuation curve of the economic growth rate in China (1950–2009)

construction and entered a period of industrialization. Until 2009, the growth rate of the gross domestic product (the GDP growth rate) experienced a total of 10 cycles of fluctuations in accordance with the "trough to trough" division approach.

When the First Five-Year Plan was implemented in 1953, the investment scale of the fixed-assets was very large, with an economic growth rate reaching as high as 15.6 percent. The overly rapid economic growth broke the equilibrium of the normal economic operation and was unlikely to last long. The economic growth rate fell to around 4 percent in 1954 and about 6 percent in 1955 and accelerated to 15 percent in 1956 after a slight adjustment. However, it was difficult to sustain at a high level and dropped to around 5 percent in 1957. The period from 1953 to 1957 constituted the first economic cycle.

When the "Great Leap Forward" movement started in 1958, the economic growth rate rose to 21.3 percent. Immediately afterwards, it declined to a great extent in the following three years of 1960, 1961 and 1962, all representing negative growth, of which the greatest decline was −27.3 percent in 1961. Thus, the peak-trough gap of the economic growth rate was nearly 50 percent from the peak of 21.3 percent in 1958 to the trough of −27.3 percent in 1961, which made up the second economic cycle.

After the adjustments were made to the economic operation, the economic growth rate rose again to 18.3 percent in 1964, during the early upsurge of the national defense construction. Then, the "Cultural Revolution" was launched in 1966 and the economic growth rate fell in 1967 and 1968, producing negative growth, which formed the third economic cycle.

The economic growth rate increased again to 19.4 percent in 1970 during the later upsurge of the national defense construction and dropped to around 3 percent in 1972, which constituted the fourth economic cycle.

Soon afterwards, entering the later stage of the "Cultural Revolution", the economic growth rate rose slightly in 1973 and fell again in 1974. It increased a little in 1975 and dropped again in 1976, feeble negative growth being represented throughout this period. The "Cultural Revolution" ended along with the crushing of the "Gang of Four" in October 1976. The two small fluctuations composed the fifth economic cycle.

If we compare the fluctuation curve of China's 60-year economic growth rate with an electrocardiogram of an economic organism, its pulse beat extremely feebly during the middle and later period of the "Cultural Revolution" from 1972 to 1976, showing that the national economy was on the verge of collapse, whereas it beat strongly and sharply before the previous period.

From the founding of new China to 1976, although the socialist construction experienced certain twists and turns, on the whole, great achievements were attained with the primary establishment of an independent and integral industrial system and a national economic system and the fundamental solution of "developing from nothing" during the industrialization process.

The report of the CPC's 17th National Congress pointed out that we should always bear in mind that the great cause of the reform and opening up was carried out on the basis that the first generation of the CPC's Collective Leadership with Mao Zedong as the core created Mao Zedong's thoughts and led the whole Party and all ethnic people to establish a new China, make great achievements in the victory of the socialist revolution and the socialist construction and draw valuable experiences from the strenuous exploration of the law of the socialist construction. The victory of China's New Democratic Revolution and the establishment of the basic socialist system paved the road for a fundamental political premise and a system foundation for the development and progress of modern China ("Upholding the Great Banner", 2007).[2]

After the crushing of the "Gang of Four" and the termination of the "Cultural Revolution", the nationwide enthusiasm for developing the economy was very high in 1977 and 1978. The economic growth rate rose to 11.7 percent in 1978 and fell to around 5 percent in 1981, which constituted the sixth economic cycle. In December 1978, the Third Plenary Session of the 11th Central Committee of the CPC brought order out of chaos and terminated the period of "taking the class struggle as the central task", shifting the Party's work focus to socialist modernization and thus commencing a new historical period of reform, opening up to the outside world and socialist modernization construction in China. It further proposed that the imbalance between major sectors of the national economy had not yet been completely resolved and the infrastructure must be developed actively in the proper sequence, without rushing and in accordance with the economy's actual capability. In April 1979, the Central Working Conference was held specifically to discuss the economic issues and formally proposed that three years should be spent on carrying out an adjustment to the whole national economy.

Promoted by the rural and urban reformation, the economic growth rate increased to 15.2 percent in 1984 and dropped to around 8 percent in 1986, forming the seventh economic cycle.

The economic growth rate rose respectively to 11.6 percent in 1987 and 11.3 percent in 1988. The residents' consumption price increased to 18.8 percent in 1988. The economic growth rate fell respectively to 4.1 percent in 1989 and 3.8 percent in 1990 during the adjustment, which made up the eighth economic cycle.

The economic growth rate recovered to 9.2 percent in 1991. In 1992, Deng Xiaoping's South Talks and the subsequent CPC's 14th National Congress generated new prospects for the reform, opening up and modernization construction. However, since it was just over 10 years since the reform and opening up, the original planned economic system had not been fundamentally transformed; therefore, problems like investment hunger and the mere pursuit of speed had not been overcome. As a result, the economic growth ascended to a peak of 14.2 percent very rapidly, producing an overheated economy. The residents' consumption price lagged behind with an increase, reaching 24.1 percent in 1994. The national economic operation successfully achieved a "soft landing" in controlling the overheated economy from the second half of 1993 to 1996, both greatly reducing the price increase and maintaining appropriate fast economic growth (Liu Guoguang, & Liu Shucheng, 1997).[3] Subsequently, it successfully countered the impact of the Asian financial crisis and overcame the insufficiency of the effective domestic demand. The economic growth rate fell steadily to 7.6 percent in 1999, which ended the ninth economic cycle.

In 2000, the economy entered the current tenth cycle, with the economic growth rate following a rising path from above 8 percent to 13 percent for eight consecutive years, 8.4 percent in 2000, 8.3 percent in 2001, 9.1 percent in 2002, 10 percent in 2003, 10.1 percent in 2004, 10.4 percent in 2005, 11.6 percent in 2006 and 13 percent in 2007, respectively. In 2008 and 2009, China was facing the overlapping of four-fold international and national adjustments, namely the overlap between the adjustment following long-term rapid growth of the national economy and the national economic periodic adjustment, the overlap with the US economic periodic recession and adjustment led by the US subprime mortgage crisis and the further overlap with the worldwide adjustment caused by the international financial crisis that was evolving rapidly from the US subprime mortgage crisis (Liu Shucheng, 2009).[4] The economic growth rate dropped to 9 percent in 2008 and is estimated to fall to around 8 percent in 2009, which will end the tenth economic cycle. China's economy will hopefully enter the rising stage of the eleventh economic cycle in 2010.

On the whole, the economic growth and fluctuation in China have presented a new steady situation at a high level for more than 30 years since the reform and opening up, which is characterized by the following five aspects.

1   The intensity of the economic fluctuation has declined rationally. The peak of the economic growth rate in each cycle reduced from around 20 percent in the previous cycles to around 11 percent-15 percent in the 1980s and 1990s after the reform and opening up. Entering the new century, the peak was controlled at 13 percent in the tenth cycle.

2   The fluctuation depth has risen significantly. The trough of the economic growth rate in each cycle was generally negative in the previous cycles. However, after the reform and opening up, it was no longer negative and presented positive growth during each adjustment.

3   The fluctuation amplitude has tended to reduce. The peak-trough gap of the economic growth rate in each cycle shrank from nearly 50 percent in the past to 6–7 percent after the reform and opening up. It is estimated to be merely around 5 percent in the tenth cycle.

4   The average height of the fluctuation has risen appropriately. During the 26 years from 1953 to 1978 (taking 1952 as the base year), the annual GDP growth rate was, on average, 6.1 percent. During the 31 years from 1979 to 2009 (taking 1978 as the base year), the annual GDP growth rate was, on average, 9.7 percent, an increase of 3.6 percent.

5   The length of the fluctuation has obviously extended. The length of the cycle was, on average, around five years in the previous eight cycles, being a short-range cycle. However, after the early 1990s, it extended to nine to 10 years in the ninth and tenth cycles, expanding to a medium-range cycle. In particular, the rising stage extended from as short as one to two years in the past to eight years in the tenth cycle, which had never occurred in the history of China's economic development for more than 60 years.

## New changes of the economic structure implied by the growth curve

There are many reasons for the economic growth and fluctuation in China to present a new steady situation at a high level. We analyze these reasons within the framework of "external impact–internal transmission" and summarize them in two categories: the constant improvement of macro regulation as an external impact and the enhancement of the growth and stability of the economic structure as an internal transmission mechanism (Liu Shucheng, & Zhang Xiaojing, 2007).[5] This article further stresses the analysis of the seven great changes in China's economic structure since the reform and opening up.

1    The variation in the systematic structure provided a significant system foundation for the high and steady economic growth.

Since the reform and opening up, significant changes have taken place in the economic structure in China, transforming the previous highly centralized planned economic system into a socialist market economy. Under the original planned economic system, enterprises did not have decision-making power in business activities, such as production, supply and sales, which were completely planned and managed by the government, leading to a rigid economy. In a socialist market economy, the market participants in the economic activities are provided with autonomy. With the introduction of market mechanisms, such as price leverage, competition mechanism and the production factor market, the market increasingly plays a fundamental role in resource allocation. This introduces unprecedented vigor and vitality into the economic development.

2    The variation in the ownership structure provided a basic economic system for the high and steady economic growth.

The variation in the ownership structure includes the change in terms of productive value and employment.

In terms of productive value, taking the ownership structure of the industrial enterprise for example, the proportions of enterprises of different types of ownership in the total industrial output value have changed significantly. In 1978, there were only two types of ownership in industrial enterprises, namely stated-owned industries and collective industries. They occupied 77.6 percent and 22.4 percent of the total industrial output value (according to the current year's price), respectively. In 2007, the form of ownership was already diversified according to the registered type (see Table 8.1) in the total industrial output value of the industrial enterprises above the designated size ("above the designated size" refers to industrial enterprises with an annual prime operating revenue of above 5 million yuan): non-corporate state-owned enterprises occupied 9 percent; collective enterprises 2.5 percent; stock cooperative enterprises 0.9 percent; associated enterprises (including state-owned associated enterprises) 0.4 percent; limited liability companies (including solely state-owned companies) 22.3 percent; incorporated companies (including state-owned holding enterprises) 9.9 percent; private enterprises 23.2 percent; other domestic enterprises 0.3 percent; Hong Kong, Macau and Taiwan merchant investment enterprises (including Sino-foreign joint ventures, Sino-foreign cooperatives and wholly foreign-owned enterprises) 10.5 percent; and foreign-funded enterprises (including Sino-foreign joint ventures, Sino-foreign cooperatives and wholly foreign-owned enterprises) 21 percent.

*Table 8.1* Proportion of enterprises of different ownership types in the total industrial output value

Unit: %

| Serial No. | Categorized By Registration | 1978 | 2007 |
|---|---|---|---|
| 1 | State-owned enterprises (non-corporate) | 77.6 | 9.0 |
| 2 | Collective enterprises | 22.4 | 2.5 |
| 3 | Stock cooperative enterprises | | 0.9 |
| 4 | Associated enterprises (including state-owned associated enterprises) | | 0.4 |
| 5 | Limited liability companies (including solely state-owned companies) | | 22.3 |
| 6 | Incorporated companies (including state-owned holding enterprises) | | 9.9 |
| 7 | Private enterprises | | 23.2 |
| 8 | Other domestic enterprises | | 0.3 |
| 9 | Hong Kong, Macau and Taiwan merchant investment enterprises (including Sino-foreign joint ventures, Sino-foreign cooperatives and wholly foreign-owned enterprises) | | 10.5 |
| 10 | Foreign-funded enterprises (including Sino-foreign joint ventures, Sino-foreign cooperatives and wholly foreign-owned enterprises) | | 21.0 |

Note. From calculated according to the data in the *China Statistical Yearbook 2008*, 2008, Beijing: China Statistics Press, p. 485.

In terms of employment, taking the ownership types of urban employment personnel for example, two main types of ownership existed in 1978, that is, stated-owned sectors and collective sectors. They respectively accounted for 78.3 percent and 21.5 percent. Individual employment only occupied 0.2 percent. The ownership structure of employment changed greatly in 2007. In urban employment, the proportion of state-owned sectors fell from 78.3 percent in 1978 to 21.9 percent in 2007; the proportion of collective sectors dropped from 21.5 percent in 1978 to 2.4 percent in 2007; the proportion of private enterprises and individuals in total reached 26.9 percent; and the proportion of other urban enterprises was as high as 32.9 percent (see Table 8.2).

The rebuilding of the micro foundation enabled various types of ownership structures to develop and expand during the reform and opening up, thus diversifying the market and investment participants and bringing their initiatives into play. This provided an important and basic economic system for the high and steady economic growth.

3  The variation in the supply structure of resources provided a necessary material condition for the high and steady economic growth.

The introduction of market mechanisms, their fundamental role in resource allocation and the variation in ownership structure revitalized the supply and basically changed the long-standing severe shortage of resources. The original

*Table 8.2* Proportion of enterprises of different ownership types in urban employment
Unit: %

| Serial No. | Categorized By Registration | 1978 | 2007 |
|---|---|---|---|
| 1 | State-owned sectors | 78.3 | 21.9 |
| 2 | Collective sectors | 21.5 | 2.4 |
| 3 | Stock cooperative sectors | | 0.6 |
| 4 | Associated sectors (including state-owned associated enterprises) | | 0.1 |
| 5 | Limited liability companies (including solely state-owned companies) | | 7.1 |
| 6 | Incorporated companies(including state-owned holding enterprises) | | 2.7 |
| 7 | Private enterprises | | 15.6 |
| 8 | Individual | 0.2 | 11.3 |
| 9 | Hong Kong, Macau and Taiwan merchant investment enterprises | | 2.3 |
| 10 | Foreign-funded enterprises | | 3.1 |
| 11 | Other urban enterprises | | 32.9 |

Note. From calculated according to the data in the *China Statistical Yearbook 2008*, 2008, Beijing: China Statistics Press, pp. 110–111.

bottleneck restraints in the resource supply, such as coal, electricity, oil, transportation and materials (important raw materials, for example steel and cement), were gradually alleviated to different extents, and some resource supplies even generated a certain conditional relative surplus. This supported the high and steady economic operation materially.

4   The variation in the industrial structure provided an industrial basis for the high and steady economic growth.

Regarding the gross domestic product, significant changes have taken place in the structure of productive value of the three major industries (see Figure 8.2). The proportion of the primary industry decreased from 50.5 percent in 1952 to 28.2 percent in 1978 and further to 11.3 percent in 2008. The proportion of the secondary industry rose from 20.9 percent in 1952 to 47.9 percent in 1978 and further to 48.6 percent in 2008, achieving relative stability since the reform and opening up. The proportion of the tertiary industry fell from 28.6 percent in 1952 to 23.9 percent in 1978 and rose to 40.1 percent in 2008 after the reform and opening up.

Since the reform and opening up, the continuous decline in the proportion of the primary industry, the relatively stable proportion of the secondary industry and the rising proportion of the tertiary industry have been favorable to a steady economic operation at an appropriately high level. In terms of the characteristics of the three major industries, the growth of the primary industry is slow and the amplitude of its fluctuation is quite small, but it is greatly affected by natural conditions. The growth of the secondary industry is fast, but the amplitude of its fluctuation is relatively large. The growth of the tertiary industry is relatively

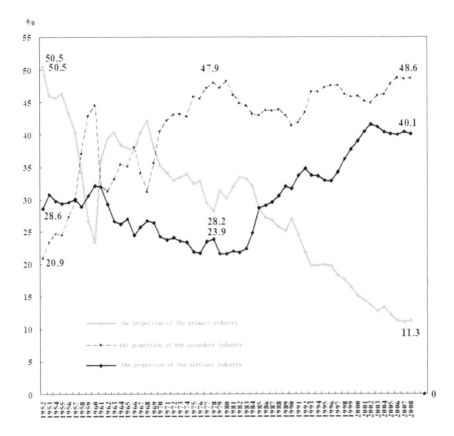

*Figure 8.2* Proportion of productive value of the three major industries in China (1952–2008)

Note. 1952–1977, from *Historical Data of GDP Accounting in China 1952–1995*, by National Economic Accounting Department of the State Statistics Bureau (Ed.), 1997, Dalian, Liaoning, China: Northeast University of Finance & Economics Press, p. 30; 1978–2008, from *China Statistical Abstract (2009)*, Beijing: China Statistics Press, 2009, p. 21.

fast and the amplitude of its fluctuation is quite small, and it is not quite affected by natural conditions. Therefore, along with the rising proportion of the tertiary industry, the stability of the whole economy will be enhanced.

5   The variation in the structure of the rural and urban population provided a strong impetus for the demand for the high and steady economic growth.

The reform and opening up promoted migration of the labor force, progress in industrialization and an improved urbanization rate (the proportion of the urban population in the total population). The improvement in the urbanization rate generates enormous demands for the construction of urban infrastructure and real estate and drives the vigorous development of various related industries. The urbanization rate in China was 10.6 percent in 1949 and increased to 17.9 percent in 1978 and 45.7 percent in 2008. Accordingly, the proportion of the rural population in the total population fell from 89.4 percent in 1949 to 82.1 percent in 1978 and further to 54.3 percent in 2008 (see Figure 8.3).

6    The variation in the consumption structure provided a new impetus for consumption for a high and steady economic growth.

Following the reform and opening up, the improvement of the average person's income promoted the upgrading of the consumption structure from food, clothing and daily necessities to dwellings and transportation and from the living type to the developmental and leisure type. This further promoted an adjustment to and optimization of the industrial structure and formed an important impetus for economic growth.

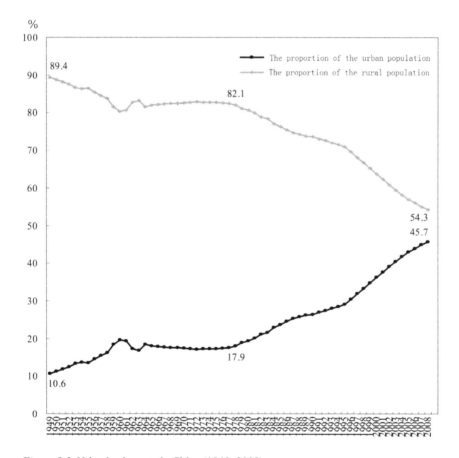

*Figure 8.3* Urbanization rate in China (1949–2008)

Note. 1949–1977, from *China Statistical Yearbook (1983)*, Beijing: China Statistics Press, 1983, p. 104; 1978–2008, from *China Statistical Abstract (2009)*, Beijing: China Statistics Press, 2009, p. 40.

*Table 8.3* Growth rate of industrial production and investment in the first half of 2009 (%)

| Indicator | Whole Country | Eastern Regions | Central Regions | Western Regions |
|---|---|---|---|---|
| Growth rate of industrial added value of enterprises above the designated size | 7.0 | 5.9 | 6.8 | 13.2 |
| Growth rate of urban fixed-assets investment | 33.6 | 26.7 | 38.1 | 42.1 |

Note. From website of the State Statistics Bureau.

7   The variation in the regional structure provided a broad geographic space for the high and steady economic growth.

Following the reform and opening up, the economic growth in the eastern coastal regions was fast in the 1980s and 1990s. The central and western regions accelerated development from the end of the 1990s. Influenced by the international financial crisis, the eastern coastal regions were strongly affected, whereas the industrial production growth and fixed-assets investment growth in the central and western regions were higher than those in the eastern coastal regions. In the first half of 2009, the industrial added value of the enterprises above the designated size nationwide increased year-on-year by 7 percent. In terms of different regions, the growth was 5.9 percent in the eastern regions, 6.8 percent in the central regions and 13.2 percent in the western regions. In the same period, the urban fixed-assets investment nationwide grew by 33.6 percent. Regarding the different regions, the growth was 26.7 percent in the eastern regions, 38.1 percent in the central regions and 42.1 percent in the western regions (see Table 8.3).

The above analysis demonstrates that many significant changes have taken place in the economic structures in China since the reform and opening up, which will be conducive to dealing with the impacts of the international financial crisis on China's economy and will continuously promote China's future economic development.

## Approaching a new economic cycle

From the perspective of coping with the international financial crisis, China's economic trends can be divided into three stages:

1   The first stage was from July 2008 to February 2009, a phase of "rapid decline". The excessive decrease in economic growth became a prominent contradiction that affected the overall economic and social development. The Party Central Committee and the State Council explicitly proposed that the maintenance of rapid and steady economic growth should be taken as the primary task of the economic work and therefore implemented a proactive fiscal policy and a moderately easy monetary policy and published a package plan for coping with the international financial crisis.

2    The second stage started in March 2009 and is estimated to continue to the end of 2009, a phase of "stabilized recovery". China's economy is currently in this stage, with a series of macro regulation measures gradually becoming effective and reversing the trend of an overly rapid economic downturn. However, the recovery foundation still needs to be further strengthened.

3    China's economy will hopefully enter the third stage in 2010, a phase of "overall recovery", by commencing the rising stage of a new economic cycle. The so-called "overall recovery" refers to the successive recovery of most industries or most economic indicators. However, in the phase of "stabilized recovery", only part of the predominant industries or part of the dominant indicators starts to recover.

The previous two stages are obvious (see Figure 8.4) in the fluctuation of the industrial production growth (the same-month year-on-year growth rate of the industrial added value of nationwide enterprises above the designated size).

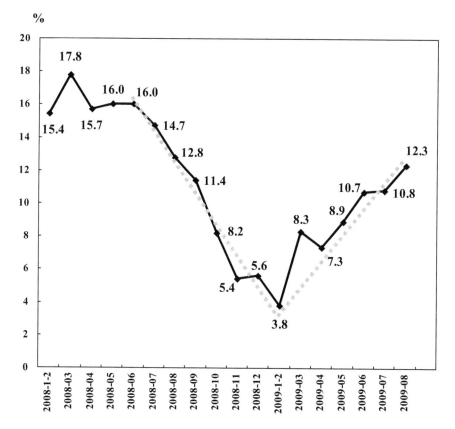

*Figure 8.4*  The same-month year-on-year growth rate of industrial added value of nation-wide enterprises above the designated size

Note. From website of the State Statistics Bureau.

*Table 8.4* Predictions for China's economic growth rate in 2010 by international financial institutions

| Name of Institution | Predicted Growth Rate (%) |
| --- | --- |
| Morgan Stanley | 10.0 |
| Barclays Capital | 9.6 |
| BNP Paribas | 9.5 |
| HSBC | 9.5 |
| International Monetary Fund | 9.0 |
| JP Morgan Chase | 9.0 |
| Asian Development Bank | 8.9 |
| UBS Securities | 8.5 |
| Overall range | 8.5–10.0 |

The industrial production growth is a representative indicator that reflects the operating state of the real economy. It was 16 percent in June 2008, fell sharply to 3.8 percent during January and February 2009, which lasted for eight months, decreased by 12.2 percent and recovered for six consecutive months from March to August 2009, forming a V-shape (see the dotted line in Figure 8.4).

International financial institutions also predicted a recovery for China's economic growth in 2010. As announced during the period from July to October 2009, the predictions for China's economic growth in 2010 made by various international financial institutions are as follows (see Table 8.4): Morgan Stanley 10 percent; Barclays Capital 9.6 percent; BNP Paribas 9.5 percent; HSBC 9.5 percent; International Monetary Fund 9 percent; JP Morgan Chase 9 percent; Asian Development Bank 8.9 percent; and UBS Securities 8.5 percent. The overall range is between 8.5 percent and 10 percent.

## Endeavors to extend the rising stage of the new economic cycle

By countering the severe impact of the international financial crisis effectively, China's economy will hopefully enter the rising stage of a new economic cycle (the eleventh cycle) in 2010. It is time to advocate that "we should endeavour to extend the rising stage of an economic cycle".

In the growth process of the tenth economic cycle, the Central Economic Working Conference, held in November 2003, proposed that "currently the economic development in China is in the ascending stage of the economic cycle" and that "we should greatly appreciate the current good momentum of the economic growth with further consolidation and development" ("The Central Economic Working Conference", 2003, p. 1).[6] This was the first time that the Central Economic Working Conference had employed the concept of the economic cycle to analyze and estimate the economic trends in China. The author wrote an article at that time, entitled "Endeavour to Extend the Rising Stage of an Economic Cycle", which was published in the *People's Daily* (Liu Shucheng, 2003, p. 9).[7] The tenth economic cycle, consisting of a rising stage of eight years (2000–07) and a descending stage of two years (2008 and 2009), is currently coming to an end. The extended rising stage of eight years occurred for the first time in the history of the economic development since the founding of new China.

A new economic cycle is approaching. Without doubt, we must continue to endeavor to extend its rising stage for as long as possible. Based on the historical experiences and lessons, we should basically understand the fluctuation profile and the appropriate growth range of the new economic cycle.

*Grasping the fluctuation profile of a new economic cycle*

In terms of the fluctuation profile of the previous 10 economic cycles, there are mainly three fluctuation patterns:

- The first pattern is "violent ups and downs", which was a representative fluctuation profile in the previous eight economic cycles from 1953 to the end of the 1980s. In particular, the second cycle, from 1958 to 1962, was a typical example of this pattern. The economic growth rate rose greatly and violently in the rising stage, which could be as short as one to two years, and immediately entered a descending stage of two to four years, with the average length of a cycle being around five years.
- The second pattern is "violent ups and slow fall". Following the early 1990s, the fluctuation profile changed from "violent ups and downs" to "violent ups and slow fall", which was reflected in the ninth cycle from 1991 to 1999. This cycle lasted for nine years, with a rising stage of two years and a descending stage of seven years. Like the previous eight economic cycles, the rising stage was still characterized by "violent ups". However, the descending stage was different from the previous ones, promptly carrying out macro regulation of a "soft landing" by drawing the historical lessons from "violent ups and downs", slowing down the excessively rapid economic growth and preventing the violent downs from following the violent ups, as occurred in the past. In 1996, the "soft landing" was proved to be basically successful. On this basis, China countered the impact of the international financial crisis and overcame the insufficiency of the effective domestic demand. Thus, the economic growth rate fell slowly from the peak of 14.2 percent in 1992 to 7.6 percent in 1999, decreasing annually by 0.9 percent, on average, over seven years.
- The third pattern is "slow rise and rapid fall". This was displayed in the tenth economic cycle from 2000 to 2009. From the very beginning, China took care to draw historical lessons from "violent ups and downs" and avoid excessively high and rapid "violent ups" to enable the economy to grow steadily. Thus, it successfully extended the rising stage of the economic cycle. Through eight years of consecutive growth, under the inertia of the domestic economic operation and the favorable international environment for economic growth, the economic growth rate rose to 13 percent in 2007 and gradually became quite rapid. Influenced by the severe international financial

crisis, following the trend of the domestic adjustment, it dropped to 9 percent at a stroke, decreasing by 4 percent within one year and forming a fluctuation profile of "slow rise and rapid fall".

In the new economic cycle, we should endeavor to achieve a new fluctuation pattern of "slow rise and slow fall", namely rising slowly for as long a time as possible in the ascending stage and falling steadily and slightly in the descending stage.

### Grasping the appropriate growth range of a new economic cycle

To achieve a fluctuation pattern of "slow rise and slow fall", the key point is to grasp an appropriate growth range in the new economic cycle, that is, to control the economic growth speed.

The issue of determining the growth speed that China's economy should maintain after economic recovery has already been discussed in the media. It is estimated that the discussion will shortly warm up and, on the whole, it consisted of five different opinions:

- The first opinion stated that China's economy should not pursue a high growth speed again in the future and should achieve an intermediate development speed of around 7 percent to 8 percent.
- The second opinion was that China's economy would still be able to maintain a high growth speed of above 10 percent following the overall economic recovery.
- The third opinion held that China's economy might maintain a growth speed of above 9 percent in more than 10 years (2008–20) in the future.
- The fourth opinion considered that the average economic growth speed would be above 9.5 percent within five years (2008–12), 8.5 percent in the following 10 years (2013–22) and 7.5 percent in another 10 years (2023–32).
- The fifth opinion was that China's economy would be able to maintain a moderately high growth speed of around 8–10 percent within the new economic cycle or in the medium term (for example, around eight years from 2010 to 2017) in the future.

This article advocates the fifth opinion, implying that the growth speed should not be excessively low or overly high. China should grasp an appropriate growth range and its relevant factors, follow the development of the economic trend closely and regulate the growth speed promptly.

### An excessively low speed is not workable

The economic growth speed in China should not be below 8 percent at the present stage. If it is below 8 percent, enterprise operation, urban employment and improving residents' income and people's life will become severely difficult; at the same time, the state fiscal revenue and the development of social undertakings will encounter great problems. This will affect the whole social security and harmony. Influenced by the international financial crisis, the GDP growth rate in China decreased to 6.8 percent in the fourth quarter in 2008, 6.1 percent in the first quarter in 2009 and 7.9 percent in the second quarter in 2009, respectively, issuing a serious challenge to enterprise production and urban employment and enabling the national fiscal revenue to grow negatively during the period from October 2008 to April 2009 (except for December 2008). It is evident that economic growth rate below 8 percent is not workable.

*An overly high speed is not appropriate*

The historical experiences and lessons of the economic periodical fluctuations in China tell us that the vital part of "violent ups and downs" is the "violent ups", because excessively rapid and high "violent ups" will easily produce enormous pressures of high energy consumption, high material consumption, high pollution and high inflation and break various equilibrium relationships that are necessary for normal economic operation, thus leading to subsequent "violent downs". In the previous 10 economic cycles, the peaks of the GDP growth rate were, respectively, 15 percent in 1956, 21.3 percent in 1958, 18.3 percent in 1964, 19.4 percent in 1970, 8.7 percent in 1975 (the later stage of the "Cultural Revolution"), 11.7 percent in 1978, 15.2 percent in 1984, 11.6 percent in 1987, 14.2 percent in 1992 and 13 percent in 2007. In terms of the experiential data in China, the economic growth rate should not be above 11 percent.

*Grasping an appropriate growth range and its relevant factors*

Why could China's economy be able to maintain a moderately high growth speed of around 8–10 percent in the medium term? The seven great changes in China's economic structure since the reform and opening up, which we analyzed previously, namely the seven factors (market economic system, ownership, resource supply, industrial structure, urbanization, consumption upgrading and regional development) that promoted high and steady economic growth, will still play a role in the new economic cycle. It is worth pointing out that the improvement of urbanization rate and the corresponding development of real estate, in particular housing development, will still be one of the most important incentive sources in the new economic cycle.

Academic circles hold different viewpoints on the improvement of the urbanization rate in the future, which can mainly be summed up as four types:

- The first viewpoint believes that the urbanization rate (45.7 percent in 2008) calculated on the basis of the current statistics is underestimated, because it does not include all the migrant workers. If they are included, the actual urbanization rate has already been relatively high (around 60 percent). Therefore, the future development space of urbanization will not be large, with merely a time span of 10 years and a space of around 10 percent.
- The second viewpoint is the opposite to the first one and holds that the urbanization rate calculated on the basis of the current statistics is overestimated, because migrant workers who live in cities for more than half a year have

already been calculated in the urbanization rate. Considering that these migrant workers have not become real city dwellers, the actual urbanization rate is still very low (less than 40 percent). Thus, the future development space for urbanization will be huge.

- The third viewpoint considers that China is in a stage of rapid urbanization on the basis of the current statistics. The urbanization rate will reach around 60 percent in 2020, 65–70 percent in 2030 and 75–80 percent in 2050, as such realizing urbanization in the middle of the twenty-first century.
- The fourth viewpoint is that the urbanization rate is not necessarily too high since China is a populous country. It will be good to have an urbanization rate reaching a little more than 60 percent in 2020.

Although the above viewpoints on the issue of improving the urbanization rate in China are different, there is at least one point in common in that the development of urbanization within the next 10 years will be relatively great. This implies an improvement not only quantitatively in the urbanization rate, but also qualitatively in the urbanization level, such as strengthening the infrastructure construction of daily life, traffic communication, culture, education, health, medical care, environmental protection and housing construction for residents (including the original urban residents and migrant workers). Currently in China, most of the general commodities are meeting the issue of surplus production capacity on the one hand, but the supply of many public goods or quasi-public goods (for example, the above-mentioned various infrastructure constructions and welfare-oriented housing) is far from sufficient on the other hand, which will provide an important impetus for future economic development in China.

To promote the smooth development of urbanization in China, in particular to enable the housing industry to become a significant pillar industry in the new economic cycle, we must effectively resolve the issue of the continuous increase in housing prices. If this cannot be settled properly, it will severely affect the development of urbanization and even social stability. The development of the housing industry in China has experienced three stages. Originally, under the highly centralized planned economic system, the government was responsible for solving the problem of urban housing, which was in severely short supply. Subsequently, housing became commercialized and fully market-oriented, thus promoting great development in the housing industry and enabling housing prices to increase continuously. Later, marketization and government responsibilities were combined to resolve the housing issue. In the current situation, to restrain the trend of the continuous increase in housing prices effectively, we must further adopt a method for "removing the burning wood from under the boiling cauldron", namely increasing the governmental welfare housing supply again, withdrawing the housing issue from the market related not only to urban low-income people but also to urban middle-income people and bringing them into the governmental guarantee category. However, we should guarantee that all urban middle-income people have a right of habitation, rather than a building property right, and that they are capable of renting a house. Moreover, this guarantee should be operated through marketization, with rental houses of high, middle and low grades for free selection.

*Closely following the development of the economic trend
and promptly regulating the growth speed*

By proposing that we should endeavor to extend the rising stage of an economic cycle, we aim to enable the economy to maintain steady growth in an appropriate growth range within a fairly long time span and fluctuate slightly, instead of increasing the economic growth rate in the ascending stage year by year, and not to go so far as to induce a significant decline in the economic growth rate quickly. We should fully note that there is inertia in economic growth in the rising stage of an economic cycle, which possesses a ripple diffusion effect or cumulative magnifying effect, during the ascending process, existing between sectors, industries and enterprises, between fixed asset investments and production and between economic expansion and price increases. Thus, these effects will cause the economic growth to face the risk of evolving from "comparatively fast" to "fast" and further to "overheating". This suggests that macro regulation sectors must closely follow the development and change of the economic trend, appropriately and continuously implement the necessary regulations to extend the rising stage of the economic cycle for as long as possible and to make steady adjustments to any overly rapid rising trend as much as possible.

[Originally published in Economic Perspectives (JingjixueDongtai), No.10, 2009]

## Notes

1 1950 to 1952, *Historical Statistical Data Collection of Provinces, Autonomous Regions and Municipalities in China (1949–1989)* (p. 9). (1990). Beijing: China Statistics Press; 1953 to 1992, *Statistical Data Collection of 50 Years in New China* (p. 5). (1999). Beijing: China Statistics Press; 1993 to 2007, *China Statistical Yearbook (2008)* (p. 40). (2008). Beijing: China Statistics Press; 2008, *China Statistical Abstract (2009)* (p. 22). (2009). Beijing: China Statistics Press; 2009, estimation of 8% by the author.
2 Hu Jintao. (2007, October 25). Upholding the Great Banner of Socialism with Chinese Characteristics and Striving for New Victories in Overall Building of a Well-Off Society. *The People's Daily.*
3 Liu Guoguang & Liu Shucheng. (1997, January 7). On Soft Landing. *The People's Daily,* p. 9.
4 Liu Shucheng. (2009). Analysis of National and International Economic Trends, 2008–2009, Economic Blue Book, Spring Issue, *Analysis of Economic Prospect in China – Spring Review of 2009,* Beijing: Social Sciences Academic Press.
5 Liu Shucheng & Zhang Xiaojing. (2007). Features of Sustained High Economic Growth in China and Reduction of Inter-Regional Economic Disparity. *The Economic Research Journal,* 10.
6 The Central Economic Working Conference Held in Beijing (2003, November 30). *The People's Daily,* p. 1.
7 Liu Shucheng. (2003, December 18). Endeavor to Extend the Rising Stage of an Economic Cycle. *The People's Daily,* p. 9.

## Reference

Shucheng, Liu. (2009). *Economic Growth and Fluctuation of 60 Years in China: Prosperity and Stability III.* Beijing: Social Sciences Academic Press.

# 9 Analysis of the next-round economic cycle

The year 2009 was the year in which China's economic development met the greatest difficulties since the beginning of the twenty-first century and China took the global lead in achieving an overall economic turnaround while effectively coping with the severe impact of the international financial crisis. The following year, 2010, is a key year in which China will continuously deal with the international financial crisis, maintain steady and rapid economic growth and accelerate the transformation of the economic growth pattern. It is an important year in which China will achieve the target of the Eleventh Five-Year Plan entirely and lay a good foundation for the development of the Twelfth Five-Year Plan. In terms of the fluctuating trajectory of macroeconomic operation, the economic growth in China crossed the trough by countering the severe impact of the international financial crisis in 2009, terminated the descending stage of the tenth economic cycle since the founding of new China and will hopefully enter the rising stage of a new cycle, that is, the eleventh economic cycle in 2010. This article will stress the analysis of three issues: the transitional course from the tenth economic cycle to a new economic cycle, namely the commencement of a new economic cycle; the features of the tenth economic cycle that just reached an end in 2009 and constituted a starting point for a new cycle; and the continuous efforts to extend the rising stage of the new economic cycle and maintain steady and rapid development of the national economy in the long term.

## Transitional course from the tenth cycle to the eleventh cycle

The tenth economic cycle in China lasted from 2000 to 2009, an entire decade, with a rising stage of eight years and a descending stage of two years (see Figure 9.1). In 1999, China successfully countered the impact of the Asian financial crisis and overcame the insufficiency of the effective domestic demand, enabling the economic growth rate (the GDP growth rate) to fall steadily to 7.6 percent and putting an end to the ninth economic cycle. In 2000, the economy entered the tenth cycle, with the economic growth rate following a rising path from 8 percent to 13 percent for eight consecutive years, respectively 8.4 percent in 2000, 8.3 percent in 2001, 9.1 percent in 2002, 10 percent in 2003, 10.1 percent in 2004, 10.4 percent in 2005, 11.6 percent in 2006 and 13 percent in 2007. In particular, according to the database of the International Monetary Fund, the GDP in China

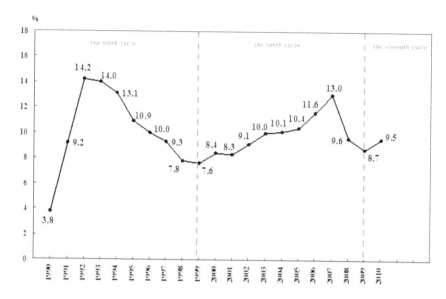

*Figure 9.1* Periodic fluctuation of the economic growth rate in China (1990~2010)

surpassed that of France in 2005, the UK in 2006 and Germany in 2007, enabling it to become the third-largest economy in the world.

In 2008 and 2009, the domestic economic adjustment and the international financial crisis overlapped, enabling the excessively rapid decrease in the economic growth to become a prominent contradiction that affected the overall economic and social development. In coping with the impact of the international financial crisis, China promptly adopted a proactive fiscal policy and a moderately easy monetary policy and implemented a package plan. Through these efforts, China effectively curbed the obvious trend of an economic downturn, crossed a trough and took the global lead in achieving an overall economic turnaround after the second quarter of 2009. The economic growth rate in 2008 was 10.6 percent in the first quarter, 10.1 percent in the second quarter, 9 percent in the third quarter and 6.8 percent in the fourth quarter, whereas in 2009 it was 6.2 percent in the first quarter, 7.9 percent in the second quarter, 9.1 percent in the third quarter and 10.7 percent in the fourth quarter. It was a real achievement that the annual economic growth rate fell to 9.6 percent in 2008 and 8.7 percent in 2009, respectively.

The domestic and international environment of the economic development in China in 2010 will be better than that in 2009. Internationally, the world economy will hopefully achieve recovery growth with the unchanged general trend of economic globalization. Great reformations and adjustments in the world's economic pattern and the brewing and rise of the new technological revolution and industrial revolution will breed new development opportunities. Domestically, the package plans and measures that were implemented to cope with the international financial crisis continuously appear to be effective. The foundation of an economic turnaround is further consolidated. China's economic development is still experiencing a period of important strategic opportunities. According to our forecast, China's economic growth rate may recover to 9.5 percent in 2010, thus entering a new economic cycle. The International Monetary Fund frequently raised the predictive value of China's economic growth rate in 2010, predicting in April 2009 a rate of 7.5 percent, in July 2009 a rate of 8.5 percent, in October 2009 a rate of 9 percent and in January 2010 a rate of 10 percent.

Although the economic development environment in China in 2010 may be better than that in 2009, the situations that it faces are extremely complicated. Various positive changes and unfavorable conditions, short-term issues and long-term contradictions, new and old issues and domestic and international factors interweave and interact with one another. A comprehensive and deliberate judgment of the situation must be made and the sense of crisis needs to be strengthened, neither regarding the trend of an economic turnaround identical to the fundamental upturn of an economic operation nor considering an improvement in the economic operation within a cycle equal to long-term sustainable economic development.

## Features of the tenth economic cycle

To grasp the new economic cycle better, we briefly review the 10 cycles since the founding of new China and illustrate the significant features of the tenth cycle that has just concluded.

At the end of 2009, the famous US economist Samuelson, who had just passed away, once vividly compared the features of an economic cycle as follows: "no two economic cycles are quite the same. When economic cycles are not identical twins, they often have a family similarity" (2005, p. 468).[1] This is because various economic cycles all present alternating movements between expansion and contraction and between peak and trough, whereas their fluctuations exhibit different lengths, heights, depths and amplitudes.

On 1 October 1949, the founding of new China opened up a new epoch in Chinese history. The national economy recovered rapidly through three years of effort in 1950, 1951 and 1952, during which the growth rate of the gross social production value was 22.6 percent in 1950, 20.1 percent in 1951 and 23.8 percent in 1952. This was the recovery growth in the early decades of the founding of new China. After 1953, China started massive economic construction and entered the period of industrialization, thus starting to step into a stage of economic periodic fluctuation. Until 2009, the fluctuation of the economic growth rate experienced 10 cycles in total (see Figure 9.2. From 1950 to 1952, the curve showed the growth rate of the gross social production value; from 1953 to 2010, the curve represented the growth rate of the gross domestic product; and the 9.5 percent growth rate in 2010 is estimated by this article).

The first cycle was from 1953 to 1957, lasting for five years; the second cycle was from 1958 to 1962, lasting for five years; the third cycle was from 1963 to 1968, lasting for six years; the fourth cycle was from 1969 to 1972, lasting for four years; the fifth cycle was from 1973 to 1976, lasting for four years; the sixth

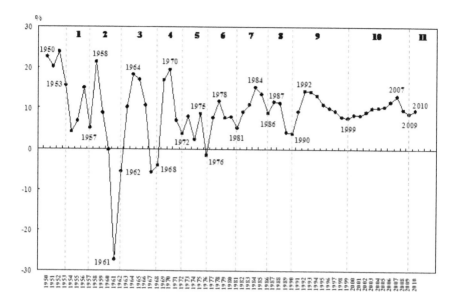

*Figure 9.2* Periodic fluctuation of the economic growth rate in China (1950–2010)

cycle was from 1977 to 1981, lasting for five years; the seventh cycle was from 1982 to 1986, lasting for five years; the eighth cycle was from 1987 to 1990, lasting for four years; the ninth cycle was from 1991 to 1999, lasting for nine years; and the tenth cycle was from 2000 to 2009, lasting for 10 years.

The 10 economic cycles presented the following distinguishing features (see Table 9.1):

1   In terms of the length of the whole cycle, it was on average around five years in the previous eight cycles, which was a short-range cycle. The ninth cycle extended to nine years, whereas the tenth cycle extended to 10 years. Both of them expanded to a medium-range cycle.

2   In terms of the length of the rising stage, it was as short as one or two years in the previous nine cycles, whereas it extended to eight years in the tenth cycle; specifically, the economic growth rate from 2000 to 2007 followed a rising path from 8 percent to 13 percent for eight consecutive years, drawing out the longest rising trajectory that has ever appeared in the economic periodic fluctuation since the founding of new China.

3   In terms of the peak position of the economic growth rate, it was very steep in the cycles of the 1950s and 1960s and reached around 20 percent, for example 21.3 percent in 1958, 18.3 percent in 1964 and 19.4 percent in 1970, respectively. Since the reform and opening up, it was controlled to a certain extent in the cycles of the 1980s and 1990s and decreased to 14–15 percent,

Table 9.1 Comparison of the previous economic cycles in China

| Serial No. of Cycle | Starting and Ending Year | Length of Cycle | Length of Rising Stage | Length of Falling Stage | Peak Year and Economic Growth Rate | Trough Year and Economic Growth Rate | Peak – Trough Gap (%) |
|---|---|---|---|---|---|---|---|
| 1 | 1953~1957 | 5 years | 2 years | 3 years | 1956 15.0% | 1957 5.1% | 9.9 |
| 2 | 1958~1962 | 5 years | 1 years | 4 years | 1958 21.3% | 1961 −27.3% | 48.6 |
| 3 | 1963~1968 | 6 years | 2 years | 4 years | 1964 18.3% | 1967 −5.7% | 24.0 |
| 4 | 1969~1972 | 4 years | 2 years | 2 years | 1970 19.4% | 1972 3.8% | 15.6 |
| 5 | 1973~1976 | 4 years | 2 years | 2 years | 1975 8.7% | 1976 −1.6% | 10.3 |
| 6 | 1977~1981 | 5 years | 2 years | 3 years | 1978 11.7% | 198 15.2% | 6.5 |
| 7 | 1982~1986 | 5 years | 3 years | 2 years | 1984 15.2% | 1986 8.8% | 6.4 |
| 8 | 1987~1990 | 4 years | 1 year | 3 years | 1987 11.6% | 1990 3.8% | 7.8 |
| 9 | 1991~1999 | 9 years | 2 years | 7 years | 1992 14.2% | 1999 7.6% | 6.6 |
| 10 | 2000~2009 | 10 years | 8 years | 2 years | 2007 13.0% | 2009 8.7% | 4.3 |

for example to 15.2 percent in 1984 and 14.2 percent in 1992. In the tenth cycle, it was further controlled and rationally declined to 13 percent in 2007.

4   In terms of the trough position of the economic growth rate, it was frequently negative in the cycles before the reform and opening up, for example being −27.3 percent in 1961, −5.7 percent in 1967 and −1.6 percent in 1976, respectively. After the reform and opening up, it was no longer negative and maintained positive growth merely with a decreasing speed. Since the 1990s, it had risen to a certain extent, for example to 3.8 percent in 1990, and fell to 7.6 percent in 1999 as a result of the Asian financial crisis. In the tenth cycle, it was a real achievement that the economic growth rate merely fell to 8.7 percent in 2009 in coping with the severest international financial crisis in a century.

5   In terms of the fluctuation amplitude of the economic growth rate, the peak – trough gap was very large in the cycles of the 1950s and 1960s. For example, the gap between the peak of 21.3 percent in 1958 and the trough of −27.3 percent in 1961 reached 48.6 percent in the second cycle. After the reform and opening up, the amplitude narrowed down distinctively, with a reduction of the peak–trough gap to around 6 percent to 7 percent. It was merely 4.3 percent in the tenth cycle.

## Continuously extending the rising stage of the new economic cycle

The rising stage of the tenth economic cycle extended to eight years and initiated a new trajectory. At present, China's economy is stepping into the rising stage of a new economic cycle. To endeavor to extend this rising stage, on the one hand, we should continuously endure the pressure exerted on China's economic development by the international financial crisis and accelerate the transformation of the economic development pattern and the adjustment of the economic structure without a moment's delay; on the other hand, we should strengthen and improve the macro regulation, continuously maintain steady and rapid economic development and avoid violent economic ups and downs according to the historical experiences and lessons drawn from the previous economic periodic fluctuations in China.

Maintaining steady and rapid economic development is of extreme significance for the stability of the overall economic and social situation in China and the promotion of the smooth development of various undertakings. Meanwhile, it provides a good macroeconomic environment for the transformation of the economic development pattern and the adjustment of the economic structure. An overheated economy will contribute to the original extensive economic development pattern and further worsen the economic structure, whereas an excessively sluggish economy requires the implementation of an expansionary policy of macro regulation to make every effort to guarantee growth and avoid a downturn, which will oppose the transformation of the economic development pattern and the adjustment of the economic structure.

To maintain steady and rapid economic development, we need to grasp well two key points in macro regulation – the control of economic growth speed and the resolving of a combination of short-, medium- and long-term issues.

## Control of the economic growth speed

The projected objective of the GDP growth in 2010 is still to achieve a rate of around 8 percent, which is a goal that has been proposed for six consecutive years since 2005. Since the early 1990s, the targets of the economic growth rate set in previous Government Working Reports are as follows: the main growth range was 8– 9 percent from 1993 to 1995, around 8 percent from 1996 to 1998, around 7 percent from 1999 to 2004 (during which no growth target was set for two years) and around 8 percent for the years after 2005. Although 8 percent economic growth was proposed as a projected objective in each of the recent six years, its implication for each year was quite different. In the previous four years, from 2005 to 2008, the 8 percent growth objective implied the prevention of an overheated economy and violent ups in the acceleration of the economic development. The 8 percent growth objective in 2009 implied the assurance of the economic growth and the prevention of violent downs in countering the impact of the international financial crisis. The 8 percent growth objective in 2010 implies a structural adjustment and a transformation of the economic development pattern – that is, mainly emphasizing sound economic development and practically guiding the shift of the work focus in various aspects to the structural adjustment and the transformation of the development pattern.

The projected objective of 8 percent economic growth is the bottom line at the current stage of China's economic development. It is a basic reference for the government to set other macro-regulation goals, such as employment, price and financial budget. China, as a developing country with a population of 1.3 billion, is obliged to maintain a certain economic development speed in 2010, which constitutes a foundation for ensuring urban and rural employment, improving residents' income and life, increasing the national fiscal revenue, developing various social undertakings and safeguarding social stability. If the growth rate is below 8 percent, it will result in a series of difficulties in enterprise operation, people's life and social development. The 8 percent growth rate is an anticipated objective that can be achieved through the efforts of all the parties involved and allows a certain leeway. In practical economic operation, the objective may be exceeded, but it will be restricted by a certain upper limit. An overly high economic growth rate will produce the pressures of high energy consumption, high material consumption, high pollution and high inflation and cause violent economic ups and downs. An appropriate range of economic growth needs to be held in practical economic operation, which is neither too low (for example, below 8 percent) nor too high. Therefore, how can the upper limit be controlled?

Recently, our research group adopted the Hodrick–Prescott (HP) filter method and derived a trend growth rate after filtering, which is shown in Figure 9.3, according to the GDP growth index of the period from 1978 to 2009 in China (Research Group of Macro Regulation, 2010).[2] It was smoother than the actual growth rate

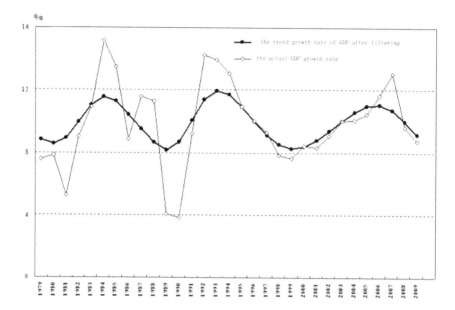

*Figure 9.3* Actual economic growth rate and filtering trend growth rate of the GDP (1979–2009)

and was generally within a range of 8 percent to 12 percent. The average annual increasing rate of the GDP growth trend was 9.87 percent after filtering, which was very close to the actual annual increasing rate of 9.78 percent, on average, during the 31 years from 1979 to 2009, with a mere difference of 0.09 percent. We can regard 8 percent to 12 percent as the appropriate economic growth range existing in China since the reform and opening up, specifically 8 percent as the lower limit, 12 percent as the upper limit and 9.8 percent as the median line of the potential economic growth rate. Currently, while entering a new economic cycle, we should consider the variations in three factors. First, great changes have taken place in the international economic environment. Following the international financial crisis, the external demand will remain depressed and sluggish for a certain period. Although the tendency of economic globalization will not change, the competition for world resources and markets will become fiercer and trade protectionism will obviously be aggravated. Second, the restraint on resources, energy and the environment will intensify continuously. Third, we should place more emphasis on improving the quality and benefit of the economic growth, transforming the economic development pattern and adjusting the economic structure. Therefore, the upper limit of the appropriate economic growth range can be lowered by 2 percent in the new economic cycle, that is, the appropriate economic growth range can be controlled at 8–10 percent and the median line of the potential economic growth rate at 9 percent. In terms of macro-regulation policy, this implies that a moderately tight macro-regulation policy should be implemented if the actual economic growth rate exceeds 10 percent; a moderately expansionary macro-regulation policy should be carried out if the actual economic growth rate is below 8 percent; and a neutral macro-regulation policy can be applied if the actual economic growth rate falls into the range of 8–10 percent.

The appropriate economic growth range of 8–10 percent needs a series of supporting factors (Research Group of Macro Regulation, 2010)[3] in the new economic cycle. First, reformation and system. The constant perfection of a socialist market economic system in reformation and the mutual development and the promotion of multiple-ownership economies with public ownership as the mainstay provided a significant system foundation for appropriate economic growth. Second, resource supply. The economic development that took place over 30 years following the reform and opening up provided the necessary material conditions for appropriate economic growth. Third, industrialization and urbanization. The acceleration of industrialization and urbanization in China provided a strong impetus for the domestic demand to achieve appropriate economic growth. Fourth, consumption upgrading. The improvement of the income level and the upgrading of the consumption structure provided a new impetus for the consumption demand to achieve appropriate economic growth. Fifth, new industries, science and technology. The development of new industries, science and technology provided new sources of growth for appropriate economic growth. Sixth, region. The adjustment and development of the eastern, central and western regions in coping with the international financial crisis provided a broad geographic space for appropriate economic growth.

### Combination of resolving short-, medium- and long-term issues

In 2010, a proactive fiscal policy and a moderately easy monetary policy should be followed continuously, maintaining the continuity and stability of policies and constantly improving the pertinence and flexibility of policies according to new situations and new circumstances. Successfully handling the relationship between the maintenance of steady and rapid economic growth, the adjustment of the economic structure and the control of inflation anticipation is to integrate the resolution of short-, medium- and long-term issues into macro regulation.

Resolving the short-term issues entails coping continuously with the impact of the international financial crisis, maintaining certain policy power and assuring a good tendency towards stabilization and recovery of the economy with the aim of maintaining the current steady and rapid economic growth.

Dealing with the medium-term issues involves controlling inflation anticipation. The consumer price index in China will not increase to a very high level in the short term. However, it is important to note that a price increase is the lagging result of excessive growth in currency credit and overly rapid economic growth. In particular, inertia is apparent in the accelerating economic growth in the rising stage of an economic cycle, which possesses a ripple diffusion effect or a cumulative magnifying effect between sectors, industries and enterprises, between fixed-assets investment and production and between economic expansion and price increases. Thus, these effects will easily cause the economic growth to face the risk of evolving from "comparatively fast" to "fast" and further to "overheating", thus risking the price changing from "deflation" to "moderately increasing" and further to "inflation". Therefore, inflation is a dynamic and medium-term process. To prevent inflation, the factors that will easily induce inflation must be controlled in advance; in particular, the issuance of currency credit and the economic growth speed must be regulated ahead of time. Attempting to control the inflation when it is already very severe will be costly. This requires the central and local governments to follow the dynamic variations in the economic situation closely and carry out the necessary regulation appropriately.

Resolving the long-term issues means continuously making efforts to adjust some long-standing structural contradictions (for example, the disequilibrium between domestic demand and external demand and between investment and consumption, the discordance between industries, the imbalanced development between urban and rural areas and between regions and the disequilibrium between economic development and social undertakings), accelerate the transformation of the long-standing extensive economic development pattern and carry out reform in those systematic and mechanism obstacles that affect sound economic development. Substantial progress should be obtained in the above to lay a solid foundation for long-term, steady and rapid economic growth constantly.

[Originally published in *Analysis of Economic Prospect in China-Spring Review of 2009*, Economic Blue Book, Spring Issue, Social Sciences Academic Press, 2009]

## Notes

1 P. A. Samuelson & W. D. Nordhaus. (2005). *Economics* (18th ed., p. 468). New York: McGraw-Hill Irwin.
2 Research Group of Macro Regulation, Institute of Economics of the Chinese Academy of Social Sciences. (2010). Analysis of Macro Regulation Objective of the "Eleventh Five-Year Plan" and Outlook for the "Twelfth Five-Year Plan". *Economic Research Journal*, 2.
3 Research Group of Macro Regulation, Institute of Economics of the Chinese Academy of Social Sciences. (2010). Analysis of Macro Regulation Objective of the "Eleventh Five-Year Plan" and Outlook for the "Twelfth Five-Year Plan", *Economic Research Journal*, 2.

## References

IMF: World Economic Outlook Database. https://www.imf.org/en/Data
Research Group of Macro Regulation, Institute of Economics of Chinese Academy of Social Sciences. (2010). Analysis of Macro Regulation Objective of the "Eleventh Five-Year Plan" and Outlook for the "Twelfth Five-Year Plan". *Economic Research Journal*, 2.

# 10 Analysis of the national and international environments of China's economic development in 2010

If we define 2008 as an extraordinary year in China's development and 2009 as the year in which China met the greatest difficulty in its economic development since the beginning of the twenty-first century, then 2010 will be a year in which China will encounter extremely complicated economic environments, both domestically and internationally. Prime Minister Wen Jiabao pointed out in the Government Working Report delivered at the Third Plenary Session of the 11th National People's Congress that "although the development environment this year may be better than that of last year, the situation we are facing is extremely complicated". The complexity lies in the interweaving and interaction of various positive changes and unfavorable conditions, short-term issues and long-term contradictions, new and old issues and domestic and international factors. This paper intends to undertake a concrete analysis of the national and international environments that China's economic development is facing in 2010.

## Analysis of the international economic environment

On the whole, the international environment of China's economic development in 2010 has a dual character, namely the tendency of turnaround overlapping with an adverse trend, indicating that the external environment is still very unstable and uncertain.

1   Expected recovery growth in the world economy, but with a fragile foundation of revival

Affected by the most serious international financial crisis in a century, the world economy presented negative growth in 2009 for the first time since World War II, producing a global economic recession. According to the latest statistics announced by the International Monetary Fund in January 2010, the world output growth was −0.8 percent (see Table 10.1 and Figure 10.1) in 2009. To cope with the crisis, all countries adopted a series of financial rescue policies or economic stimuli on an unprecedented scale and strength, which are now showing their positive impact. So far, a recurrence of the global Great Depression, which happened in the period from 1929 to 1933, has been avoided. Specifically, after experiencing a great decline during the period from the second half of 2008 to the first half

*Table 10.1* Economic growth rate of the world and the main economies

|  | Statistics of 2009 (%) | Prediction of 2010 (%) |
| --- | --- | --- |
| World output | −0.8 | 3.9 |
| Developed economies | −3.2 | 2.1 |
| United States | −2.5 | 2.7 |
| Euro zone | −3.9 | 1.0 |
| Japan | −5.3 | 1.7 |
| Emerging and developing economies | 2.1 | 6.0 |
| China | 8.7 | 10.0 |
| India | 5.6 | 7.7 |
| Brazil | −0.4 | 4.7 |
| Russia | −9.0 | 3.6 |

Note. From IMF: World Economic Outlook Database.

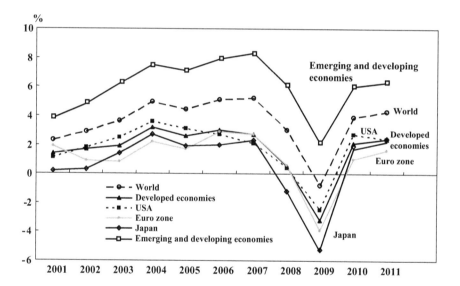

*Figure 10.1* Economic growth rate curve of the world and the main economies

of 2009, the world economy started to show signs of a revival in the second half of 2009. If no significant accident occurs in the international economy and finance, the world economic growth will hopefully change from negative to positive and achieve recovery growth in 2010. According to the latest prediction announced by the International Monetary Fund in January 2010, the world output is estimated to increase by 3.9 percent (see Table 10.1) in 2010, during which the economic growth of developed economies will recover from −3.2 percent in 2009 to 2.1 percent in 2010. The US economic growth is estimated to recover from −2.5 percent in 2009, the largest decline in the 62 years since 1947, to 2.7 percent in 2010; that of the euro zone from −3.9 percent to 1 percent; and that of Japan from −5.3 percent to 1.7 percent. The situation in emerging and developing economies may be better than that in developed countries, recovering from 2.1 percent in 2009 to 6 percent in 2010; China from 8.7 percent to 10 percent; India from 5.6 percent to 7.7 percent; Brazil from −0.4 percent to 4.7 percent; and Russia from −9 percent to 3.6 percent.

While the global economy is expected to achieve recovery growth, its foundation for revival is still fragile because it relies mainly on supernormal strong stimuli of different governments. In particular, the recovery of a real economy in developed countries is full of difficulties and an economic revival has not yet brought about an employment increase. Currently, the unemployment rate in the United States is still at a high level of around 10 percent, which is the highest rate for over 26 years. The net reduction of jobs in the United States was 208,000 in the fourth quarter of 2009. The unemployment rate was already as high as 18 percent in Spain, which had experienced a relatively serious recession. Since the economic revival in developed countries has not recovered to the potential economic growth level, the unemployment rate will stay at a high level in the short and medium term. The original consumption pattern of excessive debt in the US-led developed countries was greatly affected by the international financial crisis and is facing a deep adjustment. Together with a high unemployment rate, all these issues have caused sluggish private consumption and a low level of willingness in enterprise investment. Thus, the shrinking of the international market demand may last for a comparatively long period. As a result, the global economic revival will be a tortuous and slow process.

2   A stabilizing trend in the international financial market, but without complete elimination of risks

In the spring and summer of 2008, the US subprime mortgage crisis became increasingly fierce and rapidly evolved into a financial tsunami. At that time, many famous US large financial institutions fell into a predicament of serious deficit one after another, declared bankruptcy, or were bought or taken over by others. In January 2008, Citigroup, the largest commercial bank in the United States, and JP Morgan Chase, the second-largest commercial bank in the United States, both declared a significant deficit owing to the subprime mortgage crisis. In March 2008, Bear Stearns, the fifth-largest investment bank, was bought by JP Morgan Chase. In September 2008, two mortgage giants in the United States, Fannie Mae and Freddie Mac, were taken over by the US government and were on the verge of insolvency due to a lack of capital. In quick succession, Merrill Lynch & Co., Inc., the third-largest investment bank, was bought by the Bank of America; Raymond Brothers Co., the fourth-largest investment bank, declared bankruptcy to seek government protection from its debts; and Goldman Sachs, the largest investment bank, and Morgan Stanley, the second-largest investment bank, both declared a business transition and became commercial banks, accepting the supervision of the government. In a very short time, the international financial market was shaken violently. For over one year, it has been tending to stabilize. The global stock market has rebounded from the shocks since March 2009. Various risk indicators of the credit market have successively fallen or approached the level before the crisis. However, the financial risk has not been eliminated completely and the financial crisis has not ended yet.

The financial institutions in developed countries such as the United States have experienced a severe loss of capital. The deleveraging and liquidation of bad debts have not yet ended. New asset bubbles and financial crises are accumulating. All these will not rule out the possibility of the re-emergence of a localized financial shock. The latest report of the Federal Deposit Insurance Corporation (FDIC) demonstrated that the quantity of US "problem banks" increased from 252 at the beginning of 2009 to 702 at the end of 2009. Both the quantity and the total assets of the "problem banks" reached the peak during the 17 years since 1993. Altogether 140 US banks became bankrupt or were taken over in 2009, and another 20 banks did so from the beginning of 2010 to the middle of February. It is estimated that the quantity of bankruptcy in the banking industry of the United States in 2010 may exceed that of the previous year. The bank lending in the United States fell rapidly by 7.5 percent in 2009, which was the greatest decline during the 67 years since 1942.

In particular, instances of government debt crisis or government credit crisis in some countries took place successively, for example the recent Dubai debt crisis and especially the euro zone debt crisis. In April 2009, the fiscal debt crisis in Ireland was exposed to the public. By the end of 2009, the Greek debt crisis had been revealed as well. Subsequently, the sovereign credit rating was lowered for countries such as Portugal, Spain, Italy and Belgium, which were frequently on the list of "problem countries". It was reported by the British *Daily Telegraph* that the international media laughingly called the countries in the euro zone with serious problems, specifically Portugal, Ireland, Greece and Spain, PIGS (that is, the abbreviation of the initials of the four countries). Two-thirds of the EU member countries faced problems of fiscal deficit and a seriously low payment capacity for debt due to impermissibly high public debts. Moody's, the international credit rating agency, warned that the government credit crisis would be the biggest burden for global economic development in 2010 and would frequently create aftershocks in the financial market.

3   Certain achievements of economic stimuli, but with difficulties in their removal

In coping with the most serious international financial crisis in a century, different countries published extraordinary expansionary fiscal and monetary policies one after another, which to a certain extent played a significant role in reviving the global economy and stabilizing the financial market. However, the removal of the massive economic stimuli generated a three-dimensional problem. First, tightening fiscal and monetary policies too early may cause the economic revival to reach a premature end and induce a new economic recession. Recently, the Greek government, which was heavily in debt during the international financial crisis, published a series of retrenchment fiscal policies, such as reducing social security, laying off staff, cutting wages and increasing taxes, resulting in thousands of counter demonstrators. The public worried that the retrenchment fiscal policy may lead to a great increase in the unemployment rate and a reduction in salaries. In Spain and Portugal, the trade union constantly organized and called for strikes and protests against the government's retrenchment policies. Second, if the removal of an economic stimulus occurs too late, it may induce risks of government debt crises, inflation and asset bubbles. An excessively easy monetary policy adopted by different countries has already increased the market liquidity greatly and may give rise to a price increase during the vibrations and a sharp fluctuation in international commodities, such as oil and raw materials. Third, if the time and strength of the removal of an economic stimulus are inconsistent in different countries, it may bring about massive international interest arbitrage and aggravate the flow of international speculative capital, thus inducing a violent fluctuation in the international capital market and the main currency exchange rate.

This created difficulties for the coordination of the macroeconomic policies in different countries. At the end of 2009, Australia, India and Vietnam regarded inflation as the number one enemy of economic development. Some countries started to abandon their excessively easy monetary policy. For example, the Bank of Israel was the first in the world to raise its interest rate in August 2009. From October to December 2009, Australia raised its interest rate three times in succession, making it the earliest country among the G20 nations to cancel an economic stimulus. In October 2009, the Reserve Bank of India raised the bank's statutory liquidity ratio and began to tighten the money supply. In February 2010, the US Federal Reserve Commission announced to the public its plan to abandon an easy monetary policy and gave signs of tightening policies, but no specific schedule was published. Subsequently, it raised the discount rate for commercial banks, thus leading to worries and turmoil in the financial market.

4   An unchanged tendency of further progress in economic globalization, but an obvious rise in trade protectionism

The world opinion holds that the international financial crisis has a severe impact on the global economy and finance and generated extreme chaos; thus, the world's economic growth pattern will change. As a result, economic globalization may turn around, face stagnation or even collapse. We believe that economic globalization, namely the expansion of economic activities such as production, trade, investment and finance on a global scale, is an inevitable outcome of a high development level of modern science, technology, productive forces and international division of labor. The deep development tendency of economic globalization will not change. The international financial crisis will not fundamentally change the medium- and long-term tendency of world economic development. However, the international financial crisis and its induced global economic recession, to some extent, have led to a revival and a violent heating up of trade protectionism. To solve domestic employment issues, under domestic political and economic pressure, on the pretense of resolving the "global economic imbalance", Europe and the United States and other developed countries took many measures of trade protectionism against developing countries, including China, and caused a huge threat to the sustainable recovery of the global economy. The forms of trade protectionism were diversified, including anti-dumping and anti-subsidy, general safeguard and specific safeguard measures, an increase in import tax and imposing technical barriers on trade. In the period following the international financial crisis, all governments are liable for promoting economic globalization continuously to move forward in the direction of balanced development, shared benefits and win-win progress.

5   New development opportunities bred by a great reformation and adjustment in the world economic pattern, but with intricate global issues of industrial competition and climatic variation

The history of the world economic development reveals that every big economic crisis breeds and produces a new scientific and technological revolution. Only the key breakthroughs and innovations in science and technology are promoting great adjustments of the world economic structure and boosting the new global economic prosperity. In the period following the international financial crisis, a very important part of the great reformation and adjustment of the world economic pattern is the brewing and the rise of new scientific, technological and industrial revolutions, for example the new energy revolution symbolized by green and low-carbon technology, research and development and market exploitation of electric automobiles, advanced material, information networks, life science and biotechnology and the exploitation and utilization of space, the oceans and the earth. This will enable human society to enter an era of unprecedented intensive innovation and industry revitalization, creating significant new development opportunities. However, during the process of racing to control a commanding point of economy, science and technology, the competition in science and technology and for talents carried out around strategic emerging industries between different countries will become increasingly fierce. The one that can obtain superiority in scientific and technological innovation will be able to gain the initiative in future development. Meanwhile, intricate global issues, like climatic variation, food security and energy resources security, will also issue new challenges; for example, the battle to cope with climatic variation between developed countries and developing countries is extremely fierce, tortuous and complicated. Some developed countries are attempting to negate the principle of "common and differential liability of international environmental law" and require developing countries, especially China, to accept the indicators of quantifiable emission reduction that exceed their self-capacities and development level to create obstructions to their normal economic development.

## Analysis of the national economic environment

On the whole, the national environment of China's economic development in 2010 has a dual character as well, as favorable conditions and prominent contradictions go hand in hand, indicating that the road ahead is rough and we can never regard the tendency towards economic recovery as being identical to an ultimate turnaround in the economic operation.

1   The foundation of the current economic recovery is further strengthened, but the endogenous impetus of the economic growth is insufficient and the employment situation is still grim

Affected by the international financial crisis, China's economy was severely influenced from the second half of 2008 and the growth of the real economy apparently declined. In terms of the quarterly growth rate of the GDP, it was at a level slightly higher than 10 percent in the first and second quarters, decreased respectively to 9 percent in the third quarter and 6.8 percent in the fourth quarter in 2008 and further declined to the trough of 6.2 percent in the first quarter of 2009. However, the falling tendency was reversed in the second quarter of 2009. The GDP growth rate began to rise quarter by quarter and was, respectively, 7.9 percent in the second quarter, 9.1 percent in the third quarter and 10.7 percent in the fourth quarter in 2009 (see Figure 10.2). In terms of the same-month growth rate of the industrial added value for enterprises above the designated size on a year-on-year basis, it was 16 percent in June 2008 and fell sharply to 5.4 percent in November and 5.6 percent in December 2008, declining by more than 10 percent within as little as half a year. It reduced to the trough of 3.8 percent during the period of January- February 2009. However, the downturn trend was turned around in March 2009. It started to recover and reached 19.2 percent in November and 18.5 percent in December 2009 (see Figure 10.3). Both of these growth rates traced a standard V-shaped inversion, enabling China to take the global lead in realizing an overall economic turnaround.

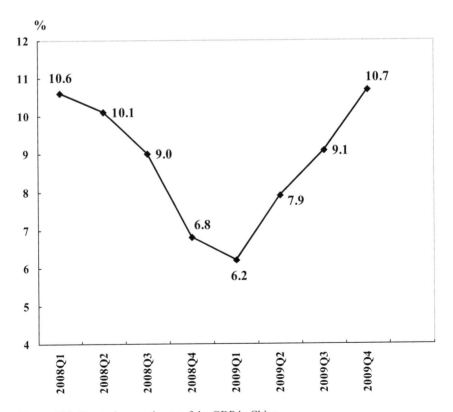

*Figure 10.2* Quarterly growth rate of the GDP in China

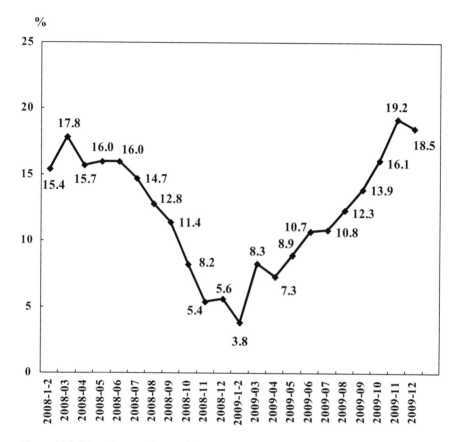

*Figure 10.3* Monthly growth rate of industrial production in China

China's GDP has recovered for three consecutive quarters and the industrial production has picked up for 10 consecutive months; thus, the foundation of an economic recovery has been further strengthened. However, the endogenous impetus of the economic growth is insufficient because the economic recovery relies mainly on the role of a package plan implemented by the government to cope with the international financial crisis. The desire for social investment has not yet been followed up and residents' consumption lacks a sustainable development capacity, creating difficulties in expanding the domestic demand. The contracted and sluggish external demand will be hard to change in the short term.

In the meantime, the employment situation is still grim, with the existence of a contradiction between the overall increasing employment pressure and the constitutive lack of a labor force, that is, overall "difficult job hunting" and a "shortage of workers". On the one hand, the aggregate labor supply exceeds the aggregate labor demand in a certain period. The scale of the newly developed urban labor forces and college graduates is quite large and the task of transferring surplus rural labor forces is still heavy. On the other hand, a certain constitutive "shortage of workers" exists in employment. In the early spring of 2010, the issue of the "shortage of workers" emerged in the coastal areas, like the Yangzi River Delta and the Zhujiang River Delta. According to a latest investigation by the Ministry of Human Resources and Social Security, 70 percent of the investigated enterprises in the eastern coastal area experienced a "shortage of workers", because enterprises, in particular the foreign trade enterprises in the coastal areas, have more orders owing to the economic recovery and require more workers, especially experienced and skilled workers, on the one hand, and migrant workers, in particular the new generation of migrant workers, have new demands for work choices, living conditions and future prospects, on the other hand. This leads to a mismatch between the employers' demands and the labor supply.

2   The policies of expanding the domestic demand and improving the livelihood of the people continuously appear to be effective, but the potential risks in finance and banking are increasing

To face the international financial crisis, China resolutely carried out a proactive fiscal policy and a moderately easy monetary policy in good time, implemented and continuously perfected a package plan in all directions and effectively expanded the domestic demand. By combining the expansion of residents' consumption and the improvement of people's livelihood, the trend of an apparent economic downturn was quickly reversed. These policies will remain effective. Meanwhile, certain financial and banking risks will be accumulated. In 2009, the monetary credit grew extraordinarily, with the newly increased credit in renminbi reaching as high as 9600 billion yuan, which was twice that in 2008 and close to 30 percent of the GDP. This produced huge pressure on the capital price increase, such as that of real estate, and the lagging consumption price increase. A platform for local government financing, taking banks as the main channel, developed rapidly. No one can afford to neglect the hidden risks in fiscal credit.

3   The enterprises' market adaptive capacity and competitiveness are continuously improving and the confidence in the market enhancing, but the independent innovation competence is not strong. The contradiction of surplus production capacity in some industries is prominent, thus creating difficulty for structural adjustments.

Chinese enterprises worked hard, showing their indomitable spirit, to cope with the unexpected international financial crisis, changed "danger" into "chance" and improved their capacity to suit the domestic and international market and their competitiveness by improving their management level, speeding up innovation, adjusting their development strategy and promoting mergers and reorganization. Some enterprises with an independent brand, independent intellectual property rights and high technology demonstrated their strong risk-resisting ability and market competitiveness. According to the data announced by the World Intellectual Property Organization, China applied altogether 7946 international patents in

2009, an increase of 29.7 percent compared with 2008. The total number of applications ranked fifth in the world, and 34 mainland Chinese enterprises entered the ranks of the global Top 500 in 2009, surpassing Great Britain for the first time. Along with economic recovery, the confidence in the market is gradually being enhanced. The confidence index of entrepreneurs dived from a high platform and plunged to 94.6 points in the fourth quarter of 2008, reaching a new low point in recent years. Later, it recovered quarter by quarter from the first quarter of 2009 and rose to 127.7 points in the fourth quarter of 2009. Another indicator that can reflect the confidence in the market is the new order index, which decreased to its lowest point of 32.3 percent in November 2008, which was far lower than the critical value of 50 percent. This illustrated a low market demand and a lack of confidence. The monthly new order index recovered to above 50 percent from February 2009 to February 2010, during which it reached a high point of 61 percent in December 2009.

However, on the whole, Chinese enterprises' capability to engage in independent innovation is not strong. At present, the output of nearly 200 Chinese products ranks first in the world. However, there are very few products that possess a brand of international competitiveness. Fewer than 10 percent of export products are in possession of independent intellectual property rights. Since most export products in China are produced under the authorization of other brands, they are at the low end of the value chain of international industrial division and provide low value-added, thus leading to a great loss in profits. The statistics show that the authorized patents that foreign companies have obtained account for more than 90 percent of the high-tech export products of communication, semiconductors, bio-medicine and computers. China applied a total of 7946 international patents in 2009, an increase of 29.7 percent compared with the previous year. The total number of applications ranked fifth in the world, among which invention patents occupied a small proportion and most of the applications were design patents and utility model patents, demonstrating that the research and development investment of the Chinese enterprises was far from sufficient. According to the evaluation report on Chinese enterprises' self-innovation announced by the China Enterprise Evaluation Association in 2009, at present, the independent research and development expenditures of Chinese enterprises only accounts for 3.8 percent of their sales income on average. The experiences of developed countries illustrate that only with more than 5 percent will enterprises be competitive. If the proportion is 2 percent, enterprises will barely survive. If it is 1 percent, it will be difficult for enterprises to continue. In terms of household appliance enterprises in China, their research and development investment merely occupies 1 percent of their sales, causing them to possess virtually no basic technology and core technology and to be dominated by others in the core technological fields, such as liquid crystal panels, semiconductors and chips. Due to the lack of a self-dominated brand, their production mainly relies on the massive consumption of resources. Therefore, the output level per unit of resource is only equivalent to one-tenth of that of the United States and one-twentieth of that of Japan. In terms of the development of infant industries, on the whole, Chinese enterprises lack core technology and leading talents. At present, China is merely a "big manufacturing country" and a "large trading nation" and is far from being a "powerful manufacturing country" and a "strong trading nation". Considerable efforts have to be made to transform "Made in China" into "Created in China".

Meanwhile, the issue of surplus production capacity in some industries is quite serious. The elimination of backward production capacity, mergers and reorganization will be restricted by huge employment pressure and an imperfect system and mechanism. As revealed by the investigation carried out by the China Entrepreneur Survey System in October 2009, 63.4 percent of the enterprises believed that there was an overcapacity in their industrial production, of which 18.6 percent held that there was a serious surplus in the production capacity and 44.8 percent thought that there was somewhat of a surplus in the production capacity. In addition, 37.1 percent of the enterprises reflected that the surplus production capacity in the whole industry was the major difficulty that they had encountered. It was reported that 21 out of 24 industries had presented a surplus production capacity up to the third quarter of 2009, in which steel, cement, plate glass, the coal and chemical industry, polycrystalline silicon and wind power equipment were the key industries. Not only are some traditional industries still expanding blindly, but also the tendency to engage in repeated construction is emerging in some new industries.

4   China has repeatedly achieved a bumper harvest with an improvement of rural incomes. However, the foundation for steady agricultural development and a sustained increase in rural incomes is not stable.

The "three-dimensional rural issues concerning agriculture, countryside and farmers" are the top priority in China and should be constantly enhanced. In 2009, in the face of the severe impact of the international financial crisis, the challenge of serious natural disasters and the violent price fluctuation of domestic and international agricultural products, through painstaking efforts, the overall situation in agriculture and the countryside in China was better than expected at the beginning of the year. The total grain output reached 530.82 million tons in 2009, hitting a new peak again and achieving an increase in the grain output for six consecutive years (see Figure 10.4). This played an important role in maintaining the market supply of agricultural products and stabilizing the overall price level. In the same year, the per capita net income of rural households broke 5000 yuan for the first time, reaching 5153 yuan, an increase of 8.5 percent in real terms, and representing rapid growth for six consecutive years as well. During the seven years from 1997 to 2003, the per capita net income of rural households only increased by around 2–4 percent in real terms, whereas it rose to around 6–9 percent in the recent six years from 2004 to 2009. The rural production and living conditions, such as water, electricity, road, firedamp construction, housing, education, health and social security, have improved and developed considerably. However, the foundation for steady agricultural development and a sustained increase in rural incomes is not stable. The infrastructures of irrigation and water conservation are fragile. The anti-disaster ability of agriculture is not strong enough because the agricultural production is greatly influenced by climatic variations. The socialized

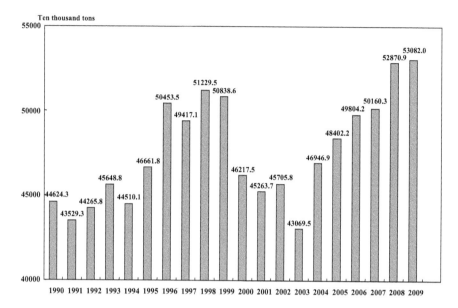

*Figure 10.4*  Grain output in China

service system at the grassroots level, such as the extension of agricultural science and technology, is still imperfect and thus is unable to support agricultural production fully. The continuously increased grain production and low comparative efficiency in agricultural planting and feeding exert huge downward pressure on agricultural product prices and create difficulties in achieving sustained increases in grain yields and rural incomes. The development of various rural public utilities still lags behind. Therefore, a rapid promotion of industrialization and urbanization will bring new circumstances and new issues of concern in balancing the economic and social development of urban and rural areas, such as the protection of cultivated land, the protection of farmers' rights and issues concerning the new generation of migrant workers.

5    China is still experiencing a period of important strategic opportunity. However, prominent issues, such as medical care, education, housing, income distribution and social management, demand prompt solutions.

In the period following the international financial crisis, China is still experiencing a period of important strategic opportunity. The international financial crisis neither fundamentally changed the medium- and long-term tendency of world economic development nor changed the improving tendency of economic and social fundamentals in the long term in China. The rapid promotion of industrialization and urbanization will provide a strong impetus for domestic demand for future economic development; the continuous improvement in the per capita national income and the corresponding upgrading of the consumption structure will provide a new impetus for the consumption demand for future economic development; scientific and technological development and the rise of infant industries will provide new sources of growth for future economic development; the adjustment and re-emergence of the eastern, central and western regions in coping with the international financial crisis will provide a broad geographic space for future economic development; the constant perfection of a socialist market economic system in reformation and the common prosperity and mutual promotion of multiple-ownership economies with public ownership as the mainstay will provide a significant system foundation for future economic development; the rapid economic growth over 30 years since the reform and opening up will provide the necessary material conditions for future economic development; and the rich experiences that the Party and central government have accumulated in leading socialist modernization and in coping with the Asian financial crisis and especially the international financial crisis will provide precious policy support for future economic development.

However, prominent social contradictions will appear in a certain period in the future. The task of social construction with a focus on improving people's livelihood is particularly tough. Conspicuous issues, such as medical care, education, housing, income distribution and social management, demand prompt solutions. According to the surveys undertaken respectively by Xinhua net and People's Daily Online on the eve of the "Two Conferences" in 2010, medical care, educational equity and the regulation of housing prices, specifically the issues of the difficulty and high cost of obtaining medical services, the difficulties and expensiveness of attending school and the difficulty and high cost involved in purchasing houses, are reported as the top 10 hot spots; in particular, the issue of the overly rapid increase in housing prices has never attracted as much attention as in 2010. Meanwhile, the excessively growing income disparity appears among the top 10 hot spots as well and ranks first in the survey result of Xinhua net. An investigation shows that most residents in China are currently willing to consume. However, due to the widening income gap, some residents have a very low income, thus leading to insufficient consumption capability. In addition, social management issues, such as household registration reform, endowment insurance, anti-corruption, judicial justice, democratic supervision and inquiry after politics in networks, are subjects of great concern by netizens and are reported as being among the top 10 hot spots.

In summary, although the national and international environment of economic development in China in 2010 may be better than that in 2009, the situations that we face are extremely complicated. We must make an overall and proper judgment of the current situation, strengthen the sense of crisis, make full use of various advantages to prepare ourselves for various risks and endeavor to achieve sound and rapid economic and social development.

[Originally published in *Economics Perspectives (JingjixueDongtai)* No. 3, 2010]

## Reference

IMF: World Economic Outlook Database. https://www.imf.org/en/Data

# 11 Analysis of the economic trend in 2010 and the economic growth during the Twelfth Five-Year Plan in China

## Main features of the economic trend in 2010

*By coping continuously with the international financial crisis, China's economy has started to enter the rising stage of a new economic cycle*

The last economic cycle in China, namely the tenth cycle since the founding of new China, was from 2000 to 2009 and followed a good trajectory with a rising stage of eight years and a falling stage of two years; it lasted altogether for ten years (see Figure 11.1). In terms of the rising stage from 2000 to 2007, the GDP growth rate followed a rising path from 8 percent to 14 percent for eight consecutive years, which was the longest rising trajectory that had ever appeared in the economic periodic fluctuation since the founding of new China. The rising stage was often as short as one or two years in the previous nine cycles. In terms of the falling stage, with the overlap between the domestic economic adjustment and the impact of the international financial crisis, the GDP growth rate decreased from 14.2 percent in 2007 to 9.6 percent in 2008, falling violently by 4.6 percent within one year. It descended to 9.1 percent in 2009, merely decreasing by 0.5 percent compared with 2008. It may recover to around 10 percent (9.8–10.2 percent) in 2010, which would be higher than that in 2009, thus entering the rising stage of the eleventh economic cycle.

In terms of the quarterly GDP growth rate, it presented an apparent declining trend and was 10.6 percent in the first quarter, 10.1 percent in the second quarter, 9 percent in the third quarter and 6.8 percent in the fourth quarter of 2008. It slid down to 6.5 percent in the first quarter of 2009 (see Figure 11.2). From the second quarter of 2009, the GDP growth rate crossed the trough, drew out a typical V-shaped recovery and took the global lead in realizing an overall economic turnaround. It produced an upward trend and was 6.5 percent in the first quarter, 8.1 percent in the second quarter, 9.1 percent in the third quarter and 10.7 percent in fourth quarter of 2009. It continuously rose to 11.9 percent in the first quarter of 2010, fell slightly to 10.3 percent in the second quarter of 2010 and was on average 11.1 percent for the first half of 2010.

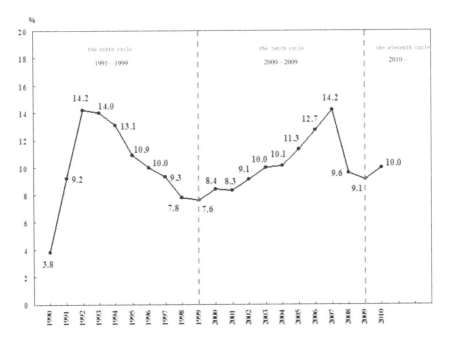

*Figure 11.1* Periodic fluctuation of the GDP growth rate in China

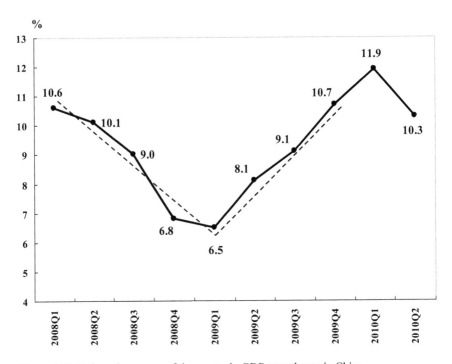

*Figure 11.2* V-shaped recovery of the quarterly GDP growth rate in China

**The growth of economic indicators, such as industrial production, appropriately slowed down, maintained a high level and became stabilized**

The growth of economic indicators, such as industrial production, fixed-assets investment and money supply, slowed down, maintained a high level and became stabilized, presenting a trend of high rises in the first half and low rises in the second half of 2010 and transforming from a turnaround when coping with the international crisis, into a normal, steady increase.

First, observing the operation situation of the industrial production, the same-month year-on-year growth rate of the industrial added value for nationwide enterprises above the designated size experienced a rapid decline from July 2008 to January and February 2009 and a turnaround from March to December 2009, followed a V-shaped trajectory and reached a new peak (see Figure 11.3) of 20.7 percent in January and February 2010. It fell to 13.4 percent during the period from March to July, rose slightly to 13.9 percent in August and stabilized at a level of 13 percent during the three months of June, July and August 2010. The high growth of the industrial production in the second half of 2009 constituted one reason for an appropriate decline in 2010. In detail, the industrial production growth was low in the first half and high in the second half of 2009; specifically, the same-month growth rate increased month-over-month in 2009 and led to a situation of high rises of the same-month year-on-year growth rate in the first half and low rises in the second half of 2010. The active adjustment of the state macro-regulation policies made up another reason for the appropriate decline in

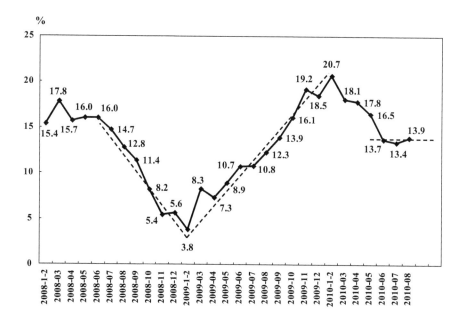

*Figure 11.3* Same-month year-on-year growth rate of industrial added value for nation-wide enterprises above the designated size

the industrial production growth. To avoid violent economic ups and downs, it was necessary to regulate the economic growth while the industrial production growth recovered to a certain high rate with the aim of saving energy, reducing consumption, eliminating backward production capacity and preventing prices from increasing too rapidly. In particular, six high-energy-consumption industries – the ferrous metal smelting and rolling processing industry, non-ferrous metal smelting and rolling processing industry, non-metal mineral product industry, manufacturing of chemical materials and chemical products, industry of oil processing and coking and nuclear fuel processing and production and supply of electricity and heat – produced a bad situation of overly rapid growth momentum, excessive release of production capacity and excessive increase in energy consumption during the rapid recovery of industrial production from the third quarter of 2009 to the first quarter of 2010. Following the deployment of further strengthening measures for energy conservation and emission reduction by the executive meeting of the State Council on 28 April 2010, energy conservation, emission reduction and the elimination of backward production capacity were intensified, enabling the industrial production growth to decrease to some extent since May 2010. Currently, it is normal for the industrial production to slow down appropriately. The total year-on-year growth rate of the industrial added value for nationwide enterprises above the designated size increased by 16.6 percent during the period from January to August 2010 compared with the same period in 2009 and remains at a high level.

Second, observing the operation situation of the fixed-assets investment, the total year-on-year growth rate in urban areas nationwide fell slightly from 26.6 percent during the period from January to February to 24.8 percent during the period from January to August 2010 (see Figure 11.4). In the previous package plan of investment implemented to cope with the impact of the international financial crisis, the total growth rate of the fixed-assets investment in urban areas nationwide was above 30 percent during the period from January–April to January–December 2009. In terms of the total year-on-year monthly growth rate from 2005 to 2008, 25–28 percent was the normal range. In 2010, in addition to the high growth in 2009, the investment growth declined appropriately, mainly due to the enhancement of the state macro regulation. On the one hand, the state strictly controlled the launching of new projects. In principle, new projects would no longer be approved. On the other hand, the investment growth in the six high-energy-consumption industries fell considerably. The total year-on-year investment growth in the six high-energy-consumption industries was 14.5 percent from January to August 2010, a decrease of 9.6 percent compared with the same period in 2009. In August 2010, the investment growth in the six high-energy-consumption industries was merely 9.2 percent. It is worth noting that private investment is accelerating, showing an increase of 31.9 percent from January to July 2010, 7 percent higher than the urban fixed-assets investment growth (24.9 percent). In addition, real estate investment and housing investment have increased rapidly since 2010 and their total year-on-year growth rates in recent months have achieved a high and steady level of 35–38 percent and 33–35 percent, respectively.

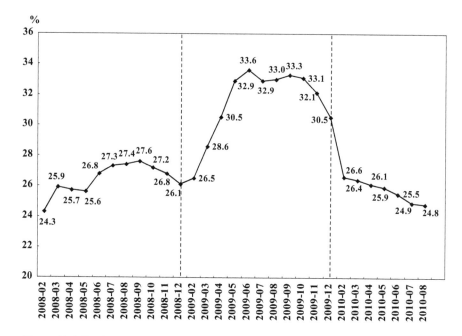

*Figure 11.4* Total year-on-year growth rate of urban fixed-assets investment nationwide

Moreover, observing the situation of variation in the money supply, the supply of broad money (M2) and narrow money (M1) experienced rises in each month of 2009 and basically presented a moderately declining trend in the year-on-year growth at the end of each month from January to August 2010 (see Figure 11.5). M2 increased by 26.1 percent year-on-year at the end of January, fell to 17.6 percent at the end of July and slightly rebounded to 19.2 percent at the end of August, while M1 increased by 39 percent year-on-year at the end of January and declined to 21.9 percent at the end of August. The moderate decline in the money supply embodied the result of an active adjustment in the state macro regulation and was related to the slowing down of the growth in foreign exchange reserves.

### Prices Slightly Rose within a Controllable Range

The same-month year-on-year rise rate in residents' consumption price increased from 1.5 percent in January to 3.5 percent in August 2010, the highest during the 22 months since November 2008 (see Figure 11.6). Residents' consumption price increased by 0.6 percent in August compared with that in July 2010. On the one hand, the price situation of a low rise in the first half and a high rise in the second half of 2009 produced a carry-over effect on the price movement in 2010; 1.7 percent of the 3.5 percent year-on-year price rise rate in August 2010 was due to the carry-over effect. On the other hand, new price increase factors led to an overall residents' consumption price increase, in which 1.8 percent of the 3.5 percent

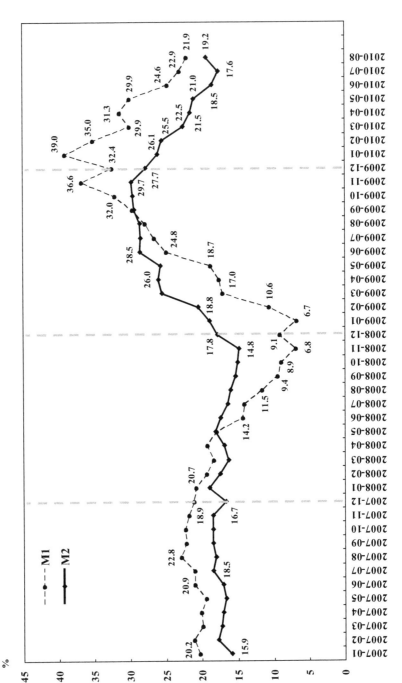

*Figure 11.5* Year-on-year growth of M1 and M2 at the end of a month

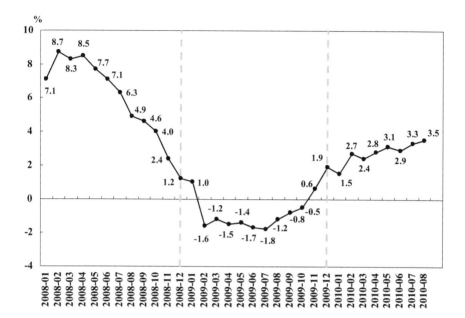

*Figure 11.6* Same-month year-on-year increase rate of residents' consumption price (January 2008–August 2010)

year-on-year price rise rate in August 2010 was due to these new factors, which mainly included the food price increase. In recent months, the weather has varied considerably from the south to the north of China and there were frequent natural disasters, such as floods, leading to a great increase in the prices of vegetables, grain and eggs. The year-on-year price increase was 19.2 percent in vegetables and 12 percent in grain in August 2010. It was 9 percent in pork, 7.7 percent in vegetables and 7.5 percent in eggs in August 2010 compared with the figures in July 2010.

The price tendency in the future is still very uncertain because the two factors of promoting the price increase and curbing the price increase coexist. The factors that promote the price increase are reported below. The price variation of agricultural products is very uncertain. In particular, the increase in the international grain price stimulates the domestic market to a certain extent. Recently, the extremely bad weather worldwide has triggered massive reductions in the grain production of the main grain-producing countries, such as Russia, Kazakhstan, Ukraine, Canada and Australia, thus leading to a new round of soaring in the international grain prices. The wage cost increase and the price increase of means of production may, to some extent, transmit to the price of residents' consumption. The factors that curb the price increase are the following. First, an appropriate decline in the economic growth curbs the price increase. In terms of the general law of price variation in China, an excessive price increase is closely related to an overly high economic growth rate. In recent years, the GDP growth rate has been stable and the price fluctuation has slowed down as well. Figure 11.7 provides the curve of the same-month year-on-year price rise rate of residents' consumption from January 1990 to August 2010. As depicted in Figure 11.7, after reaching the peak of 27.7 percent in October 1994, it reached two high points in recent years with 5.3 percent in July 2004 and 8.7 percent in February 2008, which were related to the increase in the economic growth rate at that time. There was no continuous price increase as the economic growth rate was controlled within a certain range. Historical experiences demonstrate that the price increase is easy to control as long as the economic growth is not overheated. Second, strengthening the administration of inflation expectation restrains the price increase. The supply of broad money (M2) and narrow money (M1) basically presented a moderately declining trend in the year-on-year growth at the end of each month from January to August 2010, which helped to ease the inflation pressure. The departments concerned enhanced the administration of market order and supervision of market price behavior. Third, the basic balance between the total grain supply and demand curbs the price increase. China achieved a bumper harvest for six consecutive years from 2004 to 2009. There was a good harvest in summer crops and hopefully there will be a good harvest in autumn crops as well in 2010. Fourth, an excessive supply of most industrial products restrains their price increase. The same-month year-on-year rise rate of the factory price of industrial products fell from 7.1 percent in May to 4.3 percent in August 2010, which was conducive to relieving the price pressure that was transmitted to the follow-up products. Fifth, the gradually weakened carry-over effect curbs the price increase. The carry-over effect was 2.2 percent in July, reduced to 1.7 percent in August and will decrease to 1.3 percent in September 2010. Integrating the analyses of these factors, the impact of curbing the price increase, in general, may be greater than that of promoting the price increase; thus the annual price rise will be moderate and controllable and can be maintained at around 3 percent.

### There were many dilemmas in economic and social development

The issues involving dilemmas are related to the economic fluctuation at the initial stage of a new economic cycle. Some issues bear the characteristics of both the falling stage of the last cycle and the rising stage of a new cycle, including either current prominent and urgent issues or long-standing and structural issues. The main issues are summed up as follows:

1    Macro-regulation policies face a dilemma. After a series of expansionary and stimulating policies were published to cope with the international financial crisis and obtained certain achievements, an issue arose concerning the timing of abandoning an economic stimulus. If it is attempted too early, the economic growth may fall sharply again. If it is attempted too late, the inflation pressure will be huge.

2    The control of housing prices faces a dilemma. If the high housing prices cannot be regulated effectively, social problems will easily be induced. If

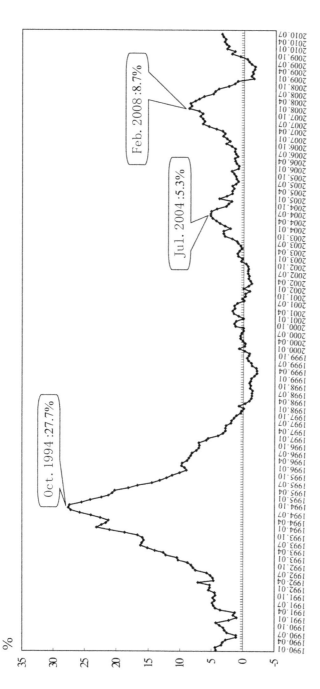

*Figure 11.7* Same-month year-on-year increase rate of residents' consumption price (January 1990–August 2010)

the real estate industry rapidly declines, it will directly affect the economic growth and the employment of a large amount of migrant workers in this field.

3    The income distribution reform faces a dilemma. To improve the contribution of consumption to the economic growth and narrow the gap in income distribution, we must increase the income of the medium- and low-income groups. However, this will increase the costs for enterprises and cause difficulties in their business operation. Meanwhile, distributing the "pie" of social wealth among the state, enterprises and individuals involves a significant taxation reform and will be extremely difficult.

4    Price regulation faces a dilemma. To transform the economic development pattern and promote energy conservation and emission reduction, it is necessary to carry out a reform of the original resources with low prices. However, in view of the current high inflation pressure, it is necessary to control an appropriate price adjustment; otherwise, it will increase the pressure of the price increase.

5    The RMB exchange rate faces a dilemma. If it appreciates too quickly, it will cause the export situation to face deterioration and exert high pressure on the employment of migrant workers. Moreover, once there is a financial impact, it will easily give rise to sharp depreciation, leading to violent ups and downs in the value of the RMB and affecting the whole economic stability. If it does not appreciate, there will be huge international pressure. Small continuous appreciations will be likely to cause an influx of a large amount of hot money.

6    Foreign trade faces a dilemma. On the one hand, as the tide of the international financial crisis is waning and the world economy is reviving, it is necessary to take this opportunity to expand exports. On the other hand, the revival of the global economy is extremely difficult. In particular, the European sovereign debt crisis is currently a small issue, but it will stir up big waves if it is not dealt with well. Therefore, the external demand instills little optimism.

### China's GDP surpassed that of Japan for the first time and it became the world's second-largest economy

In 2009, China's GDP was US$4909.2 billion, US$158.3 billion less than that of Japan, which was US$5067.5 billion. In the second quarter of 2010, China's GDP was US$1330 billion, while Japan's GDP was US$1280 billion, so China surpassed Japan by US$50 billion. China, for the first time, became the world's second-largest economy. This was a great symbolic event in the economic development of China in 2010. It is considered inevitable that the yearly GDP in China will exceed that of Japan in 2010. The overseas media reported and commented on this event. The *New York Times* reported on 16 August 2010 that China's economy had finally surpassed Japan in the second quarter of 2010 and it had become the world's second-largest economy after several decades of magnificent development. This was a landmark in the economic development of China and had long been expected. However, people were still shocked when it came true. The *World Journal* (www.chinesedailynews.com) published an article on 13 May 2010 entitled "China's Economy Surpassing Japan – A Mixture of Joys and Worries" and held that it was obviously delightful that China's economy had surpassed Japan's and become the world's second-largest economy. However, the point was that it might cause anxiety as well. We should be clear that the world's second-largest economy in terms of the GDP was not identical to that in terms of the per capita GDP. China was far from being the world's second-greatest economic power. Currently, its economic development was reaching a turning point with the urgent transformation of its development pattern.

## Analysis of the economic growth during the Twelfth Five-Year Plan in China

The Twelfth Five-Year Plan period (2011–15) is a crucial stage in which China will build an all-around well-off society and a key period in which China will deepen its reform and opening up and accelerate the transformation of its economic development pattern. Looking at the overall international and domestic situations, China's development is still in an important period of strategic opportunities, facing both historic opportunities and many foreseeable and unforeseeable risks and challenges. The main aim of the Twelfth Five-Year Plan will no doubt be to accelerate the transformation of the economic development pattern and enable it to run throughout the whole process and all areas of the economic and social development in China. Against such a background, the trends and features of China's economic growth speed during the Twelfth Five-Year Plan period are of great concern to everyone.

### *The target and actual values of the economic growth speed of each Five-Year Plan*

We first review the targets and actual rates of the economic growth in the five five-year plans from the Seventh Five-Year Plan to the Eleventh Five-Year Plan (see Table 11.1). The target for the economic growth rate in the Seventh Five-Year Plan was 7.5 percent and the actual rate was 7.9 percent, exceeding the target rate by 0.4 percent. In the Eighth Five-Year Plan, the target for the economic growth rate was originally 6 percent but was later revised to 8–9 percent. The actual rate was 12.3 percent, 6.3 percent more than the original target and exceeding the revised target rate by 4.3–3.3 percent. In the Ninth Five-Year Plan, the target for the economic growth rate was 8 percent and the actual rate was 8.6 percent, exceeding the target rate by 0.6 percent. In the Tenth Five-Year Plan, the target for the economic growth rate was 7 percent and the actual rate was 9.8 percent, exceeding the target rate by 2.8 percent. The Eleventh Five-Year Plan's target for the economic growth rate was 7.5 percent and the actual rate was 11 percent (the GDP growth rate of 2010 is calculated as 10 percent for the time being), exceeding the target rate by 3.5 percent.

*Table 11.1* Economic growth target and actual rate of various Five-Year Plans

| | Starting and ending year | Average annual economic growth target (%) | Actual rate of average annual economic growth (%) | Actual rate greater than the target (%) |
|---|---|---|---|---|
| The Seventh Five-Year Plan | 1986–90 | 7.5 | 7.9 | 0.4 |
| The Eighth Five-Year Plan | 1991–95 | 8–9 (6) | 12.3 | 4.3–3.3 (6.3) |
| The Ninth Five-Year Plan | 1996–2000 | 8 | 8.6 | 0.6 |
| The Tenth Five-Year Plan | 2001–05 | 7 | 9.8 | 2.8 |
| The Eleventh Five-Year Plan | 2006–10 | 7.5 | 11.0 | 3.5 |

Note. In the "average annual economic growth target" column, it is the GNP growth target in the Seventh Five-Year Plan, the Eighth Five-Year Plan and the Ninth Five-Year Plan. It is the GDP growth target in the Tenth Five-Year Plan and the Eleventh Five-Year Plan. The "actual rate of average annual economic growth" is the GDP growth rate.

*Table 11.2* Annual economic growth target and the actual rate

| Year | Annual economic growth target (%) | Annual actual economic growth rate (%) | Actual rate greater than the target (%) |
|---|---|---|---|
| 2005 | 8 | 11.3 | 3.3 |
| 2006 | 8 | 12.7 | 4.7 |
| 2007 | 8 | 14.2 | 6.2 |
| 2008 | 8 | 9.6 | 1.6 |
| 2009 | 8 | 9.1 | 1.1 |
| 2010 | 8 | 10.0 | 2.0 |

In terms of the yearly target for the economic growth rate (see Table 11.2), it was determined as around 8 percent for six consecutive years from 2005 to 2010 (all are GDP growth rates). All the years exceeded the target rate (the GDP growth rate of 2010 is calculated as 10 percent for the time being). On the whole, regardless of whether the target in the five-year plan or the yearly target is considered, the actual economic growth rate surpassed the target rate.

Early in 1983, Deng Xiaoping pointed out that:

according to the latest statistics, gross industrial and agricultural output in 1982 increased by 8 percent, greatly exceeding the originally planned figure of 4 percent – something that had not happened in the previous two years. This raises a question: what will come of achieving a much higher growth rate than projected in the annual plan? We must investigate and study this question right away and analyse it correctly. However, this doesn't mean we should alter our Sixth Five-Year Plan. Long-term plans should be more flexible, while annual plans should be more specific, though of course they should have some flexibility too. We should pay attention to improving economic efficiency, instead of just going after increases in the value and quantity of output. Experiences show that whenever our plans have been too ambitious, we have overreached ourselves. This has been a bitter lesson for us. We are already aware of this mistake and will continue to guard against it in future. But now we face the opposite situation.

(Selected Works of Deng Xiaoping, 1994)[1]

It has been 27 years since Deng Xiaoping put forward this issue in 1983. Now, everyone has become accustomed to the situation of the actual economic growth rate being much higher than the target rate, which is hard to change.

## *The probable features of the economic growth speed during the Twelfth Five-Year Plan period in China*

At present, the economic growth speed during the Twelfth Five-Year Plan period in China may present the following three features:

1   In terms of the position in the economic periodic fluctuation, the economic growth speed during the Twelfth Five-Year Plan period will be in the rising stage of a new economic cycle.

The first year of the Seventh Five-Year Plan period (1986–90) was in the trough of the economic growth rate. Subsequently, the economy entered the eighth cycle since the founding of new China, with two years of a high economic growth rate and two years of a falling rate, fluctuating considerably (see Figure 11.8).

The Eighth Five-Year Plan period (1991–95) entered the ninth cycle with violent economic ups and a subsequent steady decline.

The Ninth Five-Year Plan period (1996–2000) was in the continuous falling stage of the ninth cycle with the last year entering the rising stage of the tenth cycle.

The whole period of the Tenth Five-Year Plan (2001–05) followed the rising path of the tenth cycle, which was the best among all the five-year plans.

The Eleventh Five-Year Plan period (2006–10) was in the continuous rising stage of the tenth cycle. Subsequently, influenced by the overlap between the domestic economic periodic adjustment and the international financial crisis, the economic growth rate fell and entered the rising stage of the eleventh cycle in the last year.

In this way, the Twelfth Five-Year Plan period (2011–15) will be just like the Tenth Five-Year Plan period and will occur in the rising stage of a new economic cycle, with neither an overheated economy nor an economic downturn. By virtue of this advantageous trend, promoting the transformation of the economic development pattern and the economic structural adjustment will lay a decisive foundation for the construction of an overall well-off society.

2   In terms of the base year, the economic growth rate is relatively high, thus the continuous, accelerating rise will not be large. Macro regulation will mainly focus on steady economic growth and the prevention of the economic growth from overheating.

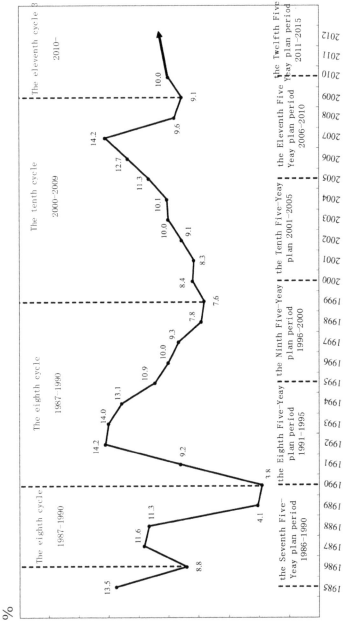

*Figure 11.8* Fluctuation curve of the GDP growth rate in China

In 1985, the base year of the Seventh Five-Year Plan period, the GDP growth rate was as high as 13.5 percent (see Figure 11.8). Therefore, China was facing national economic adjustment while entering the period of the Seventh Five-Year Plan, with a falling economic growth rate.

In 1990, the base year of the Eighth Five-Year Plan period, the GDP growth rate fell to 3.8 percent, providing the economic growth rate in the whole period of the Eighth Five-Year Plan with a huge space to rise.

In 1995, the base year of the Ninth Five-Year Plan period, the GDP growth rate was decreasing from the previous high rate to 10.9 percent, making it difficult to go up much for the whole period of the Ninth Five-Year Plan.

In 2000, the base year of the Tenth Five-Year Plan period, the GDP growth rate was just starting to recover and reached 8.4 percent, enabling the economic growth rate in the whole period of the Tenth Five-Year Plan to have a certain potential to rise.

In 2005, the base year of the Eleventh Five-Year Plan period, the GDP growth rate had already increased to 11.3 percent, generating the risk of the economic growth changing from rapid to overheating.

In 2010, the base year of the Twelfth Five-Year Plan period, the GDP growth rate is estimated to be a high rate of around 10 percent with no further space for a large and accelerating rise. The macro regulation should mainly focus on the prevention of economic growth from overheating. The macro regulation during the Twelfth Five-Year Plan period can draw on the experiences of the Tenth Five-Year Plan period and the previous stages of the Eleventh Five-Year Plan. In detail, to extend the rising stage of an economic cycle or to maintain steady national economic operation at an appropriately high rate, it is necessary to adopt multiple or multi-phase minor adjustments according to the specific situation of the economic fluctuation, enabling the economic growth rate not to exceed the peak, that is, not to break the appropriate economic growth range excessively.[2]

Recently, our research group adopted the HP filtering method and production function, made calculations according to the relevant data since the reform and opening up and derived that the appropriate economic growth range in China was 8–12 percent and the median line of the potential economic growth rate was nearly 10 percent (Research Group of Macro Regulation, 2010).[3] During the period of the Twelfth Five-Year Plan, the variations in three factors should be taken into consideration. First, great changes have taken place in the international economic environment. Following the international financial crisis, the external demand will remain depressed and sluggish for a certain period. Although the tendency of economic globalization will not change, the competition for world resources and the market will become fiercer and trade protectionism will obviously be aggravated. Second, various restraints in resources, energy and the environment will continuously intensify. Third, more emphasis should be placed on improving the quality and benefit of the economic growth, transforming the economic development pattern and adjusting the economic structure. Therefore, the upper limit of the appropriate economic growth range can be lowered by 2 percent during the period of the Twelfth Five-Year Plan, that is, the appropriate economic growth range can be controlled at 8–10 percent and the median line of the potential economic growth rate at 9 percent.

3   In terms of the economic development stages, the gross national income per capita is starting to fall into the range of medium- and high-income countries and is undergoing a period of rapid development.

According to the gross national income per capita (GNI per capita), the World Bank divides the world's economies into four groups: the low-income group, medium- and low-income group, medium- and high-income group and high-income group. The specific division standard varies annually. The statistics of the GNI per capita of the world economies is frequently revised by the World Bank as well. According to the statistics and the division by the World Bank, there were two years during which the GNI per capita in China entered the medium- and low-income group from the low-income group for the first time.

According to the statistics of the World Bank in 1997, the GNI per capita in China was US$860, greater than US$786, the lower limit of the medium- and low-income group; thus, for the first time, it entered the medium- and low-income group. However, the World Bank subsequently revised the GNI per capita in China to US$750. By doing so, it was less than US$786, the lower limit of the medium- and low-income group. Therefore, China still fell into the low-income group.

According to the statistics of the World Bank in 1998, the GNI per capita in China was US$750, less than US$760, the lower limit of the medium- and low-income group. Thus, China was listed in the low-income group. However, the World Bank subsequently revised the GNI per capita in China to US$790. Accordingly, it was greater than US$760, the lower limit of the medium- and low-income group. Therefore, according to the final revised data of the World Bank, China entered the medium- and low-income group for the first time in 1998.

Regardless of the initial statistics or the final revised data of the World Bank, China has remained in the medium- and low-income group from 1999 up to now. According to the data published by the World Bank, the GNI per capita in China was US$3620 in 2009. It is estimated that the GNI per capita in China will break US$4500 during the period of the Twelfth Five-Year Plan. China will enter the medium- and high-income group by that time.

The GNI per capita is one of the important representative indicators that indicate a country's economic development stage. Different levels of GNI per capita or different stages of economic development have different impacts on the speed of economic growth. Generally speaking, when the GNI per capita rises from a low level to a medium level along with the upgrading of the consumption structure and the corresponding industrial structure, the economic growth speed may be rapid. When the GNI per capita increases to a certain high level and while being affected by the stabilization of the consumption structure and the saturation of the basic consumption demand, the economic growth speed may tend to slow down. However, the certain high level of the GNI per capita varies with different situations in different countries.

Meanwhile, different countries will encounter different economic and social issues at different stages of low-income, middle-income or high-income levels. If these issues are dealt with well, they will continuously promote economic and social development. If they are not handled properly, they may induce stagnation in economic development. This will generate issues related to the so-called "low-income trap" (also called the "poverty trap"), "middle-income trap" and "high-income trap". The "middle-income trap" is divided into the "middle- and low-income trap" and the "middle- and high-income trap". The "middle- and low-income trap" refers to the economic and social issues that a country may encounter while stepping into the medium- and high-income group and after its GNI per capita has entered the medium- and low-income group from the low-income group. The "middle- and high-income trap" refers to the economic and social issues that a country may encounter while stepping into the high-income group and after its GNI per capita has entered the medium- and high-income group from the medium- and low-income group. In fact, regardless of the stage of the income levels, low, medium and high, corresponding economic and social issues may appear, namely the so-called "trap" issues, which may be overcome smoothly at any stage of the income levels.

In 2004, when China initially announced that its GNI per capita had broken US$1000 in 2003, academic circles focused on discussing the issue of how to avoid the "middle- and low-income trap". During the period of the Twelfth Five-Year Plan, China will enter the medium- and high-income group. Therefore, it is necessary to discuss, at present, the issue of how to avoid the "middle- and high-income trap". In terms of the international experiences, different situations occur in different countries, either striding over a "trap" smoothly or falling into a "trap" for a period of time. The key depends on whether the strategy of the economic and social development is appropriate. At the same time, the GNI per capita in China will break US$4500 and start to enter the medium- and high-income group during the period of the Twelfth Five-Year Plan. There will be huge space for development from the high-income group (it is estimated that the lower limit of the high-income group will be above US$13000). As a result, China's development is currently experiencing an important period of strategic opportunities and will continuously be in this stage for a certain period of time afterwards. It is still possible to maintain rapid economic development.

South Korea and Japan are successful examples of countries that have avoided the "middle-income trap". In terms of the situation in South Korea (see Figure 11.9; the left coordinate is the GNI per capita and the right coordinate is the GDP growth rate), the GNI per capita was merely US$110 in the early 1960s. It broke US$1000 in 1978, US$3000 in 1987 and US$10,000 in 1995 within the space of only 17 years. In other words, South Korea escaped the "low-income trap", "middle- and low-income trap" and "middle- and high-income trap" smoothly and climbed all the way to the high-income group. However, affected by the subsequent Asian financial crisis in the mid- and late1990s, the Korean GNI per capita rapidly fell to US$9200 in 1998 after reaching US$12190 in 1997 and recovered to the level of US$12680 in 2003, experiencing an adjustment for six years. It rose to above US$20000 in recent years.

The corresponding GDP growth rate in South Korea roughly experienced five stages:

1　During the period in which the GNI per capita changed from US$110 to US$500, namely the period from 1962 to 1975, the GDP growth rate was relatively high, frequently exceeding 12 percent.

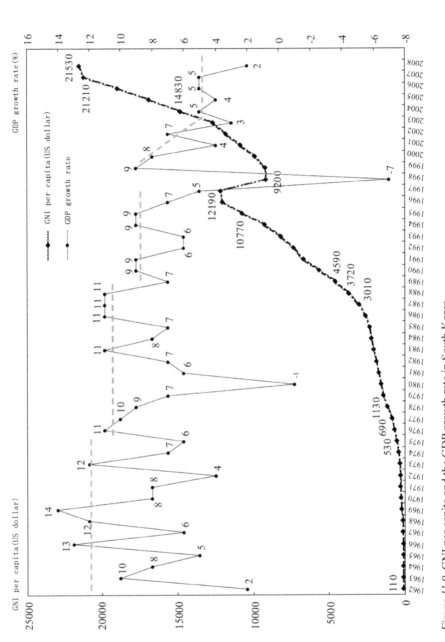

*Figure 11.9* GNI per capita and the GDP growth rate in South Korea

Note. The data in Figures 11.9 to Figure 11.13 all come from the database of the World Bank.

2   During the period in which the GNI per capita changed from US$600 to US$3700, namely the period from 1976 to 1988, the GDP growth rate was relatively high as well, frequently reaching 11 percent.

3   During the period in which the GNI per capita changed from US$4500 to US$12000, namely the period from 1989 to 1997 before the Asian financial crisis, the GDP growth rate still maintained a high level, often reaching 9 percent.

4   Affected by the Asian financial crisis, the GNI per capita fell to US$9200 after reaching US$12000 and recovered to the level of US$12000 through an adjustment over six years, that is, the GDP growth rate obviously declined during the period from 1998 to 2003.

5   During the period in which the GNI per capita changed from US$14000 to US$20000, namely the period from 2004 to 2008, the GDP growth rate was around 5 percent.

On the whole, during the 36 years when the GNI per capita in South Korea changed from US$110 in 1962 to US$12000 in 1997, the GDP growth maintained a high speed.

In terms of the situation in Japan (see Figure 11.10; the left coordinate is the GNI per capita and the right coordinate is the GDP growth rate), the GNI per capita was merely US$610 in the early 1960s. It broke US$1000 in 1966, US$3000 in 1973 and US$10000 in 1984 within the space of only 18 years, successfully evading the "middle- and low-income trap" and the "middle- and high-income trap", and climbed rapidly to the high-income group. Subsequently, it broke US$20000 in 1988, US$30000 in 1993 and US$40000 in 1995. Japan only took 11 years from breaking US$10000 in 1984 to breaking US$40000 in 1995. Since reaching US$41350 in 1996, its GNI per capita has been fluctuating between US$32000 and below US$40000. It can be said that Japan has fallen into the "high-income trap".

The corresponding GDP growth rate in Japan roughly experienced three stages:

1   During the period in which the GNI per capita changed from US$610 to US$3000, namely the period from 1962 to 1973, the GDP growth was in a high range, frequently reaching 8–13 percent.

2   During the period in which the GNI per capita changed from US$3000 to US$25000, namely the period from 1974 to 1990, the GDP growth was in a moderate range, often being 3–5 percent.

3   The GDP growth has been in a low range from 1991 until the present, since the GNI per capita exceeded US$26000, often being 0–3 percent.

On the whole, the GNI per capita in Japan rose to US$10000 in 1984, climbed smoothly to US$40000 in 1995 at a moderate speed within 11 years and surpassed that of the United States during the 12 years from 1988 to 2001.

Brazil and Thailand are examples of countries that once fell into the "middle-income trap". In terms of the situation in Brazil (see Figure 11.11; the left coordinate is the GNI per capita and the right coordinate is the GDP growth rate),

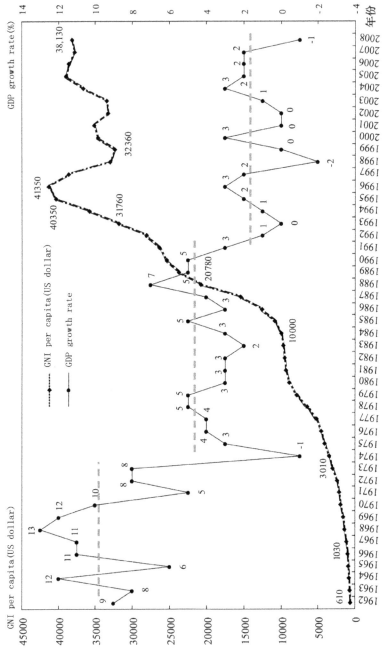

*Figure 11.10* GNI per capita and the GDP growth rate in Japan

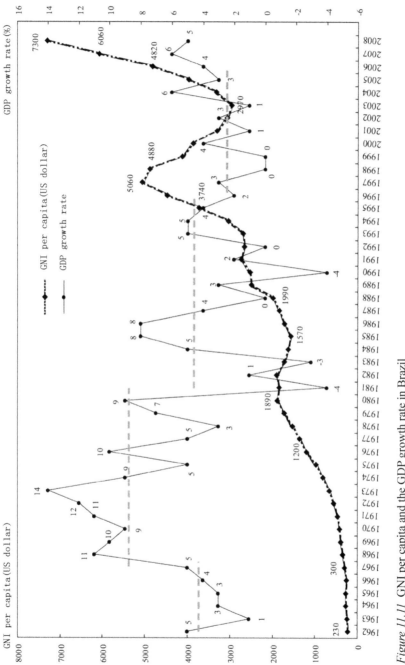

*Figure 11.11* GNI per capita and the GDP growth rate in Brazil

the GNI per capita was US$230 in the early 1960s and broke US$1000 in 1976. However, after reaching US$1890 in 1980, closing to US$2000, it fell into the "middle- and low-income trap" and declined to US$1570 in 1988, fluctuating for eight consecutive years without breaking US$2000. It reached US$2000 in 1989 and broke US$5000 in 1997, but again fell into the "middle- and high-income trap" and dropped to US$2970, fluctuating for nine consecutive years without breaking US$5000. It has risen to US$7300 in recent years.

The corresponding GDP growth rate in Brazil roughly experienced four stages:

1   The GDP growth rate was relatively low during the period from 1962 to 1967, when the GNI per capita fell below US$300, often being 3–5 percent.
2   During the period in which the GNI per capita rose from US$300 to US$1890, namely the period from 1968 to 1980, the GDP growth rate was relatively high, frequently exceeding 9 percent.
3   During the period in which the GNI per capita changed from US$1890 to US$4000, namely the period from 1981 to 1995, the GDP growth rate fell, often being 4–5 percent and experiencing negative growth.
4   The GDP growth rate further declined after 1997, when the GNI per capita broke US$5000, often being around 3 percent. It has recovered again in recent years.

In terms of the situation in Thailand (see Figure 11.12; the left coordinate is the GNI per capita and the right coordinate is the GDP growth rate), the GNI per capita was US$110 in the early 1960s, broke US$1000 in 1988 and US$2000 in 1993 and was close to US$3000 in 1996. However, it subsequently fell into the "middle- and low-income trap" and declined to US$1900. It broke US$3000 in 2007, fluctuating for 11 consecutive years during this period.

The corresponding GDP growth rate in Thailand roughly experienced four stages:

1   During the period in which the GNI per capita rose from US$110 to nearly US$500, namely the period from 1962 to 1978, the GDP growth rate was relatively high, frequently reaching 8–11 percent.
2   During the period in which the GNI per capita rose from US$500 to nearly US$800, namely the period from 1979 to 1986, the GDP growth rate declined, frequently being 5–6 percent.
3   During the period in which the GNI per capita changed from US$800 to nearly US$3000, namely the period from 1987 to 1996, the GDP growth rate rose again to 8–13 percent.
4   The GDP growth rate declined again to around 5 percent after 1997, when the GNI per capita was close to US$3000.

Now we make an overall comparison between South Korea, Brazil, Thailand and China (see Figure 11.13). In 1962, the GNI per capita was US$110 in South Korea, US$230 in Brazil, US$110 in Thailand and US$70 in China.

In terms of the time when the GNI per capita broke US$1000, Brazil was the earliest in 1976, followed by South Korea in 1978, Thailand in 1988, 10 years later than South Korea, and China in 2001, 13 years later than Thailand.

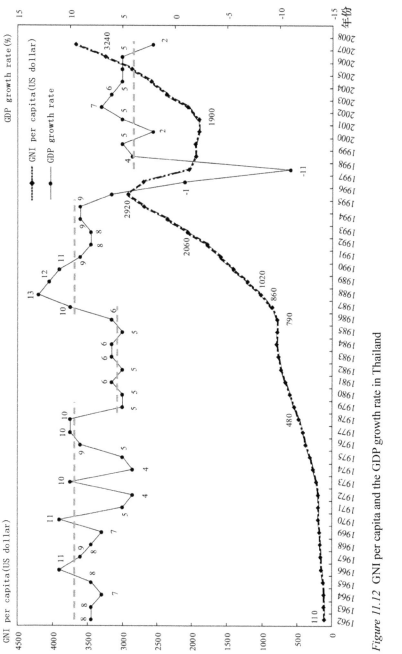

*Figure 11.12* GNI per capita and the GDP growth rate in Thailand

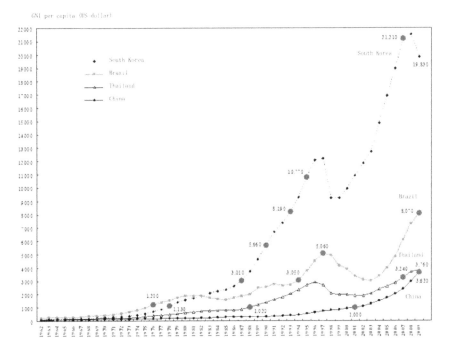

*Figure 11.13* Comparison of the GNI per capita between South Korea, Brazil, Thailand and China

South Korea was the first country with a GNI per capita to break US$3000, in 1987, followed by Brazil in 1994, seven years later than South Korea, Thailand in 2007, 13 years later than Brazil, and China in 2009, two years later than Thailand.

Regarding the time when the GNI per capita broke US$5000, South Korea was the earliest in 1990 and Brazil in 1997, seven years later than South Korea. The GNI per capita in Thailand and China has not reached the level of US$5000.

In terms of the time when the GNI per capita broke US$8000, South Korea was the earliest in 1993 and Brazil in 2009, 16 years later than South Korea.

South Korea's GNI per capita broke US$10000 in 1995. The GNI per capita in Brazil has not reached the level of US$10000.

In 2009, the GNI per capita was as high as US$19830 in South Korea, US$8070 in Brazil, US$3760 in Thailand and US$3620 in China, which was very close to Thailand.

Figure 11.13 illustrates that different countries have sometimes experienced smooth development and encountered different issues as well. At present, the GNI per capita in China is still relatively low. Thus, there is huge room for development. Recently, Robert B. Zoellick, President of the World Bank, made a speech at the symposium celebrating the thirtieth anniversary of the China – World Bank partnership and pointed out that wise leaders and officials are starting to ask how China can best avoid 'the Middle Income Trap'. Experience shows that transitioning from middle income to high income status can be harder than from low income to middle income. China's experience in moving from a low-middle income economy to a high income society may also provide insights for other middle-income economies.

(2010)[4]

[Originally published in Economic Blue Book, *Analysis and Prediction of the Economic Situation in China in 2011*, Social Sciences Academic Press, 2010]

## Notes

1 *Selected Works of Deng Xiaoping* (1st ed., Vol. 3). (1994). The Bureau for the Compilation and Translation of Works of Mars, Engels, Lenin and Stalin Under the Central Committee of the Communist Party of China (Trans.). Beijing: Foreign Languages Press.
2 The author wrote articles to clarify this issue; Multiple Minor Adjustments: No Exceeding in Economic Growth Peak. (2006). *Economics Perspectives*, 10; Grasping Feature: Multi-Phase of Macro Regulation in Economic Cycle. (2006). *Analysis and Prediction of the Economic Situation in China in 2007*. Beijing: Social Sciences Academic Press.
3 Research Group of Macro Regulation, Institute of Economics of Chinese Academy of Social Sciences. (2010). Analysis of Macro Regulation Objective of the "Eleventh Five-Year Plan" and Outlook for the "Twelfth Five-Year Plan". *Economic Research Journal*, 2.
4 R. B. Zoellick. (2010, September 13). Address at the Symposium of Celebration of the 30th Anniversary of China – World Bank Partnership. The World Bank Website.

## Reference

Zoellick, R. B. (2010, September 13). Address at the Symposium of Celebration of the 30th Anniversary of China-World Bank Partnership. The World Bank Website. World Bank: Database.

# 12 Analysis of national and international environment facing China during the implementation of the Twelfth Five-Year Plan

Both the Twelfth Five-Year Plan approved at the Fifth Plenary Session of the 17th Party Central Committee and Premier Wen Jiabao's "Government Work Report" at the Fourth Session of the 11th National People's Congress analyzed the national and international environment facing China during the period of the Twelfth Five-Year Plan in depth and emphasized that China continued to have important strategic opportunities in terms of its development, comprehensively judged based on the international and domestic situation. This article undertakes a detailed analysis.

## Implications of the thesis of an important period of strategic opportunities

Carrying out a dynamic review and a trend analysis of various domestic and international environments will lead to a scientific judgment and an accurate understanding of the national and international circumstances facing China. This will provide a premise and a foundation for formulating correctly the overall strategic goal and task. By synthetically estimating the international and domestic circumstances, it is evident that China's development is still in an important period of strategic opportunities. This thesis provides the most fundamental analysis of the domestic and international environment for formulating and implementing the ambitious targets and tasks of the Twelfth Five-Year Plan. It also sets out the scientific premise for formulating and implementing the Twelfth Five-Year Plan. Whether we can seize a significant historic opportunity, that is whether we can make full use of all the advantageous conditions at home and abroad to eliminate the effects of various adverse factors is a major issue that will determine the country's prosperity or decline and the success or failure of the Chinese revolution and its construction.

When China had just crossed the threshold of the twenty-first century, the 16th National Congress of the Communist Party of China (CPC) put forward in 2002 for the first time that based on an overview of its situation, the first 20 years of the twenty-first century will be an important period of strategic opportunities for China to which we must hold fast. The 17th National Congress of the CPC reiterated in 2007 that we should seize hold of and exploit fully an important period of strategic opportunities at the beginning of a new historic era. Examining the international and domestic situation of China after the first 10 years of the new century have passed and when the second 10 years have just started, it is apparent that China is still in an important period of strategic opportunities, facing the serious impact of the international financial crisis and its far-reaching influences, the remarkable rapid economic growth for over 30 years since the country's reform and opening up and the new contradictions induced by the rapid growth. This implies that we should form unified understanding, concentrate people's strengths and further enhance the consciousness of opportunities and the sense of crisis and urgency to seize and make good use of the strategic opportunities available at the beginning of the second 10 years of the new century and continuously strive to attain the strategic goal of building a comprehensively affluent society, elevating the economy to a new level.

## Analysis of the international environment

This section provides an analysis of the international environment in which China will operate in the period of the Twelfth Five-Year Plan, making three main points.

1   The general feature of the international environment is that the worldwide trend of multi-polarization and economic globalization continues at a considerable pace and in great depth. Moreover, there is an orientation towards peace, development and cooperation.

Multi-polarization refers to a pattern that sees multiple world powers coexisting, seeking support from each other and imposing limits on one another, working together and participating in international affairs on an equal footing. This is the inevitable outcome of the end of the bipolar structure of the Cold War, the relaxation of international relationships and the rise, decline and realignment of various powers. Following the international financial crisis, new changes are taking place in the balance of world power. The integral strength of developing countries, in particular the emerging market countries, is improving. The world is moving further towards multi-polarity, which will be conducive to further combating hegemony and power politics, promoting the establishment of a new fair and rational international political and economic order and maintaining world peace and stability. It is still possible to bring about a long period of peace in the world and avoid a new world war.

Economic globalization refers to the broad development of economic activities at the global level, including production, trade, investment and finance, and the process of the massive flow and allocation of various production factors, such as capital, technology, the labor force and information, worldwide, which is the inevitable result of the development in contemporary productivity, scientific and technological development and the significant development of the international labor division. Following the international financial crisis, the tendency towards economic globalization has gained momentum: there is greater inter-dependence and interaction in the global economy, including the growth of new transnational mergers and acquisitions, transnational investments, technical cooperation and industry transfer. The continuing development of economic globalization will help to optimize the allocation of production factors at the global level and promote economic development worldwide. It will be favorable for different countries seeking to participate in international economic cooperation and competition and expand their scope for development. Moreover, it will be conducive to world peace and stability.

Promoted by the trends of multi-polarization and economic globalization, there continues to be a tendency towards peace, development and cooperation. To preserve peace, the pursuit of development and promotion of cooperation concern the well-being of all nations and represent the fundamental interests and the common aspirations of the people of different nations. To move with the trend of the times and maintain world peace, it has become a realistic choice for increasing numbers of countries to strengthen their friendly cooperation with other nations on the basis of equality and mutual benefit, seeking and expanding the convergence of the interests of different countries and promoting common development and prosperity.

2    Under the conditions of multi-polarization and economic globalization, with the orientation towards peace, development and cooperation, the impact and influence of the international financial crisis has been far-reaching. Profound changes are taking place in the world's economic structure, which is characterized by four new features, each of which is discussed in turn in the following paragraphs.

First, adjustments to the world economic structure are accelerating. Following the international financial crisis, the world economic structure has entered a period of adjustment. Different countries are adjusting their patterns of development to seek new advantages. As the financial system suffered greatly from the financial crisis, it is difficult for developed countries to get credit normalized. Moreover, the recovery of employment is lagging behind economic resurgence, with the unemployment rate remaining at a high level and income decreasing, thus causing developed countries to have broken their former patterns of excessive debt financing and excessive consumption, which were prevalent for a long time. Such countries are attempting to restore economic growth through expanding investment and exports and reviving their manufacturing industries. As many countries are hampered in terms of implementing an export-driven pattern of economic growth, the emerging market countries are attempting to exploit new growth opportunities to further develop their economies by expanding domestic demand while simultaneously making efforts to stabilize their foreign markets. Resource-exporting countries are strengthening their exploitation and development independently by virtue of their resource advantages, extending their industrial chains and trying to move away from their former development pattern of relying solely on exporting resources. These considerable adjustments in the world's economic structure will exert a strong influence on supply and demand structures in the international market. Consumption will continue to falter in terms of demand and competition will be more challenging in terms of supply.

Second, the global economic governance structure is undergoing profound changes. The global economic governance structure refers to those organizations that discuss and resolve significant international issues – economic, financial, banking and currency – and coordinate activities internationally. Severely impacted by the international financial crisis, the traditional coordinating platform of the international economy, which was originally monopolized by few developed countries, has struggled to deal with the current complicated world economic situation. Thus, it is necessary to form a structure with more countries working together and participating in international affairs on an equal footing. For example, strengthening the functions of the G20 summit could enable it to be the major platform for discussing and coordinating macroeconomic policy in international society. As a result, the world economic governance structure is entering a period of reformation, showing that the reform of international financial supervision, the international financial organization system and the international monetary system have become significant topics of discussion.

Third, scientific and technological innovation and industrial transformation breed breakthroughs. An interesting outcome of the economic crisis is that it will help to clean up the old industrial structure and produce a new industrial structure. Under pressure from many sources, such as the impact of the international financial crisis, global climate change and increasing pressure on natural resources and the environment, global scientific and technological innovation and industrial transformation are in a new period of gestation and the whole world will likely enter into an era of unprecedented intensive innovation and industry revitalization. Many countries, one after another, are enhancing their scientific and technological innovation, strengthening basic research on the frontier, training talent and accelerating the cultivation and development of emerging industries, such as new energy, advanced materials, new information networks, biological medicine, energy conservation and environmental protection, low-carbon technology and the green economy. The above aspects are the key to a new round of scientific, technological and industrial revolutions and the strategic opportunities that countries are keen to seize for future economic, scientific and technological development. In September 2009, the US government published a report entitled "American Innovation Strategy: Promoting Sustainable Growth and High-quality Employment" and put forward its plan to expand investment and regain its leading position in the world in terms of basic research. The report emphasized the need to train the next generation of talent with knowledge and skills that conform to demands of the twenty-first century and develop a world first-class workforce. It proposed promoting market competition, encouraging innovation and entrepreneurship and making significant breakthroughs in national priority areas, such as clean energy, advanced automobiles and health care. In March 2010, the European Union issued its "European Strategy 2020" and put forward three key points for future economic development: the development of an intelligent economy based on knowledge and innovation; the improvement of efficiency in the utilization of resources and the development of green technology for the realization of sustainable growth; enhancement of the employment level and an increase in investment in skills training aimed at achieving growth together with high employment synchronizing the economy, society and regions. In addition, Japan published its "Future Exploitation Strategy", Russia put forward its "Key Orientation of National Policy" for developing renewable energy sources and South Korea proposed a "National Strategy of Green Development".

The integral strength of developing countries, in particular, the emerging market countries, is on the rise. In coping with the international financial crisis, developed countries have found themselves in trouble, with an economic downturn and a slow revival, whereas developing countries, in particular, the emerging market countries, took the lead in economic resurgence and highlighted a positive momentum in terms of rapid and steady economic growth. According to the latest "World Economic Outlook" released by the International Monetary Fund (IMF), the economic growth rate of developed economies was −3.4 percent and that of emerging and developing economies was 2.6 percent in 2009; it was, respectively, 3 percent and 7.1 percent in 2010. The IMF termed the phenomenon of the sharp contrast between the slow recovery of developed economies and the rapid recovery of the emerging and developing economies "two-speed recovery". Developing countries – and in particular the emerging market countries – have gradually become an important engine of global economic growth. Likewise, according to an IMF report and the estimation of the market exchange rate, the aggregate GDP of Brazil, Russia, India and China (BRIC) accounted for 15 percent of the total world amount in 2008.This was set to increase to 22 percent in 2015 and surpass that of the United States. The increment of the aggregate GDP of the BRIC countries will account for one-third of the world incremental amount. Developing countries are striving for more participation and discourse rights and are playing increasingly important roles in international affairs.

3   On the whole, the international environment is beneficial to China's peaceful development. However, there are still many unstable and uncertain factors that will influence peace, development and cooperation.

First, the pressure of the hegemony of developed countries and power politics will continue for some time as they continue to have the upper hand in such fields as the economy, science and technology. Second, some of the new features of the world's economic pattern identified above are both advantageous and disadvantageous, providing both opportunities and challenges. In particular, international competition focused on resources, markets, technology and talent will become more intense. Trade protectionism will worsen periodically. Moreover, although the global economy will continue to revive, the recovery is not yet strong and there are justifiable concerns for the future. All these factors will pose new challenges to China's economic and social development.

## Analysis of the national situation

This section analyzes the national situation faced by China in terms of its economy, again focusing on three main points.

1  The general overview of the national economic situation is that China's economic trend towards growth and expansion has not changed. China is in an in-depth developmental stage of industrialization, informationization, urbanization, marketization and internationalization, which promote each other. There is still much room for development.

Industrialization is the most fundamental material and technical condition and foundation for building a comprehensively affluent society in China. In light of the general situation of industrialized countries, the industrialization process can be divided into two stages. In the first stage, there is preliminary development and the proportion of industrial production exceeds that of agriculture. In the second stage, there is profound development and the proportion of agricultural production declines further, but the proportion of industrial production also decreases, being overtaken by the service industry. In terms of the proportional variation in the added value of the three major sectors in gross domestic product (GDP), in 1952 the primary industry sector, dominated by agriculture, had a 50.5 percent share, far greater than the proportion of 20.9 percent of the secondary industry sector (manufacturing) and the proportion of the tertiary industry sector (services) at 28.6 percent (see Table 12.1). In 1970, the proportion of secondary industry rose to 40.5 percent and exceeded that of primary industry for the first time. In 1978, at the beginning of the reform and opening up of China, the proportion of primary industry declined to 28.2 percent, secondary industry rose to 47.9 percent and tertiary industry dropped to 23.9 percent. In 2010, the proportion of primary industry fell continuously to 10.2 percent, secondary industry was basically stable and declined only slightly to 46.8 percent, while tertiary industry rose to 43 percent, still lower than the secondary industry. In terms of the proportion of productive value, the development of industrialization in China was still in the middle stage. However, looking at the proportional variation in employment in the three major industry sectors, although the proportion of employment in the primary industry is clearly declining at present, it is still higher than that of the secondary industry. In 1952, the proportion of employment was

*Table 12.1* Proportion of the three industries in GDP
Unit (%)

| Year | Proportion of added value of the three industry sectors in GDP | | | Proportion of employment in the three industry sectors in total employment | | |
|------|---------|-----------|----------|---------|-----------|----------|
|      | Primary | Secondary | Tertiary | Primary | Secondary | Tertiary |
| 1952 | 50.5    | 20.9      | 28.6     | 83.5    | 7.4       | 9.1      |
| 1978 | 28.2    | 47.9      | 23.9     | 70.5    | 17.3      | 12.2     |
| 2010 | 10.2    | 46.8      | 43.0     | 38.1*   | 27.8*     | 34.1*    |

Note. From *China Statistical Yearbook 2010*, China Statistics Press, 2010, p. 39. For employment, data marked * relate to 2009. The 2010 data for the share of industry sector in GDP are from "The 2010 Statistics Bulletin of the National Economic and Social Development of the People's Republic of China", by National Bureau of Statistics,2011, March 1, *The People's Daily*.

83.5 percent in primary industry, 7.4 percent in secondary industry and 9.1 percent in tertiary industry. In 2009, they were 38.1 percent, 27.8 percent and 34.1 percent in the primary, secondary and tertiary industry sectors, respectively. This pattern of variation is related to the vast population of China. Industrialization is still an arduous historical task in China's modernization. During the period of the Twelfth Five-Year Plan, we should accelerate industrialization, improve its level and quality and transform and upgrade the manufacturing industry to cultivate and develop strategically the new industries. It is necessary to develop a clean, safe and modern industrial system with an optimized structure, advanced technology, high value-added and a strong capability for creating more jobs. In other words, we should keep to the path of new industrialization with Chinese characteristics.

Informationization is a new scientific and technological revolution. The widespread application of information technology has become an important means of promoting economic and social development. China has derived an advantage of backwardness of IT-driven industrialization, which will in turn stimulate IT applications and the integration of IT applications with industrialization. This has induced transformations in production modes and economic development patterns, providing important technical support for promoting industrialization at a high starting point. The information infrastructure level in China has jumped rapidly with the nationwide installation of a trunk optical fiber cable reaching 21.20 million Core KM.[1] This makes China the largest information communication network globally. The number of fixed telephone subscribers, mobile users and internet users ranks first in the world. During the period of the Twelfth Five-Year Plan, we should improve the level of informationization comprehensively, speed up the construction of the next generation of national information infrastructure with broadband and ensure the provision of a ubiquitous, integrated and safe network. Moreover, we should propel informationization in various fields of the economy and society to promote further deep integration of informationization and industrialization, finally establishing an informationized China.

Urbanization is an important carrier of industrialization and informationization and has the greatest potential for expansion of domestic demand, in particular consumption demand. The urbanization rate (the proportion of the urban population in the total population) in China was 10.6 percent in 1949 and increased to 17.9 percent in 1978. During the period of the Eleventh Five-Year Plan, urbanization in China developed very fast, with the urbanization rate rising from 43 percent in 2005 to 47.5 percent in 2010, an increase of 4.5 percent, with an average annual increase of 0.9 percent (see Figure 12.1). During the period of the Twelfth Five-Year Plan, we must actively and steadily promote urbanization, continuously improving its level and quality and strengthening the urban carrying capacity comprehensively to prevent and govern "urban disease". By the end of the Twelfth Five-Year Plan in 2015, the urbanization rate is estimated to reach 51.5 percent, an average annual increase of 0.8 percent. In 2014, the urban population in China is set to exceed the rural population for the first time, a significant and historic change for a populous country with more than 1.3 billion people.

Marketization is an important system and mechanism in terms of guaranteeing the promotion of economic and social development. In the 30 years and more

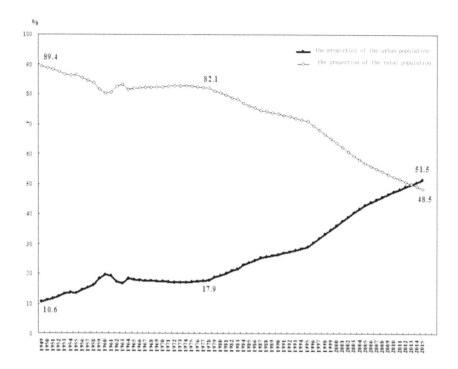

*Figure 12.1* Urbanization rate in China

Note. From *China Statistical Yearbook 2010*, 2010, Beijing: China Statistics Press, p. 95.
Data for the period during the Twelfth Five-Year Plan are estimated values.

since the reform and opening up of China, the country has successfully achieved a historic transition from a highly centralized planned economic system to an energetic socialist market economy. The introduction of the market mechanism and its fundamental role in resource allocation has improved the efficiency of resource allocation and strongly promoted rapid economic growth in China. The execution of the market mechanism is based on the establishment and development of the basic economic system, retaining public ownership as the mainstay of the economy and allowing diverse forms of ownership to develop side by side. In terms of the variation in the ownership structure of industrial enterprises, the proportions of enterprises of different types of ownership in the total industrial output value have changed significantly. In 1978, at the beginning of the reform and opening-up period, there were only two types of ownership in industrial enterprises, namely stated-owned industries and collective industries. They comprised 77.6 percent and 22.4 percent of the total industrial output value (at current year prices). In 2009, in the total industrial output value of the industrial enterprises above the designated size,[2] the form of ownership was already diversified according to the registered type (see Table 12.2): non-corporate state-owned enterprises held an 8.3 percent share; collective enterprises 1.7 percent;

Table 12.2 Proportion of enterprises of different ownership types in the total industrial output value

Unit (%)

| | Categorized By Registration | 1978 | 2009 |
|---|---|---|---|
| 1 | State-owned enterprises (non-corporate) | 77.6 | 8.3 |
| 2 | Collective enterprises | 22.4 | 1.7 |
| 3 | Stock cooperative enterprises | | 0.7 |
| 4 | Associated enterprises (including state-owned associated enterprises) | | 0.2 |
| 5 | Limited liability companies (including solely state-owned companies) | | 22.1 |
| 6 | Incorporated companies (including state-owned holding enterprises) | | 9.2 |
| 7 | Private enterprises | | 29.6 |
| 8 | Other domestic enterprises | | 0.4 |
| 9 | Hong Kong, Macau and Taiwanese merchant investment enterprises (including Sino-foreign joint ventures, Sino-foreign cooperatives and wholly foreign-owned enterprises) | | 9.5 |
| 10 | Foreign-funded enterprises (including Sino-foreign joint ventures, Sino-foreign cooperatives and wholly foreign-owned enterprises) | | 18.3 |

Note. Calculated according to the data in the *China Statistical Yearbook 2010*, 2010, Beijing: China Statistics Press, p.507.

stock cooperative enterprises 0.7 percent; associated enterprises (including state-owned associated enterprises) 0.2 percent; limited liability companies (including solely state-owned companies) 22.1 percent; incorporated companies (including state-owned holding enterprises) 9.2 percent; private enterprises 29.6 percent; other domestic enterprises 0.4 percent; Hong Kong, Macau and Taiwanese merchant investment enterprises (including Sino-foreign joint ventures, Sino-foreign cooperatives and wholly foreign-owned enterprises) 9.5 percent; foreign-funded enterprises (including Sino-foreign joint ventures, Sino-foreign cooperatives and wholly foreign-owned enterprises) 18.3 percent. During the period of the Twelfth Five-Year Plan, China will undertake further reforms in difficult areas, such as perfecting the socialist market economic system and adhering to and improving the basic economic system, to see dramatic breakthroughs in crucial areas and key links and provide a strong guarantee for scientific development.

Internationalization is a significant external condition for promoting economic and social development. A closed-door policy is unable to realize industrialization and modernization. Opening up to the outside world has become China's basic state policy. For over 30 years, China has instituted an all-dimensional, multi-layered and wide-ranging opening-up pattern, which has effectively promoted rapid economic and social development. During the period of the Twelfth Five-Year Plan, China will follow a more proactive opening-up strategy and constantly foster greater links with the outside world to stabilize and expand external demand and extend into new fields and spaces by accelerating the transformation of the development mode of foreign trade. By both "bringing in" and "going out", we should pay equal attention to the utilization of foreign capital and foreign direct investment and cultivate new advantages to participate in international economic and technological cooperation and competition. Through improving the capacity to utilize both domestic and international markets and resources, we will promote the transformation of foreign trade development from expanding its scale to improving its quality and efficiency; thus, we shall progress from low-cost advantages to comprehensive competitive advantages.

2   In addition to the trend in China's economy towards growth and expansion identified above, there is a series of favorable conditions in the current economic development.

First, in terms of demand, the potential of the Chinese market is considerable. During the period of the Eleventh Five-Year Plan, GDP per capita increased from US$1,700 to US$4,000. By the end of the Twelfth Five-Year Plan, it is estimated that GDP per capita will exceed 40,000 yuan, calculated according to 2010 prices. Converting to the US dollar at an exchange rate of 1:6.5, GDP per capita will be more than US$6,000. The improvement in per capita income will provide a broad domestic market for a populous country with more 1.3 billion people and a vast territory and will effectively push forward the upgrading of the consumption structure and the corresponding industrial structure.

Second, in terms of supply, China is generous in its funding, with an overall improvement in science, technology, education, labor quality and infrastructure. China possesses increasingly enhanced financial strength, sufficient credit funds and adequate foreign currency reserves to guarantee the money supply for economic and social development. Steady and rapid economic growth provides a tax resource for the steady increase of fiscal revenue. Therefore, the nationwide fiscal revenue has maintained strong growth. During the period of the Eleventh Five-Year Plan, fiscal revenue increased rapidly and consecutively from 3,160 billion yuan in 2005 to 8,310 billion yuan in 2010, with an average annual growth of 21 percent. The increase in fiscal revenue provided solid financial resources for promoting the transformation of the pattern of development, the adjustment of the economic structure, the overall development of both urban and rural areas and regional coordinated development to achieve the equalization of basic public services and protect and improve people's livelihoods. Various outstanding deposits of financial institutions reached 28,700 billion yuan in 2005 and 71,800 billion yuan in 2010, of which the urban and rural residents' deposit balance reached 30,300 billion yuan. In 2010, the national foreign exchange reserves exceeded US$2,800 billion; moreover, they ranked first in the world for five consecutive years.

The overall level of science, technology, education, labor quality and independent innovation is improving. The strength of science and technology has been remarkably enhanced. The total expenditure on research and development (R&D) ranks fourth in the world, calculated according to the current exchange rate. The share of the budget for R&D in GDP rose from 1.3 percent to 1.8 percent during the period of the Eleventh Five-Year Plan and should further increase to 2.2 percent at the end of the Twelfth Five-Year Plan. In 2009, the number of personnel employed in science and technology reached 51 million, jumping to first place in the world. The authorization of invention patents reached 128,000 in 2009, an increase of 142 percent compared to 2005 and ranking third in the world. Moreover, the authorization of domestic invention patents exceeded that of foreign invention patents in China for the first time in 2009. In 2010, the authorization of invention patents rose to 135,000 and international patent applications were over 12,000, ranking fourth in the world. China has achieved breakthroughs in frontier technological research, of which some have reached the international advanced level. "Tianhe-I", a quadrillion-level high performance computer independently designed and manufactured by China, reached number one in the world in terms of computing performance. Great progress has been achieved in manned space flight and China's lunar exploration program. The successful launch of the Shenzhou series of spacecraft enabled China to become the third country in the world to master the technology of extravehicular activity. The successful launch of Chang'e-1 and Chang'e-2 in succession made China the fifth country in the world to send off a lunar probe.

Overall, the education level has improved. During the period of the Eleventh Five-Year Plan, the gross enrollment rate of higher education rose from 21 percent in 2005 to 24.2 percent in 2009, with the total number of students reaching 29.79 million, placing China first in the world. The national average number of years of education increased from 8.5 years in 2005 to 9 years in 2010. The gross enrollment rate for secondary education rose from 52 percent in 2005 to 82.5 percent in 2010 and was set to increase further to 87 percent in 2015. The average number of years of education among the prime working-age population reached 9.5 years in 2009 and is estimated to rise to 10.5 years in 2015. The average number of years of education among the incoming labor force is estimated to be 13.3 years in 2015.

Infrastructure is increasingly being perfected. Transportation is no longer the bottleneck it once was for national economic development and has become a significant means of support and a forerunner for economic and social development. In 1980, at the beginning of the reform and opening-up period, the total distance of the national road network was merely 888,000 km, but it had reached 3.984 million km by the end of 2010, ranking second in the world. The distance covered by expressways expanded from 41,000 km in 2005 to 74,000 km in 2010. The port container throughput has held world first for seven consecutive years. During the period of the Twelfth Five-Year Plan, we should further promote the overall development of different modes of transportation, essentially building up a national rapid rail network and expressway network and constructing an integrated traffic and transportation system with optimal network infrastructure, advanced and practical technical equipment and a safe and efficient transportation service.

Third, in terms of policy, the capacity of the Party and the government concerning macro regulation and tackling major challenges has markedly increased, thus social stability is well maintained. During the period of the Eleventh Five-Year Plan, facing complex changes in national and international environments and significant risks and challenges, such as preventing overheated economic growth, countering the huge impact of the international financial crisis and overcoming major natural disasters like the Wenchuan earthquake, the Party and the government cool-headedly and resolutely led the Chinese people in coping with the difficult situations that arose and maintained steady and fast economic growth and social stability, thus accumulating precious experience. In terms of macro regulation, the major experiences are specified as below. We must pursue scientific development and accelerate the transformation of the economic development mode. While maintaining the integration of government regulation and the market mechanism and giving full play to the fundamental role of the market in resource allocation, we should also exploit to the full advantages of the socialist system, such as efficient decision-making, effective organization and the concentration of resources to accomplish large undertakings. The overall domestic and international situation should be considered, making the expansion of domestic demand a long-term strategy and following an open strategy of mutual benefit and win-win results. The reform and opening up of the country must be taken steadfastly as the fundamental driving force to promote economic and social development. Persisting with an integrated approach to developing the economy and improving the well-being of the people, we will enable all people to share in the fruits of reform and advancement. By bringing the initiative of the central and local government into play, we will form a powerful force to ride out the crisis. The crucial experiences garnered to date are of far-reaching significance for China in moving on continuously. Social stability is an important guarantee of development in the economy, politics, society and culture. Viewing the profound changes in the economic system, social structure and ideology, as well as the profound readjustments in the interest patterns at present, the Party and the government continue to attach great importance to strengthening and bringing forth new ideas in the social administration, resolving social conflicts and tackling social risk. Having done well in fostering mass work in the new circumstances, they have promoted social harmony, ensuring people can live and work in peace and contentment, and have laid the foundation for building a comprehensively affluent society.

3    On the whole, the domestic economic trend is beneficial to China's development. However, there are still many issues that are not yet well balanced, coordinated or sustainable.

Specifically, people are predominantly concerned with issues such as the wide disparity in income, strong expectations of price increases, high housing price increases and increasingly prominent "urban disease". Constraints on resources and the environment in economic development are intensifying. Moreover, it is difficult to rectify the imbalance between investment and consumption in the short term. The developments of urban and rural areas and that in different regions are not yet optimally coordinated. Many obstacles in terms of systems and mechanisms continue to restrict scientific development, thus the innovative capacity of science and technology is not yet sufficiently strong.

In brief, during the period of the Twelfth Five-Year Plan, China will face both rare historic opportunities and many foreseeable and unforeseeable risks and challenges. We should be efficient in making scientific judgments and grasping the opportunity afforded by the ongoing trend in national and international development, making full use of all the favorable conditions and effectively resolving any prominent contradictions and issues. Continuously, taking hold of an important period of strategic opportunities, we will strive for new victories in building a society that is prosperous in all respects and promoting the great cause of socialism with Chinese characteristics.

[Originally published in *Analysis of Economic Prospect in China-Spring Review of 2011*, Economic Blue Book, Spring Issue, Social Sciences Academic Press, 2011]

## Notes

1 An optical fiber cable consists of multiple cores and is calculated by multiplying the number of cores by the length of optical fiber cable, also termed Core KM.
2 "Above the designated size" refers to industrial enterprises with an annual prime operating revenue of above five million yuan.

## Reference

IMF: World Economic Outlook Database. https://www.imf.org/en/Data

# 13 Analysis of China's economic growth and fluctuations in 2011 and during the Twelfth Five-Year Plan

Since 2007, China's economic operation has experienced four stages of variation: rapid economic growth at a high level in 2007; a great decline in economic growth in the face of the international financial crisis; a subsequent substantial recovery in countering effectively the impact of the international financial crisis; a new economic growth within a rational and appropriate range. To be specific, China's economic trend in 2011 and during the period of the Twelfth Five-Year Plan may exhibit six features, each of which is treated in turn below.

1    In terms of the trend in periodic economic fluctuation, China's economy will operate within an appropriate range of growth in a new cycle in 2011 and during the Twelfth Five-Year Plan period.

Following the founding of the new China, China started massive economic construction in 1953 and entered a period of industrialization. Until 2009, the economic growth rate (the growth rate of gross domestic product) experienced a total of 10 cycles of fluctuations and in 2010 China entered its eleventh economic cycle.

The initial eight cycles each lasted an average length of around five years, with one or two years in the rising stage and around three years in the subsequent falling stage. On the whole, they appeared to be short-term cycles.

The length of the cycles extended to nine years in the ninth cycle and 10 years in the tenth cycle, thus expanding to a medium-term cycle. The ninth cycle experienced a rising stage of only two years, as in the previous eight cycles, but a steadily falling stage of seven years, dropping annually by 1 percent on average (see Figure 13.1). The tenth cycle established a new and sound trajectory, with the rising stage extending to eight years, the longest rising trajectory ever experienced since the founding of the new China, and the economic growth rate increasing from 8 percent in 2000 to 14.2 percent in 2007. However, the rate of economic growth was quite rapid in 2007. Influenced by the overlap between domestic economic adjustment and the impact of the international financial crisis, the economic growth rate fell from 14.2 percent in 2007 to 9.6 percent in 2008, a severe decrease of 4.6 percent within one year. In coping with the impact of the international financial crisis, China promptly adopted a proactive fiscal policy and a moderately easy monetary policy and implemented a package plan.

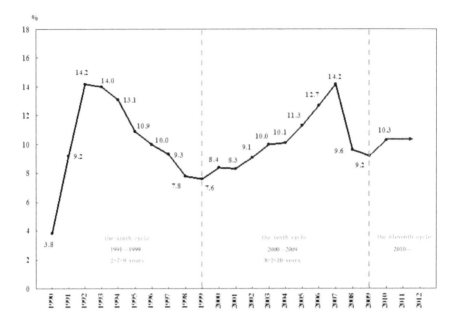

*Figure 13.1* Fluctuation of the economic growth rate in China (1990–2010)

After the second quarter of 2009, China effectively curbed its rapid economic downturn and took the lead in achieving an overall economic turnaround in the world. The economic growth rate in 2009 was 9.2 percent, falling by a mere 0.4 percent compared to 2008. It recovered to 10.3 percent in 2010, higher again than 2009, and entered the eleventh economic cycle. If macro regulation is conducted well, the eleventh economic cycle may maintain the lengths of the ninth and tenth cycles, constituting a medium-term cycle of around 10 years. Thus, China's economy may run within an appropriate range of growth in a new cycle in 2011 and during the Twelfth Five-Year Plan period.

In terms of the quarterly fluctuation in the economic growth rate (see Figure 13.2), it can clearly be seen that China's economy has experienced four stages of variation in recent years. In the first stage, in 2007, economic growth was around 14 percent in each quarter, i.e. high and rapid. In 2008, in the second stage, economic growth dropped greatly and declined all the way through to a trough of 6.6 percent in the first quarter of 2009. In the third stage, between the second quarter of 2009 and the first quarter of 2010, when coping with the impact of the international financial crisis, China's economic growth recovered significantly and rose all the way to 11.9 percent in the first quarter of 2010, drawing a trajectory of V-shaped recovery. In the fourth stage, between the second quarter of 2010 and the first quarter of 2011, the economic growth rate fell to an appropriate range of growth and became stabilized, with a rate of 9.7 percent in the first quarter of 2011. As a result, China's economy has transformed from an "abnormal

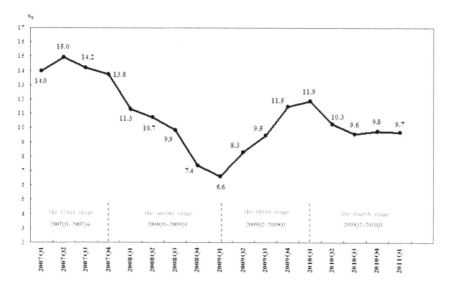

*Figure 13.2* Quarterly fluctuation of the economic growth rate in China (first quarter 2007 to first quarter 2011)

state" of considerable decline in economic growth when facing the international financial crisis and its subsequent substantial recovery to a "normal situation" of an appropriate range of growth.

2   In terms of the position of the economic growth rate in the base year, the starting point is relatively high. A continuous accelerating rise will not be anticipated in 2011 and during the Twelfth Five-Year Plan period. Macro regulation will focus mainly on steady economic growth and the prevention of overheating.

In 1990, the base year or the starting point of the Eighth Five-Year Plan period (1991–95), the economic growth rate was 3.8 percent, providing considerable scope for economic growth over the whole five-year period.

In 1995, the starting point of the Ninth Five-Year Plan period (1996–2000), the economic growth rate decreased from the previous high rate to 10.9 percent, making it difficult to increase much for the whole period of the Ninth Five-Year Plan.

In 2000, the starting point of the Tenth Five-Year Plan period (2001–05), the economic growth rate was just starting to recover and reached 8.4 percent, providing a certain scope for a rise over the period.

In 2005, the starting point of the Eleventh Five-Year Plan period (2006–10), the economic growth rate had already increased to 11.3 percent, leading to the risk of economic growth shifting from rapid to overheating.

In 2010, the starting point of the Twelfth Five-Year Plan period (2011–15), economic growth was already at a high rate of 10.3 percent with no further space for a large and accelerating rise over the five-year period. The focus of macro regulation will be on running the economy steadily, avoiding blindly going all out too soon at the beginning of the Twelfth Five-Year Plan, not engaging in massive vanity projects at the time of the change in state leadership, preventing economic growth from overheating and finally endeavoring to ensure the national economy operates within an appropriate range of growth. For this reason, in 2011 and during the period of the Twelfth Five-Year Plan, macro regulation should seek first to bring the economic growth rate steadily back within an appropriate range following its substantial recovery, while coping with the impact of the international financial crisis. Entering 2011, this normal and steady decline was interpreted by some Chinese and foreign media, as well as some of the public, as China's economy entering stagflation, or facing the risk of stagflation, or potentially falling into a "hard landing". They estimated that the economic growth rate might drop below 8 percent and even held that there might be a banking crisis in China's economy over the following three years. These interpretations do not conform to the actual situation in China.

The main basis for considering that China's economy has already fallen into or might fall into stagflation in early 2011 includes two indicators. One is that the purchasing managers' index (PMI) of the manufacturing industry in China has declined for two consecutive months. The other is that the same-month year-on-year growth rate of industrial added value for enterprises above the designated size nationwide decreased by 1.4 percent in April compared to March.

The Chinese manufacturing PMI in 2011 was 52.9 percent in April, 0.5 percent lower than March, and 52 percent in May, 0.9 percent lower than April, which was the lowest for over nine months (see Figure 13.3). In terms of the fluctuation in PMI from January 2007 onwards, it was at a high level of around 55 percent in each month and reached a peak of 59.2 percent in April 2008. Due to the impact of domestic economic adjustment and the international financial crisis, PMI declined sharply from its peak to a trough of 38.8 percent in November 2008, but subsequently recovered. During the 27 months from March 2009 to May 2011, the PMI was continuously in an expansion range above the critical point (50 percent), although there were several small fluctuations within the range of 51–56 percent. In reality, owing to various factors, the economy cannot grow in a straight line. It is normal to experience small fluctuations and these should not be a cause of surprise.

In terms of the same-month year-on-year growth rate of industrial added value for enterprises above the designated size nationwide, there were four stages of variation over the period 2007–11 (see Figure 13.4), as with the quarterly fluctuation in the economic growth rate. In the first stage, industrial production growth was running at a high level of around 18 percent in each month of 2007. In the second stage, between 2008 and January and February 2009, it dropped sharply and declined all the way to a trough of 3.8 percent in January and February 2009. In the third stage, between March 2009 and January and February 2010, when China was coping with the impact of the international financial crisis, industrial production growth recovered significantly and rose all the way to a high level of 20.7 percent in January and February 2010, drawing a trajectory of V-shaped

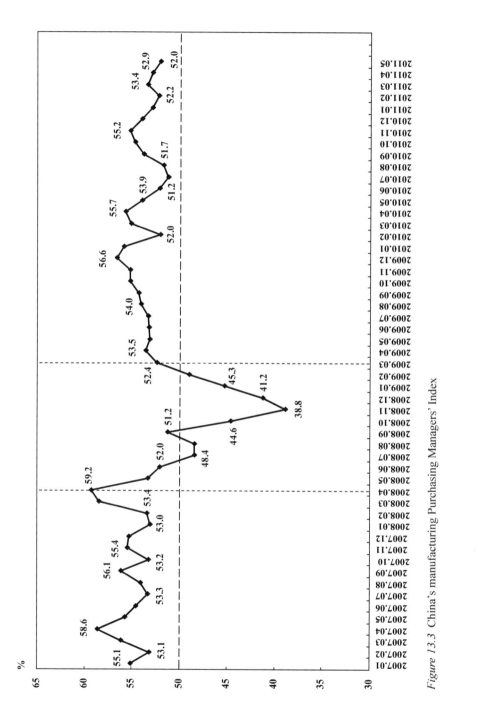

*Figure 13.3* China's manufacturing Purchasing Managers' Index

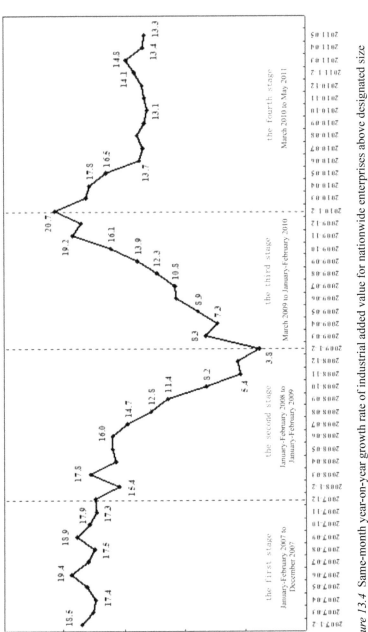

*Figure 13.4* Same-month year-on-year growth rate of industrial added value for nationwide enterprises above designated size

recovery. In the fourth stage, between March 2010 and May 2011, the industrial growth rate fell to an appropriate range of growth and became stabilized. It maintained a range of 13.1– 14.8 percent for 11 consecutive months from June 2010 to May 2011. How, then, might one argue that China's economy had already fallen into or might fall into stagflation?

3    In terms of the prime task of macro regulation, the focus in 2011 is to stabilize the overall price level. Stabilized prices and steady growth complement each other.

The same-month year-on-year rate of increase in residents' consumption prices was 4.9 percent in January, 4.9 percent in February, 5.4 percent in March, 5.3 percent in April and 5.5 percent in May of 2011 (see Figure 13.5).

In terms of the situation in the period 2006–10, the price was low and steady in 2006, slightly fluctuating below 3 percent. It started to climb and successively exceeded 3 percent, 4 percent, 5 percent and 6 percent in 2007. The Central Economic Working Conference held at the end of 2007 put forward a proposal to prevent rapid economic growth transforming into an overheated economy and avoid the clear risk of inflation evolving from a structural price increase. At the beginning of 2008, the price rose to 8.7 percent and faced a risk of exceeding10 percent. Subsequently, in countering the impact of the international financial crisis, the price declined to 1.2 percent, along with the decrease in the economic growth rate. The price was in negative growth for most of the months of 2009. It started to climb and successively exceeded 3 percent, 4 percent and 5 percent in the second

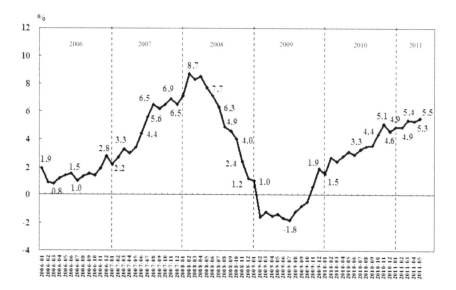

*Figure 13.5* Same-month year-on-year rise in residents' consumption prices (January 2006–April 2011)

half of 2010, mainly originating from the price increase for small agricultural products, such as garlic, beans, ginger, oil, sugar, apples and hot peppers.

I have already undertaken an analysis of the reasons for and measures of the above price increase (see Liu Shucheng, "Gaining a Profound Grasp of the Economic Situation and New Changes in Macro Regulation", *People's Daily*, 10 January 2011, p. 7). It is necessary to discuss whether people's capability of adapting to price increases has improved or diminished after 30 years of reform and the opening-up process. I believe that this capability has diminished, rather than having improved. First, a price increase directly affects the actual living standard of urban and rural residents, in particular the low-income group. Residents truly felt that the price of daily necessities, such as food like grain, vegetables, edible oil, meat, eggs and fruit, increased by 10 percent and even by above 20 percent, rather than a general price increase of 4 percent or 5 percent. For the high-income group, a price increase is nothing, but it is a heavy burden for the low-income group. Therefore, this will exacerbate the existing gap between rich and poor and easily intensify social contradictions. Second, nowadays, as the economy and a market orientation develop, general households will keep some precautionary savings for medical care, education, housing, endowment and unemployment. However, once prices increase and money depreciates, their savings will diminish and their household assets will evaporate. This will severely influence people's mood, the stability of life and trust in the government. Thus, price is a major issue that involves hundreds and thousands of households and concerns their livelihoods, sound economic development and social harmony and stability; the effects can never be overstated. The Central Economic Working Conference held at the end of 2010 proposed that the most urgent task of macro regulation at the time and in the future was to keep the overall price level basically stable and "put stabilizing the overall price level in a more prominent position". The Government Work Report of 5 March 2011 further proposed that the government must "make it top priority in macroeconomic control to keep the overall price level stable".

For the price trend in 2011, the mainstream view is that price rises could be high in the first half of 2011 and low in the second half due to the low rise in the first half of 2010 and high rise in the second half, together with the carry-over effect. The price regulation target of around 4 percent could be achieved with effort. I agree with this basic judgment. However, considering some uncertain factors working more strongly than expected, there is the possibility of a low rise in prices in the first half of 2011 and a high rise in the second half. Although this is not anticipated, such uncertain factors should never be taken lightly. These uncertain factors in 2011 and 2012 mainly include the economic growth situation, the potential for an agricultural natural disaster and international factors.

First, there is the issue of whether or not economic growth will remain fast or will overheat in 2011 and 2012. Since the reform and opening up of China, subsequent price increases have been related closely to the pulling force of demand, namely overheated economic growth. A new feature of this price increase is that economic growth is not excessively high as in the past and prices have started to climb while economic growth is not yet apparently high, rapid or overheating. Up to now, most domestic and foreign economic experts have predicted that the economic growth rate in 2011 will be lower than in 2010 at around 9.5 percent. I essentially agree with this prediction. However, it should not be ruled out that the economic growth in 2011 and 2012 may be rapid. Two main concerns are that there will be a change in office for leadership at all levels and that various regions exhibit considerable enthusiasm for going all out in the economy at the beginning of the Twelfth Five-Year Plan. Consequently, the current tasks of stabilizing prices and providing steady growth are complementary.

Second, grain production has been increasing for seven consecutive years. If there were to be a natural disaster, in particular a severe drought, in 2011, it would affect the grain harvest and promote price increases.

Moreover, if the prices of international oil, raw materials and agricultural products go up, the pressure of imported inflation will increase.

In addition to these uncertainties, we must pay close attention to and watch out for a spiraling relationship between wage increases and price increases, i.e. the relationship described in the Phillips curve. There are three expressions of the Phillips curve:

- The first one is the original curve which was first proposed in 1958 by the New Zealand economist A. Phillips, who had been undertaking research in the UK, with the longitudinal axis denoting the wage increase rate and the lateral axis expressing the unemployment rate, mainly focusing on the relationship between wage increases and unemployment.
- The second is the Phillips curve transformed by the US economists Samuelson and Solow in 1960, with the longitudinal axis altering from the wage increase rate to the price rise rate and the lateral axis expressing the unemployment rate. The reason for substituting the price rise rate for the wage increase rate was that at that time in the United States, the price increase originated primarily from wage increases, namely the rise in labor costs.
- The third curve is the common one with which we are familiar at present, with the longitudinal axis denoting the price rise rate and the lateral axis changing from the unemployment rate to the gap in the economic growth rate, namely the gap between the actual economic growth rate and the potential economic growth rate. The reason for substituting the gap in the economic growth rate for the unemployment rate was the identification of the quantitative relationship between the gap in the economic growth rate and the unemployment rate by the US economist Okun in 1962, known as "Okun's law".

Thus, in the original Phillips curve, the longitudinal axis of the wage increase rate is substituted by the price rise rate and the lateral axis of the unemployment rate is substituted by the gap in the economic growth rate.

At present, the factors that promote price increases in 2011 are increasingly related to wage cost increases. Thus, we return to the longitudinal axis of the original Phillips curve. Since 1997, the price level has been low and steady for over 10 years, a feature related to no severe overheating in economic growth and also to low labor costs and slow wage increases. Therefore, when studying the relationship of the Phillips curve in the past, little attention was focused on the relationship between price increases and wage increases. However, the era of cheap labor in China is over. In future, price increases and increases in labor costs will be more closely connected. Now many local governments propose that any increase in residents' income or staff salaries should be synchronized with economic growth. Some have even proposed a plan of doubling salaries within five years. It is necessary to pay close attention, to follow up and watch out for a spiraling relationship between wages and prices.

4   In terms of the policy mix of macro regulation, a proactive fiscal policy shall match a prudent monetary policy.

Based on the new changes in the domestic and international economic situation, the Central Working Conference held in December 2010 made adjustments to the two main policy orientations and the mix of macro regulation. This was intended to implement a continuous proactive fiscal policy and transform a monetary policy from "moderately loose" to "prudent" (see Figure 13.6). Implementing a proactive fiscal policy enables it to play an important role in stabilizing economic growth, adjusting the economic structure and income distribution and promoting social harmony. However, what is different from the previous two years is the adjustment of the scale, focus and strength of the proactive fiscal policy, along with a change in economic circumstances. Adjusting a monetary policy from "moderately loose" to "prudent" demonstrates a significant change in the macro policy orientation. This adjustment is a return from an "abnormal state", in which the country was coping with the international financial crisis, to a "normal situation" of steady economic growth. On the one hand, the adjustment appropriately tightens monetary credit, mainly for the purpose of coping with a severe surplus of international liquidity and the pressure of domestic price increases to curb asset price bubbles and stabilize inflation expectations. On the other hand, transforming to "prudent" is intended to make a change to "neutral", rather than to "tight", and will serve to maintain steady and rapid economic growth to a much greater extent.

Since the beginning of the 1990s, with the gradual establishment and development of China's socialist market economic system and the constant changes in the national and international economic situation, the fiscal policy and monetary policy, as the two main policy instruments of macro regulation, have experienced six transformations in their orientation and mix (see Figure 13.6).

The first of these was a mix of a moderately tight fiscal policy and a moderately tight monetary policy. From the second half of 1993, directed against the overheated economy and the severe inflation in the economic operation at that time, the government adopted a moderately tight fiscal policy and a moderately tight monetary policy, enabling China's economy to achieve a "soft landing" successfully in 1996 and effectively control the overheated economy and the serious inflation. This policy mix was implemented for around five years from the second half of 1993 to the first half of 1998.

The second transformation was a mix of a proactive fiscal policy and a prudent monetary policy. To cope with the impact of the Asian financial crisis that broke out in 1997, overcome insufficient domestic demand and avoid the reappearance of inflation, the government transformed the direction of the two macro-regulatory

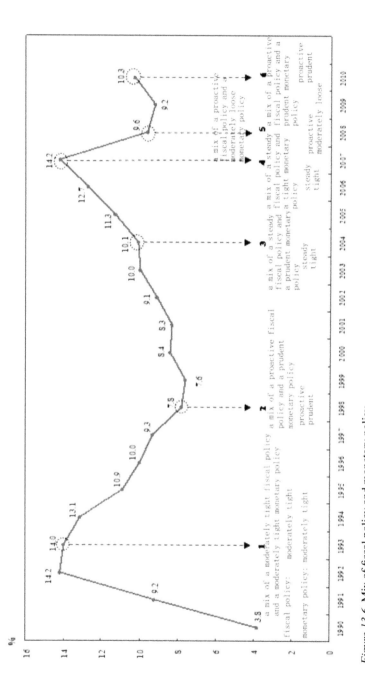

*Figure 13.6* Mix of fiscal policy and monetary policy

policies from the middle of 1998. The moderately tight fiscal policy was amended to a loose, expansionary and proactive one. The moderately tight monetary policy was changed to a tight-fitting, neutral and prudent one. A proactive fiscal policy is advantageous in expanding total demand, promoting economic growth and avoiding an economic downturn. A prudent monetary policy guarantees necessary supports for economic development and avoids the blind easing of the money supply, which is beneficial to preventing financial risks, curbs deflation and avoids comeback inflation. This policy mix was carried out for around six and a half years from the middle of 1998 to 2004, pushing China's economy to enter a rising stage of a new economic cycle at the beginning of the new century.

The third transformation comprised a mix of a steady fiscal policy and a prudent monetary policy. Upon the entry of the new century, to avoid an overheating tendency in the economic recovery, the government transformed a proactive fiscal policy to a tight-fitting and steady fiscal policy and continuously implemented the tight-fitting and prudent monetary policy. This policy mix had been carried out for about three years from 2005 to 2007, thus enabling China's economy to maintain steady and rapid growth.

The fourth transformation was a mix of a steady fiscal policy and a tight monetary policy. At the beginning of December 2007, the Central Economic Working Conference proposed preventing rapid economic growth from transforming into an overheated economy and avoiding obvious inflation evolving from a structural price increase, making these aspects top priority in macro regulation. Based on this proposition, the government continuously implemented a steady fiscal policy and transformed a prudent monetary policy to one that was tough and tight. Following the implementation of this policy mix in the first half of 2008, China turned to address the impact of the international financial crisis.

The fifth transformation was a mix of a proactive fiscal policy and a moderately loose monetary policy. In the second half of 2008, to cope with the impact of the international financial crisis that evolved from the US subprime mortgage crisis, the government transformed the direction of the two macro-regulatory policies. The steady fiscal policy was amended to adopt a proactive stance. The tight monetary policy shifted to a moderately loose mode. This was the first time that the government had implemented a mix of a proactive fiscal policy and a moderately loose monetary policy since the beginning of the 1990s. By 2010, having carried out this policy mix for over two years, China took the global lead in realizing an overall economic turnaround.

The sixth transformation is the latest, comprising a mix of a proactive fiscal policy and a prudent monetary policy. For over two years, in coping with the impact of the international financial crisis, China's economy has transformed from a great decline in economic growth to an overall economic turnaround and has further turned to a new normal growing stage. Based on the new changes in the national and international economic situation, the government has maintained its proactive fiscal policy and transformed its monetary policy to a prudent one.

China has continuously improved its macro-regulatory level and strengthened its coping capacity through rich and varied practice, thus providing strong policy support for maintaining steady and rapid economic development.

5   In terms of the potential economic growth rate, against the background of accelerating the transformation of economic development mode as the mainstream strategy, the appropriate range of economic growth can be controlled at 8–10 percent and a potential economic growth rate of 9 percent in the Twelfth Five-Year Plan period.

Our research group adopted the Hodrick–Prescott (HP) filter method and production function, calculated according to the relevant data since the reform and opening-up period and found that the appropriate range of economic growth in China from 1979 to 2009 was 8–12 percent and the median line of the potential economic growth rate was nearly 10 percent. Since the reform and opening-up period, a high price has been paid for fast economic growth, as shown by the extensive economic growth mode. This can be summarized as high energy consumption, high materials consumption, high pollution, low labor costs, low resource costs, low environmental costs, low level of technical content and low price competition. As a result, this has brought about a series of structural contradictions such as the following: an imbalance between internal and external demand; disharmony between investment and consumption; unbalanced distribution; unreasonable structures between the primary, secondary and tertiary industries; weak innovative ability in science and technology; imbalanced development between urban and rural areas and between various regions; intensified constraints on economic growth in terms of resources and the environment; discordance between economic and social development. The extensive economic growth mode and a series of structural contradictions mean that China's economic development will be conditioned to a great extent by energy, mineral resources, land, water and the ecological environment; moreover, it will be influenced by an increase in various costs, restricted by the low domestic consumption demand and affected by the international economic and financial risks. Therefore, we urgently need to transform the pattern of economic development in the Twelfth Five-Year Plan period. Against the above background, the upper limit of the appropriate range of economic growth can be lowered by 2 percent during the Twelfth Five-Year Plan period, namely, the appropriate range of economic growth can be controlled at 8 –10 percent, the median line of the potential economic growth rate at 9 percent. In terms of macro-regulation policy, this implies that a moderately tight macro-regulation policy should be implemented if the actual economic growth rate exceeds 10 percent; a moderately expansionary macro-regulation policy should be carried out if the actual economic growth rate is below 8 percent; and a neutral macro-regulation policy can be applied if the actual economic growth rate falls in the range of 8–10 percent.

6   In terms of the impetus for economic growth, the improvement in average personal income, the promotion of urbanization and adjustment and the upgrading of industrial structure become important aspects of power in the Twelfth Five-Year Plan period.

Two great historic changes will take place in the period of the Twelfth Five-Year Plan. One is that the gross national income (GNI) per capita will enter to the medium- and high-income group from the medium- and low-income group according to the standard of the World Bank. The other is that the proportion of the urban population will exceed 50 percent. This will provide an important impetus for expanding domestic demand, in particular expanding consumption demand and promoting the optimization and upgrading of demand and the industrial structure in the Twelfth Five-Year Plan period.

At the end of the Eleventh Five-Year Plan period, China's GDP reached 39,800 billion yuan (US$5,745 billion) in 2010 according to the conversion rate of the International Monetary Fund (IMF), whereas Japan's GDP was US$5,390 billion in the same year; thus, China's GDP exceeded that of Japan and China became the second-largest economy in the world. The GDP of the United States was US$14,624 billion in 2010, amounting to 2.55 times that of China, and China's GDP was 39 percent of the GDP of the United States in 2010. During the period of the Eleventh Five-Year Plan, the average annual growth rate of GDP was 7.5 percent as planned and the actual rate was 11.2 percent. In terms of GDP per capita in the same period, it rose from 14,185 yuan in 2005 to 29,748 yuan in 2010 (approximately from US$1,700 to US$4,000). The average annual growth rate of GDP per capita was 6.6 percent in the original Eleventh Five-Year Plan and the actual rate was 10.6 percent.

According to the Twelfth Five-Year Plan, the average annual growth rate of GDP will be 7 percent on the basis of an overall improvement in quality and efficiency. Calculated based on the price in 2010, GDP in 2015 will reach 55,000 billion yuan. In line with the forecast of the IMF, China's GDP will reach US$9,980 billion and the GDP of the United States will be up to US$18,000 billion by 2015, 1.8 times that of China. China's GDP will be 55 percent of the GDP of the United States, namely exceeding half of the GDP of the United States. By 2015, GDP per capita in China will reach 39,600 yuan and exceed US$6,000 based on an exchange rate of US$1.00 equaling 6.5yuan.

Figure 13.7 displays the growth of the GNI per capita in China from 1962 to 2010 according to the World Bank database. The data for 2011–15 are calculated based on the Twelfth Five-Year Plan. In 1962, the GNI per capita was US$70, lying in the low-income group globally. In 1978, at the beginning of the reform and opening up of China, the GNI per capita rose to US$190 and to US$790 in 1998, entering the medium- and low-income group. It exceeded US$1,000 at the beginning of the new century. During the period of the Eleventh Five-Year Plan, it rose from US$1,760 to US$4,050. The GNI per capita is estimated to reach US$4,450 in 2011, the first year of the Twelfth Five-Year Plan period, starting to enter the medium- and high-income group.

In terms of residents' income, during the period of the Eleventh Five-Year Plan, urban per capita disposable income increased from 10,493 yuan in 2005 to 19,109 yuan in 2010. The average annual growth rate in the original plan was 5 percent and the actual rate was 9.7 percent. Rural per capita net income rose from 3,255 yuan in 2005 to 5,919 yuan in 2010. The average annual growth rate in the original plan was 5 percent and the actual rate was 8.9 percent. The Twelfth Five-Year Plan proposes that the government should make efforts to synchronize residents' income growth with economic development and increase in labor remuneration

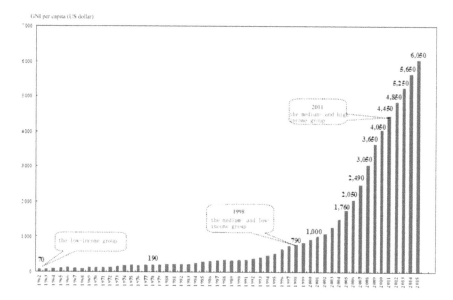

*Figure 13.7* GNI per capita in China (1962–2015)

with an improvement in labor productivity and gradually raise the proportion of residents' income in the distribution of national income and the proportion of labor remuneration in the first distribution of national income to accelerate the formation of a rational system of income distribution. According to the Twelfth Five-Year Plan, urban per capita disposable income will increase from 19,109 yuan in 2010 to above 26,810 yuan in 2015, at an average annual growth rate of 7 percent. Rural per capita net income will rise from 5,919 yuan in 2010 to over 8,310 yuan in 2015, also at an average annual growth rate of 7 percent.

Regarding the promotion of urbanization, the urbanization rate (the proportion of the urban population in the total population, see Figure 13.8) in China was 10.6 percent in 1949 and increased to 17.9 percent in 1978. During the period of the Eleventh Five-Year Plan, the urbanization rate rose from 43 percent in 2005 to 47.5 percent in 2010 (according to the latest data from the sixth national population census in 2010, the urbanization rate was 49.68 percent and the proportion of the rural population was 50.32 percent). During the period of the Twelfth Five-Year Plan, we must actively and steadily promote urbanization, continuously improving its level and quality and strengthening the urban carrying capacity comprehensively to prevent and govern "urban disease". According to the Twelfth Five-Year Plan, the urbanization rate will reach 51.5 percent in 2015. During the period of the Twelfth Five-Year Plan, the urban population in China will exceed the rural population for the first time, which will be a significant and historic change for a populous country with more than 1.3 billion people.

Concerning the adjustment and upgrading of the industrial structure during the period of the Twelfth Five-Year Plan, the significant changes in the industrial

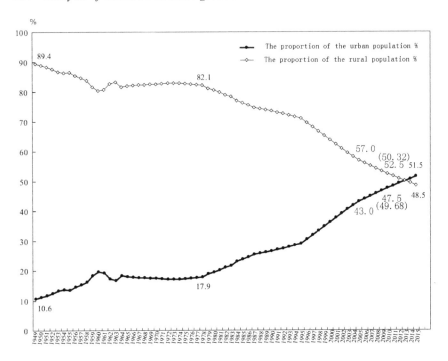

*Figure 13.8* Urbanization rate in China

structure will include accelerating the development of modern agriculture, transforming and upgrading the manufacturing industry, cultivating and developing strategic emergent industries, promoting changes in energy production and energy utilization, constructing an integrated traffic and transportation system, improving informationalization comprehensively, advancing the development of the marine economy, promoting the development of the service industry and accelerating the development of the cultural sector (see Table 13.1). This will inject new impetus into economic development during the period of the Twelfth Five-Year Plan.

*Table 13.1* Industrial structural adjustment during the period of the Twelfth Five-Year Plan

| | Related Industry | Main Content |
|---|---|---|
| 1 | Accelerating the development of modern agriculture | Ensuring national food security as the primary goal. |
| 2 | Transforming and upgrading the manufacturing industry | Developing advanced equipment for the manufacturing industry; adjusting and optimizing the raw materials industry; transforming and upgrading the consumer goods industry; promoting the manufacturing industry from large to strong. |

| | Related Industry | Main Content |
|---|---|---|
| 3 | Cultivating and developing strategic emergent industries | Energy conservation and environmental protection industries; next generation information technology industry; biology industry; high-end equipment manufacturing; new energy industry; advanced material industry; new energy vehicles. |
| 4 | Promoting changes in energy production and energy utilization | Building up a modern industrial system with safe, stable, economical and clean energy. |
| 5 | Constructing an integrated traffic and transportation system | According to the principle of appropriately advanced development, promoting the overall development of different modes of transportation, basically building up a national rapid rail network and expressway network and preliminarily forming an integrated traffic and transportation system with supporting and connecting network facilities, advanced and practical technical equipment and a safe and efficient transportation service. |
| 6 | Improving informationalization comprehensively | Speeding up the construction of the next generation of the national information infrastructure with broadband and an integrated, safe and ubiquitous network. |
| 7 | Advancing the development of the marine economy | Offshore oil and gas; transportation; fishery; tourism; sea creatures; seawater utilization; marine engineering equipment manufacturing. |
| 8 | Promoting the development of the service industry | Including productive and living service industries. |
| 9 | Accelerating the development of the cultural sector | Pushing the cultural sector to become a pillar of the national economy. |

[Originally published in *Economic Perspectives (JingjixueDongtai)*, No.7, 2011]

# References

Shucheng, Liu. (2011a). Analysis of National and International Environments Facing China during the 12th Five-Year Plan. In *Economic Blue Book, Spring Issue, Analysis of Economic Prospect in China-Spring Review of 2011*. Beijing: Social Sciences Academic Press.

Shucheng, Liu. (2011b, January 10). Profoundly Grasping Economic Operation Situation and New Changes in Macro Regulation. *The People's Daily*.

# Index

Note: Page numbers in italic indicate a figure or table

For Product Safety Concerns and Information please contact our EU
representative GPSR@taylorandfrancis.com
Taylor & Francis Verlag GmbH, Kaufingerstraße 24, 80331 München, Germany